Building a Cyber Risk Management Program
Evolving Security for the Digital Age

Brian Allen and Brandon Bapst
with Terry Allan Hicks

Beijing · Boston · Farnham · Sebastopol · Tokyo

Building a Cyber Risk Management Program

by Brian Allen, Brandon Bapst, and Terry Allan Hicks

Published by O'Reilly Media, Inc., 1005 Gravenstein Highway North, Sebastopol, CA 95472.

O'Reilly books may be purchased for educational, business, or sales promotional use. Online editions are also available for most titles (*http://oreilly.com*). For more information, contact our corporate/institutional sales department: 800-998-9938 or *corporate@oreilly.com*.

Acquisitions Editor: Simina Calin	**Indexer:** BIM Creatives, LLC
Development Editor: Sara Hunter	**Interior Designer:** David Futato
Production Editor: Katherine Tozer	**Cover Designer:** Karen Montgomery
Copyeditor: nSight, Inc.	**Illustrator:** Kate Dullea
Proofreader: Dwight Ramsey	

December 2023:   First Release

Revision History for the First Release

2023-12-04:   First Release

See *http://oreilly.com/catalog/errata.csp?isbn=9781098147792* for release details.

978-1-098-14779-2

LSI

Table of Contents

Preface

In our professional journeys, we encounter pivotal moments—be it a change of job, a new career path, or the adoption of an innovative perspective—that significantly alter our course. For us, a keen and focused curiosity sparked numerous enlightening discussions. These discussions laid the groundwork for an essential framework and a proactive, value-centric approach to managing security risks. This evolution of ideas and strategies culminated in the creation of a structured and comprehensive cyber risk management program.

Brian's Story

A few years ago, on a flight to California with my wife as we headed off for vacation, I found myself asking a simple question that turned out to be a eureka moment (for *me* anyway). "What is a cyber risk management program?" It seemed simple at the time. But with a slow internet at 30K feet, I did some searching and couldn't find an authoritative answer. What had raised the question was the document I was reading: the 2018 Securities and Exchange Commission (SEC) guidance to boards and corporate officers on cybersecurity oversight matters. In that guidance, the SEC stated that boards of directors and corporate officers must have oversight of a cyber risk management program. A satisfying answer to the question wasn't in the guidance, nor any other material I could find. With the SEC's expectation that companies had these answers, and with accountability hanging in the balance, it was an important question not to have an answer to.

Let me back up and explain why I was reading SEC guidance on my vacation. For more than a decade, I was the chief security officer (CSO) for Time Warner Cable, a Fortune 130 provider of critical infrastructure (telephone and internet services). Building on my experience, I'd written an earlier book, *Enterprise Security Risk Management: Concepts and Applications*, with my longtime associate Rachelle Loyear. The concept of enterprise security risk management is based on the fundamental premise that, at its core, security is a risk function, and every task a security practitioner executes could and should be viewed through the lens of five core risk concepts that apply to any risk paradigm: 1) What is your asset? 2) What are the risks? 3) How could you mitigate these risks? 4) How could you respond to incidents? 5) What consistent continued learning can you pursue about your environment? It doesn't matter if you practice cybersecurity, physical security, business continuity, fraud management, or any related security discipline. Every tactic, in every discipline, fits into one of those five core principles. I went to the consulting firm EY to build out in practice the concepts of that book and to work with boards and executives. It was during that part of my career that I was curious about the executive's security risk management role. Though the SEC document might sound boring, it produced a career-changing revelation. Curiosity got me again.

During the next few years, Brandon and I researched the heck out of that question and had a ton of conversations with colleagues, which led to even more questions. We both developed significant experience assessing and building cyber risk management programs at large institutions. After I left EY, we spent time mapping out a broad array of risk-related standards. We evaluated the guidance that boards were receiving, looked at the case law that establishes executive-level accountability, and generally considered the value and role of security as a strategic function—beyond its tactical necessity.

Here are some of the findings of all that research:

- Security is a risk function (we knew that).
- Risk management is a mature practice (the risk practice in the security field is not that mature).
- Most security organizations and practitioners take an ad hoc approach (the law, regulators, and the changing economy are demanding a changed expectation of enterprise security practices, all pointing to the maturing of the risk function as the path forward).
- A cyber risk management program can be clearly defined as a standalone program, which is frankly not optional at this point.

There is true value in building a cyber risk management program, but it needs structure and a commitment to executing risk management as a formal program.

The journey with Brandon has been amazing, and it continues. We have reciprocal respect and continually challenge each other...a necessary step to move from what security was in our minds to something that it needs to be. I learn from him every time we speak. I appreciate Brandon as a colleague and close friend.

Brandon's Story

As a consultant in EY's Cybersecurity practice, I've had the privilege of partnering with top executives, CSOs, CISOs, and security practitioners from some of the world's largest and most recognized brands across a broad range of industries. This journey, which involved guiding companies in their shift from tactical security practices to holistic security risk management programs, has been a fulfilling venture into addressing their most intricate challenges.

My progress on this path has been shaped by invaluable experiences, and especially by the influence of several key individuals. My entry into the world of cybersecurity began 15 years ago, thanks to an introduction by my uncle, Jim Mazotas, a serial entrepreneur and founder of multiple cybersecurity companies. What followed was an academic foundation at Malone University and subsequent certifications. My journey has been further enriched by the mentorships of several leaders and colleagues through my time at EY.

I've learned through my time serving clients how every company's cybersecurity journey is unique. Some are at the early stages of change, grappling with fundamental challenges and working with varying degrees of support from leadership. Others, especially in sectors like financial services and healthcare, have more mature cybersecurity risk practices. But a common thread has been evident throughout: the rapid digitalization of business operations and increasing regulatory pressures means an enterprise's approach to security must continue to evolve.

This book is a distillation of insights, experiences, and best practices Brian and I gathered over the years. It extends beyond theory to offer security practitioners—and many others with a role in risk management—a blueprint for professional growth, enhanced job security, and greater personal and professional satisfaction in their roles. And it presents a guide for a fast-changing world, because while technology and threats are constantly evolving, the principles of sound risk management we've outlined remain timeless.

Teaming up with Brian, whom I hold in high regard as a mentor, has been an illuminating experience. Writing this book, I've found further clarity about the "why" of our professional convictions. Our combined expertise—my hands-on consulting exposure and Brian's invaluable experience as a CSO and consultant—ensures that this book presents a holistic view on building a cyber risk management program.

Bringing It Together

We (Brian and Brandon) have been on a multiyear mission to better define a cyber risk management program. This journey has been driven by curiosity and an intentional effort to challenge existing notions. We hope this book will also inspire you to embark on a new or continued journey, hopefully one that stirs your own curiosity and thoughtful approach to maturing your practice, but also your department, or your personal career. This book not only defines risk management but describes how to build your own cyber risk management program. Ideally, this program would be supported by existing standards, laws, and authoritative guidance. It should stand on its own as a true foundation for the strategic elements of a security practice. It also has expected outputs and is defendable. Lastly, it can support security's practice through the unknowns of digitalization, and it can drive strategic decisions, protect against budding liability, and communicate security's value as a strategic partner.

As we started breaking down the SEC's guidance to support our definition of a cyber risk management program, a bigger picture emerged. Not only was the SEC formalizing an obligation, but the courts were beginning to close in on corporate-officer-level liability, including the CISO. In addition, every industry experienced digital risks, with new threats and breaches appearing constantly. Security organizations struggled to communicate the value of their efforts, and tried to avoid finger-pointing should something happen. These organizations were continuously fighting the perception that everything is protected because budgets have been approved.

Today, all of these challenges are increasing, in degree and complexity. Every enterprise is digitalized, increasing the surface area of risks exponentially, with increasing speed and without the necessary or appropriate conversation of risk balance. All the while, business leaders are starting to get budget fatigue, putting even more pressure on the security organizations as they look over their shoulders at even bigger threats—competition and even more serious consequences if they don't move fast enough in this new economy.

Our journey has led us to map a variety of authorities that helped clearly define a cyber risk management program. It turns out, there's a lot to pull from. It just hasn't been organized. We mapped the SEC guidance, international risk standards, regulatory approaches, case law, and guidance from the National Association of Corporate Directors (NACD) into a cyber risk management program (CRMP) framework. The framework covers four core components that make up a formal program along with supporting principles that provide more detailed guidance for implementation. This framework supports the concepts in this book and can be found at CRMP.info. When implemented, it should result in a standalone formal program—a needed program that answers the question that stirred this all up.

Our collective vision for this book is clear: to empower you with a structured and authoritatively defined cyber risk management program, with built-in concepts and guidance to assist with your individual approach of implementation.

Who Should Read This Book

We've designed this book to deliver real-world value to the broadest possible range of readers, while at the same time making it clear at every stage which readers will be most impacted by which content. The key roles we see benefiting from the book are:

Security practitioners at every level
> Risk management is a highly mature practice, one that's been developed, practiced, and refined for decades, but not usually as a comprehensive, formalized program for security. Developing a program will help to drive the maturity, intent, and purpose of the practice.

Security practitioners in every function
> As much as this book is focused on cybersecurity, if you take the word "cyber" out, you have the fundamental elements that could be applied to programmatically managing risks in physical security, fraud management, business continuity management, and operational resilience.

Boards of directors
> This book is designed to provide directors with a comprehensive understanding of their vital role and responsibilities in overseeing a cyber risk management program. It offers insights into the expectations for management's role in the program's establishment. The underlying principles highlight the importance of viewing cybersecurity as a business risk, providing a perspective that empowers directors to ask more relevant questions and provide better guidance to management. By moving the focus from the technical details of cybersecurity tactics and operations to a wider strategic risk oversight role, directors can improve their cyber risk management program's effectiveness while strengthening defenses against increasing legal and regulatory liabilities.

CxOs and line-of-business leaders
> These high-level decision makers will gain a clear understanding of the need for security to mature as a risk practice; this will help them understand and protect themselves against increased liability. These decision makers will also learn how to set security expectations, so they can make appropriate and informed security risk decisions that align with their overall strategies.

Regulators

> Regulatory bodies can use the guidance in this book to help develop well-defined regulations based on reasonable, consistent, and repeatable expectations. A common taxonomy and shared expectations will make their efforts more efficient, effective, and synergistic.

Auditors

> Audit professionals typically focus on best practices, evaluating the effectiveness of an enterprise's or an organization's security controls and processes against established policies, standards, frameworks, and regulations. This book provides a comprehensive structure for auditors to use in evaluating a cybersecurity risk management program, because it focuses on security execution in relation to the business's expected risk appetite and tolerance.

Business leaders and professionals whose work may be impacted by the risks introduced by digitalization

> The impacts of digital transformation are far-reaching, complex, and unpredictable. As a result, professionals in many different disciplines—most business leaders and decision makers across most enterprise functions—will find real value in learning about how to identify digitalization's risks and make informed decisions about balancing risk and reward.

Final Thoughts

This is a journey. There's no quick fix, and there is endless learning and nuance to this conversation—but it's worth the ride. What it will take is challenging our notions with what's currently in place, how we've practiced in the past, and an eagerness to be curious.

As much as this book is written specifically for a cyber practice, remove the word "cyber" and the concepts of the cyber risk management program can be applied to any security risk practice.

We're confident that the insights you'll gain will empower you in your professional journey.

For feedback, questions, or to join the conversation, visit us at *CRMP.info*.

Conventions Used in This Book

The following typographical conventions are used in this book:

Italic

> Indicates new terms, URLs, email addresses, filenames, and file extensions.

This element signifies a general note.

O'Reilly Online Learning

O'REILLY® For more than 40 years, *O'Reilly Media* (*https://oreilly.com*) has provided technology and business training, knowledge, and insight to help companies succeed.

Our unique network of experts and innovators share their knowledge and expertise through books, articles, and our online learning platform. O'Reilly's online learning platform gives you on-demand access to live training courses, in-depth learning paths, interactive coding environments, and a vast collection of text and video from O'Reilly and 200+ other publishers. For more information, visit *https://oreilly.com*.

How to Contact Us

Please address comments and questions concerning this book to the publisher:

O'Reilly Media, Inc.
1005 Gravenstein Highway North
Sebastopol, CA 95472
800-889-8969 (in the United States or Canada)
707-829-7019 (international or local)
707-829-0104 (fax)
support@oreilly.com
https://www.oreilly.com/about/contact.html

We have a web page for this book with errata, examples, and additional information. You can access this page at *https://oreil.ly/building-a-cyber-risk-management-program*.

For news and information about our books and courses, visit *https://oreilly.com*.

Find us on LinkedIn: *https://linkedin.com/company/oreilly-media*.

Follow us on Twitter: *https://twitter.com/oreillymedia*.

Watch us on YouTube: *https://youtube.com/oreillymedia*.

Acknowledgments

We have so many to thank for guiding and supporting us on this journey, in both our careers and in writing this book. A special thanks to our supportive families, especially our respective loving wives, Maria and Sarah, and our encouraging parents who throughout our lives have built a foundation for us to be respectfully curious. Our gratitude also extends to our friend, writer, and thought-provoker, Terry Allan Hicks; to Sara Hunter at O'Reilly, who provided wisdom throughout this process; our copyeditor Adam Lawrence and his meticulous attention to detail; and the thoughtful reviewers, all of whom artfully helped shape this book.

CHAPTER 1

Cybersecurity in the Age of Digital Transformation

A worldwide pandemic brings manufacturing plants in China to a standstill, causing supply shortages and slowdowns at factories from Detroit to Yokohama. An Ethiopian airliner mysteriously nosedives minutes after takeoff, killing everyone on board; and less than six months later, on the other side of the world, the same make and model of aircraft crashes in almost exactly the same way. An unknown person tampers with the control systems at a water plant in Florida, increasing the amount of a chemical that's ordinarily safe to use in water treatment but lethal at higher levels by more than 100 times. An extortionist uses artificial intelligence (AI) to convincingly re-create an individual's voice to fake a kidnapping, and election officials worldwide worry that the same "deepfake" techniques—which can also manipulate images—will be used to undermine democratic elections. A Russian cyberattack on a satellite navigation system used by the Ukrainian military brings wind turbines hundreds of miles away in Germany to a standstill. And a lone attacker holds a major pipeline system for ransom, creating massive fuel shortages up and down the US East Coast.

These events are dramatic examples of how very fragile our daily lives, and the systems and processes they rely on, are today. This complex, intricate set of interconnections is created by the world's overwhelming reliance on digital technologies for communication and collaboration, and the unprecedented risks they've introduced—and continue to introduce—at a radically accelerating pace. Enterprises everywhere now face threats that would have been unimaginable just a few short years ago. The threats can be acutely damaging to financial interests and, in some cases, even drive companies out of business—and not just because of failures dealing with cyber threats, but because of competition: the ability of one company to take risks and move faster than its competitor, both of whom are digitalizing at a competitive pace.

The security organizations are struggling to keep pace with the significant challenges those threats and vulnerabilities represent, often falling short.

This book presents a way forward in this radically different and threatening new business and technology landscape. The approach, which draws on the authors' decades of experience in the field, is based on the premise that the way for an enterprise to protect itself today and tomorrow is to develop a comprehensive, enterprise-wide cyber risk management program. The book speaks to a broad range of enterprise stakeholders—not just security practitioners—to guide strategic decisions and execution parameters throughout the enterprise. The key is defining, developing, and implementing a cyber risk management program.

Regulators worldwide are focusing more intensely on how enterprises are managing their cyber risks, how they establish their risk tolerance, whether they're executing to that tolerance, and whether there is proper oversight of this programmatic approach. Courts are narrowing their focus on the personal liability of boards of directors, CEOs and other corporate officers, including chief information security officers (CISOs), as it relates to their oversight of cyber risk management. The lack of a program, and the outputs of a program by themselves, can be the basis of that liability.

Many readers, especially experienced security professionals, will recognize some or all of the components of a cyber risk management program as we present it, and they'll likely be practicing some of them already, at least in part. Security practitioners are by definition risk practitioners (that's an important concept that we'll be returning to again and again). Their experience in risk management will prove invaluable in designing and implementing a cyber risk management program. What sets our approach apart is that it brings together all these components and more in a comprehensive, formal program designed to protect the entire enterprise and many of its stakeholders against the entire range of risks in the present and in the future.

In this book, we'll be taking a deep dive into defining a formal cyber risk management program through a variety of authoritative sources, aligning global standards, regulations, court cases, and influential sources with a framework to support the foundational elements of the defined program. Though the book will not be a how-to approach to risk management tactics, it will nevertheless reference many risk practices and provide examples that could be implemented in the program.

Why a cyber risk management program now? Digital transformation has introduced a cyber *element* into every aspect of security and has made cybersecurity one of the most urgent concerns for enterprises worldwide in recent years—and not only for the security professionals, but for every leader as well.

The Fourth Industrial Revolution

The term *Fourth Industrial Revolution*—sometimes called *Industry 4.0*[1]—was popularized in the 2010s by the economist Klaus Schwab, founder of the World Economic Forum (WEF). The concept is commonly defined as rapid, and rapidly accelerating, change in systems and processes driven by the increasing interconnectivity and automation of technologies in ways that blur the distinctions between the physical and digital worlds. These technologies include artificial intelligence (AI), advanced robotics, machine-to-machine (M2M) communication, the networks of autonomous devices that make up the Internet of Things (IoT), and many more that are on the horizon. And as these technologies interact in new, unexpected, and unpredictable ways, they are driving social, political, economic, and cultural changes at a velocity never before seen in human history.

 A 2016 WEF report on the Fourth Industrial Revolution says, "The speed of current breakthroughs has no historical precedent. When compared with previous industrial revolutions, the fourth is evolving at an exponential rather than a linear pace. Moreover, it is disrupting almost every industry in every country. And the breadth and depth of these changes herald the transformation of entire systems of production, management, and governance."[2]

To understand the dramatic changes we're experiencing now, let's take a step back to look at how we got here, specifically at the historical changes that preceded them:

- The First Industrial Revolution used water—rivers turning millwheels and coal-fired boilers feeding steam boilers—to drive manufacturing production (steel mills and textile mills) and transportation (trains and ships).

- The Second Industrial Revolution electrified these processes, making true mass production possible.

- The Third Industrial Revolution was—and is, because it's still going on—based on electronics, using automation and information exchange to drive improvements in operational efficiency.

- The Fourth Industrial Revolution delivers operational efficiency and innovation at a velocity that was unimaginable a few years ago. It's driven, above all, by the

---

1 This German terminology reflects the country's importance in manufacturing and other industries.

2 Klaus Schwab, "The Fourth Industrial Revolution: What It Means, How to Respond," (*https://oreil.ly/oR73c*) World Economic Forum, January 14, 2016.

digitalization of existing systems, applications, devices, and processes, and—crucially—by the continuous, ongoing, rapid creation of *new* digital technologies.

In the future, the world will likely look back on the Fourth Industrial Revolution as a more radical, dramatic, and fundamental change than all three of its predecessors taken together. It builds on all of them, especially the Third, with previously unimaginable speed, scope, and impact. It's as if all the major technology developments that had come before—the electric light bulb, the automobile, radio and television, everything—were occurring at the same time.

There are five key trends impacting enterprises and the risks they face:

Industry convergence
Every industry is changing, and the cycle of change is constantly accelerating. New ecosystems, business models, and consumer behaviors are blurring industry lines across every market segment. And enterprises collaborating with third parties in industry ecosystems—sometimes even with direct competitors—face previously unknown risks, because they inevitably give up some degree of control to the other parties.

Globalization
When the people and organizations involved in the value chain—manufacturers, suppliers, partners, customers—are spread across the entire world, enterprises have to recognize that the risks they face are different, highly unpredictable, and on a scale they've never before had to deal with.

Expectations of oversight
Enterprises are being watched more closely than ever by legislators, regulators, industry and consumer organizations, and a broad range of other interested parties. And all those parties expect—and in many cases demand—greater oversight of enterprise business practices.

Legal action challenges
Often enterprise actions—and failures to act, as in the case of cybersecurity events like data breaches—result in damaging lawsuits.

A changing regulatory landscape
Regulatory requirements are becoming ever more complex and more rigorous—and often more contradictory. This increases both the risks of noncompliance and the difficulty and expense of managing those risks.

All these trends are characterized by two radically disruptive factors: *velocity* and *volatility*. Everything is happening at a dramatically accelerated pace, and the acceleration itself is constantly accelerating—markets, politics, consumer behaviors—making everything more complex, unstable, hard to predict, and harder to manage. The result is that enterprises have no choice but to become more agile than ever and keep refining and enhancing their agility through their risk decision making.

Digital transformation has made it possible for manufacturers to achieve operational and logistical efficiencies that would have been unthinkable only a few years ago. Let's take a look at a simple example of how this works: the design, testing, manufacture, shipping, and installation of a semiconductor for use in an electric vehicle (EV). The process begins with a design team in California delivering the specifications for the chip, probably with an endless series of last-minute updates, to a facility in China that's tasked with developing a prototype. When the prototype is ready, it's sent to the auto manufacturer in Michigan for testing. If the prototype is satisfactory, the specs are sent to another plant, in a different location in China, where a different manufacturer begins sourcing the rare earths and other materials that go into the chip and planning a manufacturing schedule. And here's an important point that we'll be returning to later: all these different points in the process can be handled by different entities. They don't have to be part of the same organizational structure, and they don't have to be all part of the same company—and in most cases, they won't be. They will, however, all be part of the digitalized world, forcing all involved to rethink processes and interaction, with digitalized risks built in along the way.

Let's say the manufacturing process has gone off without a hitch, and the first shipment of semiconductors is ready to go. Digital technologies make it possible to track that shipment to the most granular level. That means that at any given moment, the manufacturer knows exactly where a specific semiconductor is, not just in the world, but in which shipping container in which hold of which ship in which port. Why does this matter? Because it lets the manufacturer plan its production schedule with absolute precision. The chip will arrive just in time to be inserted into the dashboard of the EV. Production won't be delayed, and the manufacturer won't have the added costs and risks of keeping unnecessary supplies on hand—supplies that could be stolen or damaged while sitting in a warehouse. And this efficiency is made possible by digital connectivity, which drives this "just-in-time economy" and the real-time communication and information exchange it enables.

Just how fast are the changes these trends are driving? One excellent indicator of the velocity of change is the Standard and Poor's 500 (S&P 500), one of the oldest and most important stock market indexes in the US. In 1969, not much more than half a century ago, traditional industrial companies, essentially manufacturing concerns, made up a third of the 500 companies listed. Today, only 68 industrials are listed, tied for first place with information technology companies. Even more breathtaking is the change in the *lifespan* of S&P-listed companies—the period when S&P thinks they're important enough to represent a benchmark of the economy. According to Innosight (*https://oreil.ly/6a7T5*), a company's average S&P listing period was 33 years in 1964, and S&P predicts it will have dropped to just 12 by 2027.

What's the takeaway here? Enterprises need to move fast. Moving fast also means taking risks. Some of the equilibrium in the risk-reward dialogue involves maintaining a balance between different risks. In this case, the risk of cyber can be at the cost of efficiency and financing other projects, as well as at the cost of losing ground to competitors who may be willing, or capable, of taking more risks. A good cyber risk management program, delivering timely and trusted risk information, should allow companies to go faster, knowing what's around the corner. They'll identify risks more quickly, and they'll be more aware of the latency of their brakes should they need to use them. This clearly represents a strategic advantage in this digitized environment.

The radical changes created by the Fourth Industrial Revolution—new technologies and new business models being born, and old ones dying—represent the latest and most extreme example of the process the Austrian economist Joseph Schumpeter called "creative destruction." And the global economy has never experienced a more intense period of creative destruction than the one it's going through right now, driven almost entirely by digital transformation. Digital technologies are opening up creative opportunities for innovative, forward-looking businesses, even as they're literally destroying businesses that have failed to innovate or even just failed to innovate fast enough. Most importantly for the security decision makers reading this book, digital technologies have made enterprises, their operations, and their processes more vulnerable than ever before. This vulnerability and fragility was made painfully clearer by an event that was literally unprecedented in living memory, one we'll discuss in detail later in this chapter: the COVID-19 pandemic.

The penetration of digital technologies into our professional and personal lives is now so complete that most of us take it for granted. And all too often, that means we don't recognize the radical changes it's brought about, the dramatic impacts it's having on our professional lives, and above all, how dependent we are on all those technologies. Without that recognition, we can't adequately protect against, or even identify, the constantly growing risks that digitalization introduces. This of course also now extends beyond the enterprise to third parties.

> In a world transformed by digital technologies, security risk management must change dramatically to keep pace with constant digital-driven changes to the enterprise environment.

Cybersecurity Is Fundamentally a Risk Practice

In this complex, fast-changing, intricately interconnected world, there's no such thing as a zero-risk environment. From the very beginnings of civilization, ships sank, crops failed, caravans on the Silk Road linking Europe and Asia—an early example of what we've come to call the supply chain—were attacked by bandits. Enterprises have *always* needed to take on risks in order to adapt, innovate, compete, and survive. Every aspect of business, in one way or another, involves risk management. (That, too, has always been true. Merchants in ancient Egypt were taking out insurance on their shipments more than three thousand years ago.) Here's a more current example: a CFO's budget decisions represent a process of risk management, as she decides how to apportion resources to manufacturing, research and development, marketing, stock buybacks, and, of course, security. Every dollar, euro, rupee, or yen allocated to one area has to be taken away from some other area, and the CFO has to walk a fine line between costs on the one hand and risks on the other.

> There is no such thing as a zero-risk environment. The role of a cybersecurity risk management program is to help enterprise decision makers understand the risks they face—and guide them through a risk-informed decision-making process.

This is as true for the security professional as it is for the CFO. Security professionals, whatever their role, whatever their position in the enterprise, shouldn't be trying to eliminate all risk—not only because it can't be done, but because it's an unconstructive waste of their valuable time and resources. (This is a concept that most people understand intuitively, because we all make risk-based decisions constantly in our daily lives. One simple example: someone who's late for a business meeting may have to balance the risk of a speeding ticket against the reward of a new client.) Instead, they should be working with key enterprise stakeholders to define the right balance between risk and reward, establish acceptable levels of risk, and develop appropriate security and risk management measures.

A security professional is by definition a risk management professional.

Security practitioners have always practiced risk management, of course. But they've tended to approach risk management on an ad hoc basis, addressing risks and threats and vulnerabilities when and if they emerge and are identified. That's natural, because risks have always been difficult to predict and prepare for, but it's no longer an adequate approach in a world turned upside down and inside out by digitalization. Many security professionals already recognize this and are working to mature their practices, but a tremendous amount of work still remains to be done. We believe that security and risk management as professional disciplines need to mature significantly, and that a security organization can only achieve this by putting formalized security risk management programs in place.

Security has to mature to address the necessary speed of emerging risks and to meet changing enterprise needs—and this can only be accomplished through a comprehensive cyber risk management program.

This represents a set of fundamental changes in the way security works, and there's no question that addressing them will be challenging for many security professionals. Change is always difficult, and changes as radical as those brought about by digital transformation are certain to be especially difficult. It's important that the security professionals reading this book recognize that new risk-based security approaches driven by digital transformation don't just present challenges. They also mean new opportunities for professional and personal engagement and development.

Security professionals who view their role as working with key stakeholders to identify and achieve the right balance of risk and reward won't simply be helping to protect the enterprise better—although they'll definitely be doing that. They'll also be helping to ensure that those stakeholders view them as peers and fellow strategic decision makers, not simply technical personnel installing antivirus software or implementing VPNs. In short, this means that security should have a seat at the table where the important decisions are made. But getting there won't necessarily be easy. It will require that security professionals build on and augment their already extensive technology skill sets. They'll likely also need to develop skills in areas that haven't historically been considered "security" or "technology"—for example, learning how to communicate with business leaders in terms they'll understand and find accessible. And that will require that they cultivate a richer, more nuanced understanding of the changes that are reshaping the world, the enterprise, and the mature discipline of risk management.

Cyber Risk Management Oversight and Accountability

> *Clearly, the thing that's transforming is not the technology—it's the technology that is transforming you.*
>
> —Jeanne W. Ross, MIT Sloan Center for Information Systems Research

> *In today's era of volatility, there is no other way but to re-invent. The only sustainable advantage you can have over others is agility, that's it. Because nothing else is sustainable, everything else you create, somebody else will replicate.*
>
> —Jeff Bezos, "Digital Transformation and Becoming an Agile Business"

The practice and oversight of managing these risks has captured the attention of regulators and the courts.

A new set of rules released by the SEC, for example, requires that public companies report material cybersecurity incidents within a set period, and report on their cybersecurity governance, risk management, and strategies. Digital transformation makes every "malicious" event a cyber event, meaning cyber is central to every aspect of enterprise security and enterprise-wide business risk decision making. Industry regulators are also increasingly focused on cyber risk management and oversight of their programs.

As we'll discuss in detail in Chapter 2, courts have also been narrowing their focus on who has responsibility for establishing enterprises' efforts to manage these risks—not necessarily the day-to-day decisions, but the actual risk programs. Boards of directors and corporate officers, including the CISO, are experiencing a new responsibility they need to execute that is in addition to their expected responsible tactical execution: cyber risk management.

The "why now" question is also driven by these oversight responsibilities. A cyber risk management program can assist in helping to provide a more defensible program, based on existing standards, prior case law, and guidance provided by board-level education providers, specifically the National Association of Corporate Directors (NACD) and the WEF.

Digital Transformation and Maturing the Cyber Risk Management Program

In recent years, we've seen an astonishing increase in cyberattacks—in their volume, severity, and sophistication. There are plenty of reasons including a few listed here: a dramatic increase in remote work, increased exposure due to the use of employee-owned devices, and growing reliance on the IoT. And the impact is being felt. A study released in November 2021 (*https://oreil.ly/NFg6f*) showed that 81% of global organizations had experienced increased cyberthreats and had suffered downtime due to cybersecurity risks (McAfee Enterprise and FireEye). And the worldwide revenue from cybercrime for 2022 has been estimated (*https://oreil.ly/9mt57*) at a staggering *$8.4 trillion.*

The ever-increasing pace of the creation of new technologies presents enterprises with an equally fast-changing set of risks. This clearly shows that cybersecurity as a function and a discipline has moved far beyond simply protecting systems and data, and that it's not just the security organization's problem anymore.

Cybersecurity Isn't Just a "Security" Concern

While cybersecurity is obviously a major focus for enterprise security professionals, it impacts an enormous range of enterprise roles and functions, because cyber risks impact all those functions. That's why we hope this book will be read by, and will influence, not just security professionals, but also many other enterprise decision makers. Let's take a look at some of those individuals, and talk about why they need to take action to address cybersecurity issues (see Table 1-1).

Table 1-1. The position-specific benefits of a cyber risk management program

Position	Risk-related roles and responsibilities	Cyber risk management program benefits
Director (board member)	Produces oversight of corporate practices and ensures independence.	A defendable system in place for exercising cyber risk management oversight obligations with an understanding of business-critical risks.
Corporate officer (CxO)	Provides oversight and informs the board of critical risks that may be material to the enterprise. Reviews and approves recommended mitigation plans.	Properly informed of risks with the data and insights available to maintain relevance and competitiveness in the market, provides strategic guidance throughout the business on proper execution to a defined tolerance.
Business unit leader	Provides insight into risks specific to business units and corporate functions.	Delivers access to risk information relevant to business unit decision making.
Chief information security officer	Makes it possible to monitor the risk environment, guide the business in establishing acceptable risk levels, and ensure alignment with established mitigation strategies.	Offers an ongoing budget business case with alignment to the enterprise's risk appetite.
Compliance or risk manager	Offers frontline risk identification and mitigation recommendations.	Acts as an established channel for escalation and business visibility.
General counsel/legal	Guides the organization's legal strategy and approach to cybersecurity (reviewing regulatory requirements, managing legal risks related to cybersecurity, and overseeing the organization's response to any cybersecurity incidents from a legal perspective).	Provides the legal team with a clear understanding of the organization's cyber risk posture, enabling them to be proactively informed and address potential legal issues. This clarity allows them to provide more accurate and informed legal advice.
Cyber function owner or practitioners	Provides risk information from their specific security risk areas that can be aggregated. Executes the agreed-on mitigation strategy and tracks performance against it.	Aligns organizational goals with daily tactical operations (giving greater purpose to the role).
Auditor	Independently tests the design and operation of the cyber risk management program.	Clearly defined program with a design that can be assessed.

Cybersecurity is also a broader concern, involving entire enterprises, industries, and the organizations that represent them. Here are some of the most critical (see Table 1-2).

Table 1-2. Cyber risk management program needs by industry sector

Sector[a]	Illustrative examples of technology adoption	Examples of what's at stake
Energy production and distribution	IT and operational technology (OT) assets are connected to the internet to improve productivity and operational efficiency.	Everything. All other sectors depend on a stable energy supply. Without it, the economy can't function and people's health and welfare are threatened.

Sector[a]	Illustrative examples of technology adoption	Examples of what's at stake
Financial services	Digital technologies including blockchain, robotics, and artificial intelligence (AI) / machine learning (ML) are streamlining the financial system in an attempt to provide better service.	Society can't function without overall confidence in capital markets and the ability to store and transfer monetary value.
Transportation and logistics[b]	Next-generation communications technology, such as connected vehicles that exchange information in real time with nearby vehicles and infrastructure, are designed to make travel safer, more efficient, and less environmentally destructive.	Unauthorized access to vehicle systems could result in loss of drivers' personal data or manipulate vehicle functionality, causing accidents or death.
Industrial	Digital solutions including automation, AI, 3D manufacturing (additive manufacturing), and other technologies are driving efficiency, scale, and faster time to market.	Legal, safety, and environmental responsibility for these technologies are still evolving, and internet hackers have easier access to manufacturing blueprints more so than ever before, increasing attack surface exposure and potential for loss.
Healthcare	Cognitive systems generating insights across connected environments, wearable sensors, and robotic surgical processes are advancing and centralizing a once decentralized industry, helping to improve care and control costs.	Breach of protected health information and even disruption to critical health services provided due to targeted attacks from advanced adversaries (e.g., cyber criminals performing ransomware).
Education	Knowledge and information can be shared instantly and made available at scale, enabling educational institutions to reach wider populations.	Increased risk or lack of privacy along with misinformation spreading and being consumed at greater speeds.
Public sector	Rapid collection and analysis of data, increasing the participation of citizens and providing better services.	The overall complexity of the threat landscape as a result of technological advancement will test governments across the world where there is an increasing lack of skills and capacity to tackle the challenges effectively.
Communication	5G, AI/ML, IoT, and resulting data-driven insights are transforming the customer's experience and driving higher expectations for services (including speed, connectivity, and resilience).	Enabling billions of connected devices has increased the attack surface, making it possible for larger and more dangerous attacks.
Chemical	An increasingly complex global supply chain enables the conversion of raw materials sourced worldwide into more than 70,000 diverse products essential to modern life.	Chemicals must be secured against a growing and evolving set of threats, both because they're potentially dangerous and because other critical infrastructure relies on them.

[a] "Critical Infrastructure Sectors," (*https://oreil.ly/H0DVp*) CISA, accessed October 10, 2023.
[b] "How the U.S. Department of Transportation Is Protecting the Connected Transportation System from Cyber Threats," (*https://oreil.ly/1CJUg*) US Department of Transportation, accessed October 10, 2023.

Cyber Risk Management Program: An Urgent Enterprise Concern

The purpose of a security risk management program is to help guide the enterprise, its leaders (at the highest levels), and other key stakeholders in the security risk decision-making process. *Security does not make the decisions, but it informs them with its expertise and experience.* The result, ideally, is a set of risk-informed decisions that thoughtfully balance risk and reward.

> An enterprise security risk program is an essential prerequisite for success in the digital world.

The entire enterprise—the security organization, lines of business, and individual contributors—need to take part in the process of continuously maturing this security risk program. Why? Because the effort has to be strategic, not tactical. This is an important consideration for the success of the program, but also for the professional and personal development of the security professionals involved. Everyone wants a seat at the table, everyone wants to be involved in important decisions. Executives put strategic folks around the table; individuals who are seen as tactically oriented rarely are offered that seat.

That perception—that security is essentially a tactical function or, worse, merely a cost center—is one of the most significant problems the discipline faces. It will not be easy to overcome this perception, and it will take time, but it can and must be done. The key is practicing strategic risk management programmatically, and being seen to do so, on an ongoing basis.

We've developed a framework for establishing a cyber risk management program (CRMP) (*http://www.crmp.info*), mapping it against core elements of globally established and accepted risk standards, established regulations, and opinions from case laws that are starting to hold executives and boards accountable for risk oversight. The framework identifies four core components and supporting principles to help guide a security or risk practitioner, auditor, or regulator through what a CRMP is and which components should be considered for adoptions. The application is adaptable and flexible for all sizes or maturity levels of organizations. Any program needs some structure to help with stability and consistency. We've found through our research that all risk management programs are consistent in their approach. They use different words and processes to describe them, but the fundamentals are, well, fundamental to the program.

A CRMP has four essential components, which are defined by international standards bodies, court decisions, regulatory frameworks, and accepted board-level principles:

- Chapter 3, "Agile Governance"
- Chapter 4, "Risk-Informed System"
- Chapter 5, "Risk-Based Strategy and Execution"
- Chapter 6, "Risk Escalation and Disclosure"

Within the framework (*http://www.crmp.info*) you'll find the principles and a set of informative references that support each component and principle.

This Book's Roadmap

The journey we're going to take in this book will be primarily to talk about how to define and develop a cyber risk management program, and to consider its value. We'll establish what exactly makes up the program in Chapter 2. We'll define and cover in detail the four core components and the guiding principles in Chapters 3–6. In Chapter 7, we'll be offering guidance on implementing a program that has an appropriate starting point and that aligns with the enterprise's state of maturity, operating environment, and industry-specific requirements. We'll talk about the ways a program can contribute to organizational resilience by coordinating with other operational risk practices (e.g., physical, supply chain and third-party security, business continuity management, and disaster recovery) to develop a holistic enterprise risk posture in Chapter 8. We'll close this out in Chapter 9 with a look into emerging technologies and how risk management will continue to be the leading practice; we'll also go a bit deeper into AI. Not all examples in the book relate to pure cyber; some examples are very relevant to risk management in any form.

The Bottom Line

Throughout this first chapter, we've been discussing the radical changes—transformative, disruptive, exciting, and challenging all at once—that are reshaping the enterprise risk environment. In the next chapter, we'll go into much deeper detail about why enterprises need—and, in many cases, are legally required—to establish a formal, systematic cyber risk management program that can be clearly defined and defended, and that can stand alone and provide urgently needed strategic guidance in a world utterly transformed by digital technologies.

CHAPTER 2

The Cyber Risk Management Program

In the last chapter, we discussed many of the factors—social, political, economic, and especially technological—that are driving constant and accelerating change in the risk environment. In this chapter, we're going to describe in detail the cyber risk management program (CRMP). A formal approach, represented by a clearly defined and established program, is the only way enterprises can hope to address the speed and criticality of the risks they face, and do it with the consistent and trusted outputs they need.

Regulatory bodies worldwide are making it increasingly clear that they will no longer accept a lax or nonexistent cyber risk management program.

The SEC Speaks—and the World Listens

One regulatory announcement in particular sent shock waves through the business world on July 26, 2023: the Securities and Exchange Commission (SEC) introduced a new set of rules concerning disclosures related to reporting major cyber incidents, cybersecurity risk management, strategy, and governance. The new rules, which are designed to standardize and improve companies' disclosure practices, apply to all public companies operating in the US, and to many smaller and foreign companies. The SEC is highly influential in the development and adoption of regulatory standards worldwide, because regulators in other countries and jurisdictions often follow its lead, meaning enterprise risk stakeholders everywhere should be aware of its new rules and their likely impact.

The SEC took this step to ensure individuals and enterprises have "more consistent, comparable and decision-useful information"[1] when making investment decisions. In its simplest terms, this is "materially relevant" information. The SEC's longstanding definition of material information is "information [pertaining to] those matters to which an average prudent investor ought reasonably to be informed before purchasing the security registered."[2] This is a well-established principle, and the new rules don't change it. Instead, they make it clear that materiality extends to cyberspace, because, as the SEC stated in its announcement, "an ever-increasing share of economic activity is dependent on electronic systems, such that disruptions to those systems can have significant effects on [companies] and, in the case of large-scale attacks, systemic effects on the economy as a whole."[3] The SEC went on to state that "evidence suggests companies may be underreporting cybersecurity incidents" and that "investors need more timely and consistent cybersecurity disclosure to make informed investment decisions."[4]

The new SEC rules cover two basic types of disclosure, which we'll discuss in the following sections.

Incident Disclosure ("Current Disclosures")

The SEC has made fundamental changes in the requirements for disclosing security incidents including cyberattacks, data breaches, and other failures. This includes the following:

- The definition of a "cybersecurity incident" has been significantly expanded to include "a series of related unauthorized occurrences." This reflects the reality that cyberattacks and other security failures don't necessarily happen in isolation and can take place over an extended period.

- The information required in cybersecurity incident disclosure is now spelled out more clearly to include: when the incident was discovered and whether it's ongoing; a brief description of the nature and scope of the incident; whether any data was stolen, altered, or otherwise accessed or used for unauthorized purposes; and the incident's effects on the company's operations.

---

1 Gerbrand Haverkamp, Letter to Gary Gensler, (*https://oreil.ly/jtaVg*) May 19, 2022, World Benchmarking Alliance.

2 Roberta S. Karmel, "Speech to the National Investor Relations Institute, New York Chapter, New York, New York, April 2, 1978," (*https://oreil.ly/vaNa7*) SEC, April 26, 1978.

3 SEC, "Cybersecurity Risk Management, Strategy, Governance, and Incident Disclosure," (*https://oreil.ly/M2bb0*) September 5, 2023.

4 SEC, "Cybersecurity Risk Management, Strategy, Governance, and Incident Disclosure."

- Companies covered by the rules are now required to disclose a material cybersecurity incident within four business days of their having determined that the incident is material. (There are certain exceptions based on a federal government determination that disclosure may harm national security or public safety.) The SEC also states that companies must make their materiality decisions "without unreasonable delay."

- Incident disclosures should focus primarily on the material impacts of an incident—that is, any damage it may have caused—rather than on the details of the incident itself. The SEC specifies that companies should consider qualitative factors, like reputational damage and loss of customer or partner trust, not just quantitative ones, in determining materiality. Once again, the key criterion is whether or not the information would affect an investor's decision making.

Risk Management, Strategy, and Governance Disclosures ("Periodic Disclosures")

We believe disclosures regarding a company's cybersecurity risk management program and how the board of directors engages with management on cybersecurity issues allow investors to assess how a board of directors is discharging its risk oversight responsibility in this increasingly important area.

—SEC, "Commission Statement and Guidance on Public Company Cybersecurity Disclosures," 2018

The new SEC rules cover far more than incidents alone, taking into account the entire range of a company's cybersecurity practices. Here are the key changes in these areas:

- Companies are required to make periodic disclosures of the processes they have in place for assessing, identifying, and managing cybersecurity risks. This includes whether and how cybersecurity processes are integrated into a company's overall risk management practices; whether consultants, auditors, or other third parties are involved; and whether processes are in place to identify materially relevant third-party risks.

- Companies must disclose the board of directors' role in overseeing risks from cybersecurity threats, and specifically any board member or committee that oversees these risks. (Note: The SEC did not adopt a proposal to require disclosure of board members' cybersecurity expertise, taking the view that cybersecurity processes are more likely to be handled effectively at the management level.)

- Management's role in assessing and managing material risks from cybersecurity threats is also required.

The implications of the new SEC rules, and related announcements from other regulatory bodies worldwide, are clear: cybersecurity and cyber risk are much too complex, far-reaching, and important to be addressed on an ad hoc, improvisational, and incident-focused basis. These issues require a formal, systematic approach that takes into account not only cybersecurity but also the overall management of cyber risk and its enterprise-wide impacts. And that can only happen in the context of a CRMP.

The Cyber Risk Management Program Framework

In 2018, the SEC provided guidance to public companies on cybersecurity risk disclosures, including comments on the expected oversight from boards and corporate officers regarding how a company manages its cyber risks. The statement from the SEC underscores the critical importance of public companies taking proactive measures to inform investors promptly about cybersecurity risks and incidents. This includes the specific mention of the board's role in fulfilling their oversight obligation through a cybersecurity risk management program.

The statement from the SEC begs a follow-up question: "what is a cybersecurity risk management program?" This next section is designed to holistically define and establish a CRMP. Authorities and regulatory bodies have highlighted the pressing need for organizations to ensure effective communication to stakeholders about cyber risks. Boards and executives must be able to provide proper oversight of their cyber risk environment through a programmatic approach. Many existing standards and references, when viewed in isolation, may fall short of what's required for a comprehensive program that truly serves the business. This gap underscores the critical need for a unified framework that harmonizes and interprets the authoritative guidance, regulations, and standards to ensure businesses can properly manage and oversee their cyber risks.

The CRMP framework synthesizes insights from leading practices and standards, providing a structured and comprehensive approach to cyber risk management. The framework can be tailored to the unique needs and regulatory landscape of the individual enterprise. It serves as a guide for enterprises to operationalize their own CRMP in order to make informed risk decisions and evolve their security strategies to ensure they thrive in the digital age.

The CRMP framework is organized into four core components (see Table 2-1): Agile governance, risk-informed system, risk-based strategy and execution, and risk escalation and disclosure.

Each of these components is further broken down into multiple supporting principles, providing considerations for implementation. In each of the following four chapters, we'll be taking a deep dive into each of these components and the corresponding principles and relevant informative references. For a comprehensive view of the framework, see the Appendix. The CRMP framework is also available online (*http://www.crmp.info*).

Table 2-1. CRMP framework

CRMP component	Principles	Informative references
Agile governance	See "Seven Principles of Agile Governance" on page 49.	• SEC Final Cyber Rule (*https://oreil.ly/o2TGU*) • NIST CSF 2.0 (*https://oreil.ly/xngbU*) • 2023 NACD Director's Handbook (*https://oreil.ly/8enA4*) • ISO 27001:2022 (*https://oreil.ly/0ID28*) • NIST 8286 (*https://oreil.ly/WOC5f*) • IIA Three Lines Model (*https://oreil.ly/00AQ6*) • SEC 2018 Guidance (*https://oreil.ly/SVwOx*) • ISO 31000:2018 (*https://oreil.ly/vuqzY*) • AICPA CRMP (*https://oreil.ly/d5n8o*)
Risk-informed system	See "Five Principles of a Risk-Informed System" on page 66.	• SEC Final Cyber Rule (*https://oreil.ly/o2TGU*) • NIST CSF 2.0 (*https://oreil.ly/xngbU*) • 2023 NACD Director's Handbook (*https://oreil.ly/8enA4*) • ISO 27001:2022 (*https://oreil.ly/0ID28*) • IIA Three Lines Model (*https://oreil.ly/00AQ6*) • ISO 31000:2018 (*https://oreil.ly/vuqzY*) • AICPA CRMP (*https://oreil.ly/d5n8o*)
Risk-based strategy and execution	See "Six Principles of Risk-Based Strategy and Execution" on page 88.	• SEC Final Cyber Rule (*https://oreil.ly/o2TGU*) • NIST CSF 2.0 (*https://oreil.ly/xngbU*) • 2023 NACD Director's Handbook (*https://oreil.ly/8enA4*) • IIA Three Lines Model (*https://oreil.ly/00AQ6*) • ISO 31000:2018 (*https://oreil.ly/vuqzY*) • AICPA CRMP (*https://oreil.ly/d5n8o*)
Risk escalation and disclosure	See "Five Principles of Risk Escalation and Disclosure" on page 114.	• SEC Final Cyber Rule (*https://oreil.ly/o2TGU*) • NIST CSF 2.0 (*https://oreil.ly/xngbU*) • 2023 NACD Director's Handbook (*https://oreil.ly/8enA4*) • IIA Three Lines Model (*https://oreil.ly/00AQ6*) • SEC 2018 Guidance (*https://oreil.ly/SVwOx*) • AICPA CRMP (*https://oreil.ly/d5n8o*)

Many security and risk professionals believe they already have a security risk management program in place, and it's probably true that at least some of the necessary *components* of a program are already there. These may include a governance model, a risk register, and a set of mitigation efforts. Those mitigation efforts might cover anything from multifactor authentication (MFA) for employees and contractors to penetration (pen) testing for IT vulnerabilities to standards and practices for physical security at enterprise facilities. But in reality, these are simply tools, technologies, techniques, and processes—all useful and necessary, but inadequate if they're not brought together in a formalized standalone program to execute a true risk management practice.

Cyber Risk Management Program: Key Drivers

It's important to recognize that these four components aren't abstract concepts or arbitrary areas of focus. In fact, every one of them is critical—and in many cases *required*—by a complex and fast-growing set of legal, regulatory, political, and environmental factors that enterprise decision makers can't afford to ignore. Let's take a look at the most important of these drivers:

Regulatory compliance frameworks

Governments worldwide—at the regional, national, state, and sometimes even local levels—have established sets of regulations covering risk areas ranging beyond good cyber hygiene and focusing more on risk oversight and the formalized processes designed to manage risks. And the government agencies and other bodies set up to enforce those regulations have shown that they're increasingly willing to take serious action to ensure compliance—and to punish failure to comply, by both enterprises and responsible individuals. One important example is the SEC, which has authority over all publicly traded companies with operations in the US. The failure to follow SEC guidance (for example, in accurately reporting materially relevant financial information) can have serious consequences for a company's decision makers at the very highest levels—all the way up to boards of directors, but also including senior corporate officers, including the CISOs. See Table 2-2 for the three major cybersecurity frameworks.

Legal liability

In recent years, a series of high-profile court rulings—several of which we discuss in this chapter—have clarified the security risk practices that are required of enterprises and the people who run them. They aren't demanding perfection, but they are making it clear that they expect good-faith efforts in assessing, managing, and reporting security risks. They're also making it clear that they're prepared to hold accountable entities and individuals that don't act in good faith, with civil penalties like fines and civil judgments, and even prison time.

Influential authorities providing guidance on cyber risks to board and executive-level audiences

Many nongovernmental authorities—some focusing on specific industries, others on particular regions, and still others with worldwide scope—offer enterprises practical guidance for addressing cyber risk issues. An example for directors of publicly traded companies in the US is the National Association of Corporate Directors (NACD), which has published various versions of its "Cyber-Risk Oversight Handbook," and the World Economic Forum's international guidance.

Industry-recognized standard and framework organizations

Several cybersecurity frameworks have been developed to help organizations establish and report on the effectiveness of their cybersecurity programs, including the Cybersecurity Framework (CSF) of the National Institute of Standards and Technology (NIST), ISO 27001/2 from the International Organization for Standardization (ISO), and the American Institute of Certified Public Accountants (AICPA) Cybersecurity Risk Management Reporting Framework. NIST CSF 2.0 is planning an early 2024 release that will extend beyond technical security controls to include more guidance on strategic risk governance and risk management practices. Some industry frameworks apply broadly to virtually any enterprise, while others are specific to a particular industry or a particular region.

Table 2-2. Major cybersecurity frameworks

Organization	Framework	Description
NIST	NIST CSF 2.0 (planned release early 2024)	The NIST CSF 2.0 provides guidance to industry, government agencies, and other organizations to reduce cybersecurity risks. It offers a taxonomy of high-level cybersecurity outcomes that can be used by any organization—regardless of its size, sector, or maturity—to better understand, assess, prioritize, and communicate its cybersecurity efforts.[a]
ISO	ISO/IEC 27001:2022	ISO/IEC 27001 is the world's best-known standard for information security management systems (ISMS). It defines the requirements an ISMS must meet. The ISO/IEC 27001 standard provides companies of any size and from all sectors of activity with guidance for establishing, implementing, maintaining, and continually improving an information security management system. Conformity with ISO/IEC 27001 means that an organization or business has put in place a system to manage risks related to the security of data owned or handled by the company.[b]
AICPA	Cybersecurity Risk Management Reporting Framework	The AICPA has developed a cybersecurity risk management reporting framework that assists organizations as they communicate relevant and useful information about the effectiveness of their cybersecurity risk management programs. The framework is a key component of a new System and Organization Controls (SOC) for Cybersecurity engagement, through which a CPA reports on an organization's enterprise-wide cybersecurity risk management program.[c]

[a] "The NIST Cybersecurity Framework 2.0," (*https://oreil.ly/Uq1rp*) NIST, August 8, 2023.
[b] "ISO/IEC 27001 Information Security Management Systems," (*http://iso.org/standard/27001*) ISO, October 2022.
[c] "SOC for Cybersecurity," (*https://oreil.ly/tPczC*) AICPA & CIMA, accessed October 10, 2023.

A comprehensive risk management program is driven by a broad array of laws, regulatory compliance requirements, and industry protocols, which must be integrated into the design and execution of the program.

Satisfying Obligations and Liability

Enterprise decision makers can adapt these four key components of the CRMP to their specific environments and requirements (see the Appendix). Throughout this book, we look at these drivers as well as their relevance to, and impact on, specific areas of security and risk—including cybersecurity—and we show you how specific drivers align with the requirements of your role, your enterprise, and your industry. But for now, let's consider a few of the most important drivers and how they relate specifically to the four program components:

Agile governance
> One of the most urgent drivers of governance is the SEC's guidance, which is backed up by a long series of important and binding court decisions at the highest levels. Failure to follow SEC guidance can have serious consequences for a company's decision makers at the very highest levels, including corporate officers and boards of directors.

A risk-informed system
> A series of court cases, which will be covered later in this chapter, have established that in order for a board of directors to be acting in good faith and avoid personal liability, they need to have a risk-informed system in place and it must apply to everything mission critical.

Risk-based strategy and execution
> Risk always has a dollars-and-cents impact, of course, and that makes it a key concern for CFOs and others responsible for an enterprise's fiscal well-being. Regulators and courts often point to the need for organizations to understand their risk environment and make decisions that define their appropriate appetite and tolerance before they define what adequate resources are necessary to execute to that appetite and tolerance.

Risk escalation and disclosure
> As you'll see from real-world examples later in this chapter, the courts have made it absolutely clear that when things go wrong, or can reasonably be expected to go wrong, the right people—inside and outside the enterprise—*must* be informed. An unmistakable sign of the importance of this issue is that bodies (including the AICPA, NIST, and SEC) have *all* provided risk escalation and disclosure guidance.

It's worth noting that these drivers, and the guidance developed to address them, shouldn't be seen as exclusively, or even primarily, threats, challenges, or problems. This isn't intended to align drivers on a one-to-one basis but to explore how the totality of the drivers are necessitating a holistic and coordinated CRMP to resolve these drivers. It may seem that we're talking here only about the adverse consequences of failing to do what needs to be done, and that's obviously important. But the regulatory, legal, and industry guidance available to security and risk practitioners also offers valuable protections to everyone involved in risk decision making, if the applicable advice is followed—and, crucially, *shown* to be followed.

Risk Accountability and Liability: An International Phenomenon

The growing calls for responsibility, accountability, and liability at the highest levels aren't limited to the US. This is an international phenomenon, because digitalization has made almost every enterprise an international enterprise. For example, the World Economic Forum (WEF), an organization that promotes public/private cooperation worldwide, has been working on cybersecurity issues for more than ten years. In 2017, the WEF, together with the Boston Consulting Group and Hewlett Packard Enterprise, published *Advancing Cyber Resilience Principles and Tools for Boards* (*https://oreil.ly/M0LCb*), a practical framework for boards of directors working to address cyber issues. The document makes clear just how high the stakes are: "Cyber resilience and cyber risk management are critical challenges for most organizations today. Leaders increasingly recognize that the profound reputational and existential nature of these risks mean that responsibility for managing them sits at the board and top level executive teams."

There are many frameworks and standards created by various national and international entities, far too many to discuss in detail here. There are, of course, many variations between them, reflecting regional, jurisdictional, and other differences, and there are still many remaining gaps in them. Nonetheless, they collectively show the most urgent cyber risk management components and issues.

When Risk Management Fails Completely: The Boeing 737 MAX Disasters

The fundamental premise of this book is that a formal cybersecurity risk management program—with the four components we've defined, and based on established regulations, standards, and protocols—is essential in the digital world. And the best way for us to make this clear is to show what happens when this *doesn't* happen. We've chosen to focus on a catastrophic failure at one of the world's largest, most important, and, until recently, one of the most respected multinational corporations: Boeing. This isn't a cybersecurity example, but it shows how digitalization changes risks within an enterprise. More importantly, it can provide learning opportunities to any risk program, including a CRMP.

On October 29, 2018, a Boeing 737 MAX—introduced to the manufacturer's line only the previous year—crashed minutes after takeoff from Djakarta, Indonesia, and all

189 people on board were killed. Less than six months later, another 737 MAX crashed under disturbingly similar circumstances in Ethiopia, with 157 deaths.

An urgent series of investigations by regulators worldwide showed that both crashes were caused by the failure of a critical digital component of the plane's flight control system—and, crucially, by Boeing's failure to manage risk appropriately, which allowed key decision makers at the company to carry out what the US government alleged was a long-running criminal fraud.

The fallout for Boeing was brutal. It goes without saying that the loss of 346 lives is horrific under any circumstances. Additionally, the business impact on Boeing was disastrous. Airlines worldwide grounded their 737 MAX fleets, and other carriers canceled orders for the aircraft. The US Federal Aviation Administration (FAA), after initially resisting calls to ground the plane worldwide, finally caved in March 2019, and no 737 MAXes flew from then until November 2020. The damage to Boeing's once-stellar reputation was staggering. Some online trip planners gave travelers the option to avoid flying on the 737 MAX. Boeing was even reported to be considering discontinuing its iconic 7 series brand, which dated back to the introduction of the 707—the aircraft credited with beginning the age of air travel in the late 1950s.

The monetary costs to the company have been enormous, and not just in terms of lost business: they'll keep mounting for years to come. As of January 2023, Boeing had paid out more than $500 million to the families of the crash victims and $1.7 billion more to airlines for lost compensation. But the financial damage to the company didn't end there. Boeing was actually charged with fraud for its representations to regulators and others, and the company avoided *criminal* prosecution only by agreeing to pay a fine of more than *$2.5 billion* (*https://oreil.ly/dYkzy*). When the dust finally settles on all the court cases and regulatory actions, the cost to Boeing is likely to be $20 billion or more—a stunning blow for any company, even one as deep-pocketed as Boeing. The company's pattern of dishonesty clearly contributed to that cost:

> The misleading statements, half-truths, and omissions communicated by Boeing employees to the FAA impeded the government's ability to ensure the safety of the flying public.
>
> —US Attorney Erin Nealy Cox[5]

Boeing's troubles began with a basic design flaw: the failure of a digital sensor and its associated software to help correct flight irregularities from engineering changes. The placement of the 737 MAX's engines tended to make the aircraft unbalanced and unstable, and technology designed to correct the problem—digitalization of the airplane—showed a troubling likelihood to send the plane into a sudden nosedive.

---

5 "Boeing Charged with 737 Max Fraud Conspiracy and Agrees to Pay over $2.5 Billion," Office of Public Affairs, US Department of Justice, January 7, 2021.

People throughout Boeing, at all levels, were aware of the problem, and aware that it could be disastrous. Some raised the issue with their management, but some tried to ignore it. And others actively worked to conceal the truth from regulatory bodies like the FAA, from the carriers buying the planes, and even from the pilots flying them, to the point of deleting critical information about the flawed system from training manuals.

Even with a risk management system in place, there is no guarantee that Boeing would have recognized and acknowledged the problems or taken the steps necessary to fix them. It's possible that the company's senior management, if properly informed, would have decided that the cost of the required rework—which would certainly have run to millions of dollars, and possibly hundreds of millions—made the risk worth taking, but in hindsight that seems highly unlikely. And even if they had made a risk-informed decision to keep the 737 MAX in the air, and the first crash happened, established lines of responsibility and accountability would have been in place that would likely have discovered the problem rapidly, possibly preventing the second crash. In any case, the company, and the many employees involved in the design and manufacture of the 737 MAX, would have had at least some protection from legal and regulatory liability. This is because they would have been able to point to their efforts to properly identify, escalate, and manage these critical risks—even if those efforts failed.

Risk Management Program Applied to the Boeing Disasters

Let's examine the Boeing disasters through the lens of the four risk management program components:

Agile governance
> Any enterprise needs to have a structure in place to provide overall risk governance over a risk management program, including the scope, depth, and expectations of that program, with clearly identified roles and well-established authority and accountability. And that structure needs to be responsive and adaptable to changing circumstances. The entire Boeing catastrophe might have been prevented if a governance body had stepped in early in the design and manufacturing process and determined that the risk associated with the flight management system was unacceptable. And as the problems mounted and the risks became clearer (especially after the first crash), it is difficult to imagine that an agile, fast-moving governance body wouldn't have taken far more serious action than Boeing ultimately did in order to prevent the *second* crash. Governance essentially defines culture: what the enterprise values and what its priorities are. It's worth noting that the 737 MAX investigation showed that some of the 737 MAX's designers and engineers felt that Boeing's corporate culture had changed,

especially following the company's 1997 merger with McDonnell Douglas, resulting in profits being favored over safety.

> It would be fair to assume that a good program would have at least grounded the 737 MAX after the first crash and saved the lives of the 157 people who died in the second one.

A risk-informed system

This means a systematic, enterprise-wide approach to the identification, acceptance, management, and mitigation of risk—*all* risks, of all types—across the entire enterprise and in an increasingly complicated, digitally driven environment. Remember, there's no such thing as a zero-risk environment, and it's pointless and sometimes even counterproductive to try to achieve that objective. All enterprises accept some risk, and Boeing, operating as it does in one of the world's most intensely competitive industries, is no exception. (It's worth noting that some industries require trying to get as close as possible to zero risk than others—and aviation, because of the lethal consequences of risk failure, is certainly one of them.) One of the risks Boeing faced early on, as the problems with its onboard flight management system began to emerge, was that the necessary fix was likely to be extremely expensive. An added expense of that size would have cut deep into Boeing's profitability, but not nearly as deep as the eventual costs to the company. And it would have helped to protect those decision makers from some of their liability, because Boeing would have been able to show that it had at least made more systematic efforts to take risks into account.

Risk-based strategy and execution

This is defining and executing to a defined appetite and tolerance. Once again, a zero-risk environment is unachievable, and an enterprise-wide strategy informed by risk assessment and acceptance wouldn't necessarily have resulted in Boeing making all the right decisions. But it would almost certainly have prevented at least some of the cascading series of bad decisions Boeing employees at all levels clearly made. A clearly defined risk posture allows an enterprise's employees and internal organizations—design, manufacturing, safety, legal, and so on—to develop and execute a business strategy built around established risk tolerance. Every aspect of a company's operations—from product design to resource allocation to manufacturing to interaction with regulators and more—should be designed around that tolerance.

Risk escalation and disclosure

It's probably in this area that Boeing could have benefited most from a well-functioning risk management program. The investigations into the 737 MAX

---

crash (*https://oreil.ly/Ok7UA*) made it clear that many different people at Boeing, in many different roles and at many different levels, knew about the problems with the aircraft, and knew how serious they were. In the aftermath of a tragedy, it seems almost impossible to believe that anyone would ignore a potentially lethal problem, but the reality is, many did ignore it. And crucially, Boeing seems not to have had a system in place to ensure that risk concerns would be shared with the right person in a formal way—not dependent on personal relationship—with the right level of accountability and proper transparency. Appropriate escalation and disclosure wouldn't have eliminated all the risks associated with the aircraft, but it would likely have saved at least the 157 people who died on the Ethiopian Airlines flight. If Boeing executives, at the most senior levels, had been open and honest after the first crash, the FAA and the world's other regulatory bodies would almost certainly have grounded the 737 MAX, and that flight would never have left the ground.

Boeing's failures were the result of an overreliance on technology, people and departments at Boeing under so much pressure to meet production targets that they cut corners, certain management that looked the other way when problems were identified, or an undefined risk tolerance leading to a corporate culture where people were willing to do anything—even break the law and risk people's lives—so that the company could keep making money.

"Essential and Mission Critical": The Boeing Case

Boeing did not implement or prioritize safety oversight at the highest level of the corporate pyramid. None of Boeing's Board committees were specifically tasked with overseeing airplane safety, and every committee charter was silent as to airplane safety.

—Court of Chancery of the State of Delaware, "In Re the Boeing Co. Derivative Litig"

The impact of Boeing's failure on the company, its employees, its airline customers, and, most importantly, its passengers is obviously important. But the 737 MAX disasters have effects that extend far beyond Boeing and far beyond the aerospace industry. They help to clarify why an effective CRMP is absolutely essential for every enterprise and every industry segment. The most immediate impact is the court decision holding Boeing responsible for its systemic failures—and its reason for doing so.

In a shareholder lawsuit against Boeing, the court held that aircraft safety is "essential and mission critical"[6] to its operations. For this reason, Boeing's board had a responsibility to rigorously exercise its oversight of safety issues. The board didn't have a system in place for monitoring, discussing, or regularly reporting on aircraft safety. (It did have a risk oversight function, but—almost unbelievably—it focused primarily

---

6 *In re* C. A. 2019-0907-MTZ (Del. Ch. Sep. 7, 2021), *https://oreil.ly/gihKl*.

on financial risks.) The directors did receive ad hoc reports from management, but they were not systematic enough or transparent enough to represent a risk-informed process. And even though "red flags" were presented to management, they weren't reported to the board, because of the lack of an appropriate escalation structure.

Why does this finding matter to enterprises beyond the aerospace industry, and what makes it relevant in terms of cyber risk management? It all comes down to that simple yet powerful phrase *essential and mission critical*. As we've already established in the digital world, all risks are digital risks, and all digital risks create cyber risks. The inescapable conclusion is that cyber risks, like any other types of risk, are "essential and mission critical." And that means enterprises, their boards of directors, and their senior executives have the same responsibility, and liability, for cyber risks as for any other critical risks.

Cyber and Digital: The Crucial Difference

When navigating the world of risk management, it's necessary to differentiate between the concepts of the "cyber" environment and "digitalization." It may be useful to think of cyber as a distinct, discrete environment. Just as there are domestic, international, internal, external, and physical environments—among others—there's the cyber environment. It represents a digital realm where electronic data traverses networks and businesses conduct operations like communication, data exchange, and more. Early on, the primary asset thrust into this realm was information. But as technology evolved, so did the types and amounts of assets in the cyber environment. Digitalization defines the process of converting traditional or physical systems, processes, and information into a digital format. The primary goal? Improving performance and efficiencies and broadening the scope of what's possible in business operations and communications. As companies transition from physical paperwork to cloud databases, or from in-person meetings to virtual conferences, they're participating in digitalization. So how do the two connect? Digitalization introduces potential vulnerabilities into the cyber environment. As more and more processes are converted to and support digital formats, the potential attack surface expands dramatically. These vulnerabilities, when matched with the intentions of threat actors, can pose severe risks—these are our cyber risks. They can be exploited to cause significant harm to business, individuals, and broader society, hence the need for a cyber risk management program.

Benefits of a Security Risk Program

A security risk program represents a strategic approach to the risks the enterprise faces. Without a risk management program, security is essentially *seen* as a tactical function. The issue of perception is one of the biggest problems security practitioners face. People have "one-off" interactions with the security organization. For example, an executive is asked to change her password, someone else needs virtual private network (VPN) access to a sensitive application, or a visitor to a facility has to present ID to a security guard. But there is no sense of the reasoning behind those control measures. When people have only occasional interactions with the security organization, they may see "security" as little more than unwanted friction—one more irritating obstacle between them and whatever it is they're trying to get done.

> Security professionals want and need to be recognized as strategic business partners, not just technical personnel. If they're going to get a seat at the table where the important decisions are made, they're going to have to change the perception of what they do and what they're capable of doing.

It's absolutely clear that the expectations of security risk management efforts and outputs need to change. Executives should establish a clear expectation that security will mature its risk function through a formally designed program. It should expect consistent and transparent risk information, so that business leaders—collaborating with security—make risk-informed business decisions. They should expect the security teams to be seen and to interact with the business as strategic business partners. This fundamental change in perception of security will take time to overcome, but it has to happen.

Cyber Risk Management Program: Key Benefits

Implementing a robust cyber risk management program is pivotal in today's digital landscape and offers a multitude of benefits:

Board- and executive-level protections
Senior decision makers have a mandated oversight of cyber risk management activities—with enterprise-wide business engagement—ensuring that they're receiving sufficient and appropriate risk information. That means they can explain and, if necessary, defend the risk function that's been established and the risk decisions that have been made.

A shift in the perception of security as a tactical function to a strategic risk role
Faster decision making and prioritization, enabled by an agile risk operations model, makes it possible for the enterprise's security risk decision to keep pace with an evolving landscape and execute against its overall business strategy and provide a clear strategic advantage over its competitors. The result is that the security and risk organization is engaged with strategic conversations and

---

increasingly seen as a business enabler rather than just a cost center tactical function.

Defendable budgets
> Security risk management based on the established appetite and tolerance and a balance of risk and reward makes it easier to justify the cost of personnel and other resources.

Security practitioner career satisfaction and protection
> An established program gives the CISO or other senior security practitioner a "seat at the table" where decisions are made, and it provides protection against post-incident fallout and unnecessary finger-pointing and blame.

It's worth taking a little time to consider how some of these benefits will be realized in the day-to-day operations of the enterprise as a whole and the security organization in particular.

Benefit 1: Strategic Recognition of the Security Risk Function

One of the most important benefits of a clearly defined security risk program is that it gives the security organization and its activities recognized standing as a critical strategic undertaking.

As we pointed out earlier, a defined CRMP leads to outputs that are consistent, expected, and trusted. Let's take a closer look at what those three words mean and why they're so important:

Consistent
> Consistency is critical to the success of any enterprise program. Risk management is fundamentally concerned with anticipating, managing, and mitigating unexpected events, and that makes consistency in the risk management program itself essential. There will always be improvisational elements to risk management, because new and unanticipated threats and vulnerabilities will always have to be dealt with, but those on-the-fly decisions (large and small) will be simpler, less demanding on your resources, *and* more effective if you have a clearly defined program, with consistent processes and expectations that lead to more reliable outputs.

Expected
> All of the stakeholders in the cybersecurity risk program—from the board of directors to the CxOs to line-of-business leaders—have to be able to expect timely risk information that's appropriate to their specific needs and delivered in a timely fashion. Timeliness may mean, for example, risk information is delivered at the beginning of a software implementation, early in the design process for a new product, and/or as a part of the scheduled quarterly update. But the

stakeholders have a right to expect much more from the program. They should see it as a strategic function, not a tactical one, and certainly not one that's an impediment to their jobs. And they should be fully engaged, for example, at the start of and throughout a new project, so that they can work together with the security organization to guide decision making and find the right balance of risk and reward.

Trusted

The establishment of a clearly defined program means its outputs can be trusted. The risk assessments and operational guidance it provides aren't coming from a single individual on a one-off basis but are based on core risk management practices that have been refined over decades. Stakeholders can trust what they are relying on because it's the result of a program that's been defined, approved, communicated, and, crucially, subject to oversight by a governing body. (We talk much more about the critical importance of governance in Chapter 3.)

When these three key components are in place, their positive impacts begin to be felt throughout the enterprise, and success builds on itself. For example, defining the enterprise's risk appetite and tolerance makes it possible to develop an executable enterprise-wide security strategy and justify requests for resources.

Benefit 2: Ensuring the Cyber Risk Function Has an Effective Budget

The question of budgets deserves detailed consideration. IT budgets are always highly constrained, and security budgets even more so, because security functions have historically been seen as cost centers—or, let's face it, obstacles to the efficient running of the business—rather than contributors or strategic partners. Security budgets have tended to be based on a percentage of the enterprise's budget, or of the IT budget, with new resources allocated on an ad hoc basis when a new threat was identified or, worse, after an incident. The reactive, ad hoc approach is especially damaging, because digital transformation is resulting in an ever more dangerous threat environment, with attacks constantly increasing in number, velocity, and negative business impact. (Paradoxically but understandably, budget requests are also difficult to define when there's a quiet period without a major incident.) The result, predictably, is budget fatigue and resistance to spending money on a function that doesn't seem to be delivering real-world business value.

A CRMP addresses this problem by helping the enterprise's budgetary decision makers define a risk appetite and tolerance—recognizing that a zero-risk environment isn't a realizable or even desirable goal—that can form the basis of a pragmatic, realistic, and actionable security strategy.

Benefit 3: Protections for Risk Decision Makers

When, inevitably, a cyber incident happens, having an established program in place makes it easier to avoid the usual unproductive and unhelpful finger-pointing. When a risk has been identified and acknowledged, and measures taken based on established risk tolerance, it will be far more difficult for anyone to blame an individual or a single department. It may be necessary to make adjustments to the defined tolerance, and that tolerance should, of course, always be reconsidered after a major incident of any kind, but that reevaluation will be based on the CRMP's established processes.

> A well-defined and clearly communicated cyber risk security program protects the entire enterprise against certain legal and regulatory liabilities.

A well-designed CRMP doesn't just protect the individual security practitioner, at whatever level, or even the security organization as a whole, against being blamed when things go wrong. It protects the entire enterprise—including line-of-business business leaders, CxOs, the CEO, and even the board of directors—against all kinds of fallout, including legal and regulatory liability.

CRMP: Systematic but Not Zero-Risk

You might well ask, "How can having a program protect me if it doesn't stop all the problems?" In case after case, the courts have made it clear that they expect enterprises, and their key leaders, to take responsibility for managing security risks. That doesn't mean they expect a board to have oversight over every technology decision, or that they expect the enterprise to protect against every threat. The courts have recognized what we've said repeatedly—that there's no such thing as a zero-risk environment—and they don't expect any enterprise to be incident-free. But there are some very important things that they *do* expect:

- The enterprise must meet acceptable standards and good security hygiene.
- Leaders need to have established, implemented components, and have proper oversight of a CRMP, including a risk-informed decision-making process and a governance structure, stakeholder engagement, and appropriate risk escalation procedures.
- The risk program must be systematic. This ensures that risk management practices are implemented and managed consistently across the entire enterprise.

The risk management decision-making aspect will take more work, more structure, and ongoing commitment from a great many stakeholders. To protect against liability based on a lack of oversight, the enterprise and its leaders will need to show that they've asked themselves some basic questions and developed sound cyber risk management practices based on the answers. Here are some of the most important questions we've identified:

- "Does the governance body represent business decision makers, does it have proper independence and an established charter, and is it aligned to an enterprise risk management or audit committee if one is established?"
- "Has the governance body established risk appetite and tolerance, as well as a mechanism for holding the business accountable to it? Is the security strategy and budget aligned to the appetite and tolerance?"
- "Do we have at least quarterly risk reporting that indicates a specific business appetite and tolerance that has been approved by the governance body and that the business is executing to? Are they updated on a timely basis?"
- "Does the governance body regularly talk about systemic cyber risks?"
- "Do the board and executive cyber reports have established key risk indicators (KRIs) representative of the tolerance and whether the security team and business are executing to that tolerance?"
- "Is there a formal risk escalation process aligned to established risk levels?"
- "Does the audit function audit the existence and appropriateness of the cyber risk management program?"
- "Does the audit process not only audit security operational controls and capabilities but also confirm whether the business is executing and meeting the defined appetite and tolerance?"
- "Is the board confident that its cyber risk management program is existing, established, and mature enough to satisfy its cyber risk oversight obligations?"
- "Is there a process in place to properly identify and disclose cyber risks that are material to the business?"

If you don't have clear answers to these questions, you probably don't have a properly defined and executed CRMP. And if your enterprise is a public company, the board and the C-suite probably aren't meeting their cyber risk management oversight obligations.

Board Accountability and Legal Liability

Board-level legal liability is also starting to shape the definition of a board's oversight obligations and what constitutes a CRMP. One reason is that court decisions in shareholder class action lawsuits are beginning to erode boards' once-formidable protections, lowering the bar to liability and driving boards to change how they approach and execute their cyber risk oversight obligations. The event that definitively established the "good faith effort" principle of board-level liability was a 1996 court decision (*https://oreil.ly/Hx45f*) involving Caremark International, a major provider of healthcare services. A group of shareholders had sued Caremark's directors, claiming the company had failed to implement adequate risk controls over the company's employees, making it possible for some to commit large-scale fraud. Some Caremark employees were signing contracts with doctors for consulting services that were never performed, in return for referrals for Caremark products and services. The lawsuit led to a four-year investigation by the US Department of Health and Human Services (HHS) and Department of Justice (DOJ) that resulted in multiple criminal charges being laid. The company ultimately pleaded guilty to a single felony indictment.

Caremark paid a high price for its failure, with criminal and civil fines and payouts to litigants totaling approximately $250 million (*https://oreil.ly/FxbdW*)—not to mention the damage to its corporate reputation and its brand, both of which are critically important in the healthcare industry. And the implications of the Caremark case extend well beyond the company and healthcare. The court established that boards of directors can, at least under certain circumstances, be held responsible for failing to make a good-faith effort to exercise due care over a company's actions.

That term *good-faith effort* is a high bar for liability. The Caremark judgment made it clear that boards wouldn't be held responsible for every action taken by every company employee—and in fact the Caremark board members *weren't* found to be liable—only that they make a serious effort to have controls, governance, and accountability in place. The decision actually was seen as offering them protections against legal action, but decisions in later cases have begun to chip away at those protections. And Caremark did establish an important precedent for future court decisions, including Marchand v. Barnhill:

> Although Caremark may not require as much as some commentators wish, it does require that a board make a good faith effort to put in place a reasonable system of monitoring and reporting about the corporation's central compliance risks.
>
> —Marchand v. Barnhill, 212 A.3d 805

The question of what constitutes "good faith" was at the heart of another court case—this time in the food industry—that sent shockwaves through boardrooms. In 2015, an outbreak of food poisoning that killed three people in Kansas was traced to listeria bacteria in ice cream from a Blue Bell Creameries production facility in Oklahoma.

Blue Bell was forced to order the first product recall in its one-hundred-year history, shut down the Oklahoma plant and at least one other facility for an extended period, and send more than eight million gallons of product to landfills. A Food and Drug Administration (FDA) investigation determined that the company had failed to follow standard industry practices to prevent the contamination of its products, and that traces of listeria had been found repeatedly at the Oklahoma facility for years before the fatal outbreak.

The most significant aspect of the Blue Bell outbreak was, of course, the tragic loss of life. Additionally, the consequences for the company were also extremely damaging, and set an important precedent for corporations and their boards of directors. The company's production capabilities were so heavily restricted that it actually withdrew completely from operations in multiple states. Thousands of the company's employees were laid off permanently or temporarily, and many more had their compensation cut. (Blue Bell has never explicitly confirmed that these measures were the result of the listeria outbreak.) The company and its CEO/president at the time of the outbreak faced criminal charges, including conspiracy and fraud, as a result of what the DOJ alleged was a cover-up of the outbreak. The company pleaded guilty to two charges of distributing adulterated food (the ex-president's cases had not yet come to trial at the time of this writing) and agreed to pay criminal fines, civil penalties, and reimbursement totaling $19.5 million.

The Blue Bell listeria scandal actually threatened the century-old company's very survival. It was so short of cash that it had to accept a massive private equity investment that sharply reduced the value of Blue Bell stock. A shareholder brought a lawsuit against the company's board of directors and two senior executives, including the ex-CEO, for failing to exercise the standard of care established by the Caremark decision, and in 2019, the courts agreed:

> A board's 'utter failure to attempt to assure a reasonable information and reporting system exists' is an act of bad faith in breach of the duty of loyalty.
>
> —Marchand v. Barnhill, 212 A.3d 805 (Del. 2019)

The significance of the Blue Bell case, and the court decision that settled it, lies in its clarification of what would constitute a breach of good faith. The courts have now made it clear that good faith requires the implementation of a systematic risk-informed program for informing about and reporting of risk. In the Blue Bell case, the company's failure was seen as so egregious that it was impossible to accept that it was acting in good faith. The court found that:

- There was no board-level committee tasked with addressing food safety issues.

- There was no regular process or protocols requiring that the board be made aware of food safety compliance practices, risks, or reports.

- The board didn't have a schedule for considering food safety risks on a regular basis (for example, quarterly or biannually).

- In the key period leading up to the three customer deaths, Blue Bell management received reports that contained serious concerns about the safety of the company's products, but the minutes of board meetings showed no evidence that they were disclosed to the board. In fact, the board was given favorable information about food safety, but not shown reports that presented a very different picture.

The connection: the Caremark case established that a board has to act in good faith to avoid liability. The Marchand case established that in order to be seen as acting in good faith, a risk-informed system—the second core component of the CRMP—must be in place or there could be personal liability. This decision essentially expanded on the Caremark case, by defining a new standard of good faith and board-level liability. It established that a company's board of directors, and its individual members, have increasing responsibility for risk management decisions systematically, and increasing liability when they don't address their risk management responsibilities appropriately. How does this tie to cyber? That's where Boeing comes back in.

The Boeing Ruling and Cyber Risk Oversight Accountability

The process of defining and expanding board-level liability doesn't stop there. The Boeing class action lawsuit continues to define the board's obligation as requiring a programmatic approach to everything "mission critical," and brings board-level liability one step closer to cyber oversight liability. Boeing's shareholders brought a derivative suit accusing the board of failing to fulfill its oversight duties regarding safety issues. The court denied the company's request to dismiss the case, and expanded on refining the Caremark and Marchand cases rulings, reasoning that airplane safety was "essential and mission critical," and that because of that, the board was required to rigorously exercise its oversight function with regard to safety risk issues. The court held that the board failed to implement any reporting or information system to inform the board or monitor airplane safety risks in any sufficient manner, specifically finding that:

- The board didn't have a system in place to monitor, discuss, or regularly report on airplane safety.

- Although the board had a risk oversight function, its oversight was primarily focused on financial risks and didn't cover airplane safety that was "essential and mission critical."

- The board received ad hoc management reports that weren't transparent enough to satisfy an informed process, and didn't ask for additional information or demand a more thorough or regular reporting process.
- Red flags were presented to management, but weren't escalated appropriately to the board, indicating the failure to have a proper reporting system in place.

Boeing settled the shareholder's lawsuit for $237.5 million.

The court repeatedly pointed to the expectation that the board operate its risk management oversight programmatically. It pointed to the need for governance, a systematic risk-informed process, and expectations that the company execute to an appropriate appetite and tolerance, and escalate risks in a timely and transparent fashion—the four core components of a CRMP.

There's another important takeaway from the Boeing case that focuses on applying the board's oversight specifically to "mission critical" functions. The court's opinion reads, "Boeing did not implement or prioritize safety oversight at the highest level of the corporate pyramid. None of Boeing's Board committees were specifically tasked with overseeing airplane safety, and every committee charter was silent as to airplane safety."[7]

It continues, "for mission-critical safety, discretionary management reports that mention safety as part of the company's overall operations are insufficient to support the inference that the Board expected and received regular reports on product safety. Boeing's Board cannot 'leave compliance with [airplane] safety mandates to management's discretion rather than implementing and then overseeing a more structured compliance system.'"[8]

Why is this distinctly important? In the first chapter, we discussed digitalization—the beginnings of the Fourth Industrial Revolution. In this context, it's difficult to imagine that digitalization and all the business processes and risks that come along with it will not be seen as "mission critical." The association between digitalization and risk is clear, and so is the expectation of what digital risk oversight obligations will entail. Oversight will require a defined and systematic CRMP applied to "mission critical" functions—and that unquestionably includes cyber functions.

---

7 *In re* C. A. 2019-0907-MTZ (Del. Ch. Sep. 7, 2021), *https://oreil.ly/3rxul*.

8 *In re* C. A. 2019-0907-MTZ (Del. Ch. Sep. 7, 2021).

CISOs in the Line of Fire for Liability

As we were writing this book, there was an action by the SEC that sent shockwaves through the cybersecurity community. SolarWinds, a company that experienced a landmark data breach, disclosed that the SEC had notified its top executives of potential legal action. What's particularly noteworthy is that the company's CISO was among those who received a notice.[9] Jamil Farshchi, CISO at Equifax, remarked on LinkedIn that this might be the first time a CISO has ever received such a notice.

These SEC notices, known as Wells notices, indicate the commission's potential intent to bring charges against the recipients for SEC violations. The SEC violations would be focused on their core remit and directly tied to the conversation regarding cyber risk management oversight, execution, and proper transparency through timely risk escalation. The escalation of formal rules released by the SEC, along with ongoing enforcement efforts, should cause CISOs real concerns. The Wells notices clearly represent a new milestone, indicating that CISOs will now be held more accountable for their cyber risk management oversight and execution responsibilities.

The notices come about two and a half years after the discovery of the SolarWinds breach, which was one of the most extensive and sophisticated hacking campaigns against the federal government and the private sector. The breach affected numerous federal agencies and over 100 companies. The hackers exploited an update to Solar-Winds' Orion IT management platform, allowing them remote access to infected computers. The US government identified Russia's Foreign Intelligence Service as the responsible party.

This heightened scrutiny of CISOs and other cybersecurity executives follows the sentencing of Uber's former CSO, Joseph Sullivan, for concealing a 2016 cyberattack on the company. (More on that in Chapter 3.) Such actions indicate a growing trend toward holding individuals accountable for cybersecurity failures in companies. The evolving legal landscape suggests that CISOs, because they're at the forefront of cybersecurity, will likely find themselves increasingly in the crosshairs of accountability.

As we write this book, current events demonstrate the urgency of the issue. In October 2023, the SEC charged SolarWinds Corporation and its Chief Information Security Officer (CISO), Timothy G. Brown, with fraud and internal control failures. The charges stem from the company's alleged misrepresentation of its cybersecurity practices and the nondisclosure of known risks and vulnerabilities, particularly during the period between its 2018 initial public offering (IPO) and the revelation of a significant cyberattack in 2020. Despite internal acknowledgments of security weaknesses

---

9 Tim Starks (with research by David DiMolfetta), "SEC Notices Spark Alarm for Cyber Executives," (*https://oreil.ly/oF1Kb*) *Washington Post*, June 29, 2023.

and the potential for severe financial and reputational damage, public disclosures to investors described only generic risks, omitting specific known deficiencies. The SEC's complaint details instances where Brown and other employees recognized the company's vulnerabilities but failed to adequately address or escalate these issues, leading to a failure to protect critical assets and to fulfill Brown's duties under the SEC rules to escalate and disclose material risks.

This case highlights a pivotal shift in the role and responsibilities of CISOs, extending well beyond maintaining good security hygiene. The SEC's action against Brown signifies a new layer of liability for CISOs in managing cybersecurity risks. It is no longer sufficient for CISOs to solely implement tactical measures; they must also ensure that their companies' disclosures to investors accurately reflect the true state of cybersecurity risks and practices in a timely and programmatic manner. The SEC's enforcement underscores the expectation that CISOs and their companies not only implement robust cybersecurity measures calibrated to their risk environments, but also maintain transparency with investors about known issues. This new scrutiny places CISOs in a position where they are accountable for both the execution of controls and, in addition, their strategic management of cybersecurity risks.

The Bottom Line

In the first two chapters of this book, we've discussed the reasons why a comprehensive cyber risk management program is an urgent enterprise necessity. We've detailed the social, political, economic, cultural, and technological changes that are driving radical changes in the enterprise risk environment, as well as the legal decisions and regulatory compliance requirements that are making cyber risk management a critical concern for an ever wider range of enterprise stakeholders.

Let's turn to the four fundamental components that work together and form a cyber risk management program: Agile governance, a risk-informed system, risk-based strategy and execution, and risk escalation and disclosure. In the next four chapters, we'll discuss the core components in detail and how they're defined by authoritative guidance, including regulatory compliance frameworks and industry standards and protocols. We'll also expand on the principles that support each core component and provide a basis of considerations when building out a CRMP appropriate for your enterprise.

In the next chapter, we'll start by defining, designing, and implementing an Agile governance program—the heart of any risk management program.

CHAPTER 3

Agile Governance

In the preceding chapter, we discussed the urgent and growing need for a comprehensive, enterprise-wide cyber risk management program (CRMP), focusing on the social, political, economic, and cultural changes that are driving this need. And we outlined the four core components of a program. Now we're going to go into detail about the first of those components—Agile governance—and the key principles we defined as a part of the CRMP framework aligned with authoritative guidance. But first, let's take a look at some real-world examples of what can happen when adequate risk governance practices, including cyber risk governance practices, are *not* in place. (For more information on the comprehensive framework itself, see the Appendix. For more information on specific Agile governance implementation considerations, see Chapter 7.)

A worldwide ride-sharing service tries to cover up an enormous data breach by paying off the hackers responsible. The company then repeatedly lies about it, gets caught, and ends up paying nearly $150 million in fines and other penalties, while its CSO faces federal criminal charges. A social networking service descends into chaos when its new management abruptly changes its moderation policies and its advertisers leave the platform en masse because their brands are repeatedly compromised by fake accounts.

These two ultrahigh-profile enterprises—Uber and Twitter—are very different. A fast-growing ride-sharing service is working in an industry so new it barely existed a decade ago, and has to be adaptive, agile, and prepared to take on significant risks to be competitive. In contrast, a social media platform depends entirely on its users' and advertisers' willingness to use its services, in a market that's crowded and volatile, so it faces a highly unusual set of challenges in balancing risk against reward. And yet, the crises that caused so much damage to these disparate enterprises have at least two things in common. The first is that the two companies' problems were driven, deepened, and accelerated by the forces of digitalization that we discussed in the first two chapters. The second is that in their different ways they represent complete failures of one of the components of a risk management program: Agile governance.

Few areas of risk management—in cyber or anywhere else—are more complex or more challenging than establishing an appropriate risk governance model. And yet few areas are more important to protecting a company's reputation, its brand image, its competitiveness, and in some cases even its very survival. Effective governance is key to establishing enterprise processes for managing potential problems, preventing problems that can be identified, and dealing with problems appropriately when they occur. It's also key to protecting the enterprise's decision makers—from the board of directors on down—from legal and regulatory liability when things go wrong, by demonstrating that appropriate governance measures were in place for addressing, mitigating, and reporting potential problems.

Nobody expects enterprises to be perfect in dealing with risk, and certainly nobody expects them to eliminate risk entirely. As we've already established, every enterprise has to take risks to succeed, and every enterprise has to find the right balance between risk and reward. But a large and growing array of authorities—governments, courts, regulatory bodies, industry organizations, and others—*do* expect enterprises to have agile risk governance practices in place. These practices must reflect an agile —as opposed to a fixed—mindset throughout the enterprise. This is required so that stakeholders are prepared and empowered to manage processes that enable them to respond rapidly and effectively to risk issues when they arise, and so that they are held accountable for the risk decisions they make. The threat environment is changing at unprecedented speed, and decision making can't be slowed by bureaucracy for bureaucracy's sake. And crucially, Agile governance practices must represent an integral part of a formal cyber risk management program of the type we've been discussing. The simple reality is, enterprises (like the two examples we've introduced here) that can't show they have Agile governance at the heart of a security risk program are likely to find themselves and their leadership unable to properly navigate risk decision making, and to potentially find themselves in very serious trouble.

That's why this chapter takes a deep dive into *agile* risk governance: what it is, why it's so important, and how to implement and manage it as a key component of a CRMP.

Agile Governance Defined

There are many definitions of the term Agile governance. The following are two definitions—from widely recognized, well-respected sources—that align closely with one another and with the principles laid out in this book.

The World Economic Forum (WEF) (*https://oreil.ly/hVs-b*) defines Agile governance as "adaptive, human-centred, inclusive and sustainable policy-making…the continual readiness to rapidly navigate change, proactively or reactively embrace change and learn from change, while contributing to actual or perceived end-user value."

The Project Management Institute (PMI) (*https://oreil.ly/IcAc-*) defines agile team governance as the governance of agile or lean teams in a manner that reflects and supports agile and lean ways of working. PMI has identified the following principles for effective Agile governance:

- Collaboration with teams is more effective than trying to force them to conform.
- Enabling teams to do the "right thing" is more effective than trying to inspect and enforce compliance after the fact.
- Continuous monitoring provides more timely insight than quality gate reviews.

The Uber Hack Cover-Up

In 2014 and 2016, hackers stole the personal data of an estimated 57 million Uber drivers and users worldwide. That's a spectacular information security failure, even in a world where data breaches are literally an everyday occurrence. But it's what followed—how the company handled the breach and its aftermath, in ways clearly defined by its corporate culture—that turned a serious but comparatively straightforward security issue into an absolute nightmare.

Uber was legally required to disclose the breach in a timely manner to regulators and shareholders. There was never any question that the company was aware of its obligations in this area: Uber's data handling practices were already under scrutiny, the subject of negotiations with the US Federal Trade Commission (FTC) and a lawsuit from the State of New York. Even so, the company's leadership—including CSO Joseph Sullivan, *a former federal prosecutor*—not only didn't disclose the breach but spent years trying to cover it up (*https://oreil.ly/JDOXt*). Uber technical personnel installed "kill switches" on its servers in at least six countries to keep investigators from finding compromising data, in an unmistakable attempt to obstruct justice. The company also paid the hackers $100,000 in hush money, passing it off as a payment from a "bug bounty" program meant to reward researchers for finding security flaws, and then concealed it from both regulators and the board of directors.

The cover-up was eventually exposed, and the consequences for Uber were brutal. The company's reputation and brand suffered, of course. And attorneys general from all 50 states and the District of Columbia sued the company, which eventually paid out $148 million (*https://oreil.ly/xWYYK*) to settle the suits. The damage didn't end there, either. The company's founder was forced to resign as both CEO and board member, and the now ex-CSO was convicted (*https://oreil.ly/MhJRP*) on two felony counts and only narrowly escaped a prison sentence. During Sullivan's sentencing hearing, the judge stated, "When you go out and talk to your friends, to your CISOs, you tell them that you got a break."[1]

The obvious question is, how could a nightmare like the Uber hack and its aftermath happen? How could serious, experienced, astute business leaders and security professionals risk their company's reputation, their own careers, possibly even their freedom, in this way? The possible answers are endless. We could talk about a toxic corporate culture that leads individuals to think they can get away with unethical or even illegal behavior (or behavior that's actually what the enterprise expects of them). Perhaps it's a question of weak oversight, with higher-level decision makers unaware, perhaps by choice, of what's going on below them. Or it could be a security practice that's not aligned with the business's priorities.

The reality is that enterprises and the people who work for them can get themselves into trouble in a million different ways. (They can also succeed in a million different ways, which is why it's so important for them to establish an appropriate and acceptable balance between risk and reward.) It's impossible to anticipate every possible way things can go wrong, or to have mitigation processes in place to deal with them all. But it is critical to establish Agile governance practices that position the enterprise to deal effectively with both risks that are predictable and risks that are impossible to anticipate. These practices, when implemented effectively as part of a CRMP, systematically inform and guide decision making at all levels, promote an open culture with a defined risk tolerance, and protect both the enterprise and its employees from legal and regulatory liability and other adverse impacts, like the ones already discussed.

What Does Good Governance Look Like?

Governance as a concept can take many different forms, but true governance always has the same underlying purpose: to guide the enterprise in its risk-based decision making, in all areas and at all levels. It does this by setting the tone for the enterprise, from the highest levels of leadership, and establishing clear processes, systems, roles, and accountability. In a very real sense, this is an issue of enterprise culture—the standards the enterprise sets for itself, its employees, and its many other stakeholders.

It may be useful to make the distinction between governance and governing. The term *governance* refers to the systems, processes, and structures that are put in place to guide and direct an organization. It includes the rules, regulations, roles, responsibilities, and policies that shape how decisions are made, as well as the authority given to the governance body. In essence, governance is simply the framework within which an enterprise operates and makes decisions.

---

1 Sam Sabin, "Ex-Uber Security Chief Gets Probation for Concealing 2016 Data Breach," (*https://oreil.ly/Fz1I8*) Axios, May 4, 2023.

Governing, on the other hand, refers to the actual act of making decisions and implementing policies within the framework of governance. It is the process of using the systems and structures in place to lead and manage an organization through these risk issues. The governing includes defining the risk organization's budget and other resources, setting goals and objectives, and ensuring that the enterprise is implementing its established policies and procedures.

There are examples of high-profile governance failures in the media seemingly every day, and it's inevitable that we'll be focusing in this chapter on enterprises that got governance wrong and faced serious consequences for their failure. But it's important to note that there *are* enterprises that get this critical area of risk management right. This means they have in place appropriate risk governance practices that let them respond to serious problems in ways that protect the enterprise, its decision makers, and all its other stakeholders.

The gold standard in this area remains the 1982 Tylenol poisoning case. (It may be an indicator of how poor enterprise governance practices are, and how little they've improved, that the gold standard is more than 40 years old.) Seven people in the Chicago area died from taking Tylenol-branded acetaminophen that had been deliberately tampered with, and copycat crimes followed. There was worldwide panic, and understandable fear about the safety of Tylenol and other over-the-counter medications from its manufacturer, Johnson & Johnson.

The crisis could have been disastrous for Johnson & Johnson if the company hadn't handled it in exemplary fashion, immediately recalling all the Tylenol in stores worldwide, opening up its manufacturing facilities to investigators, creating tamper-proof and tamper-evident packaging, and, crucially, being completely transparent with investigators, regulators, and the public. The result of this truly agile response: it soon became clear that Johnson & Johnson was not at fault, and that the poisonings were the work of a criminal or criminals with no connection to the company. And even though the crimes were never solved, Tylenol and Johnson & Johnson's many other products remain among the world's most trusted brands to this day. The reason is that the company definitively established it deserved the public's trust, and it did so by demonstrating quality corporate culture.

Aligning with the Enterprise Governance Strategy

Agile governance—whatever risk management model is used, whatever approach is taken—can't be effective if it isn't clearly and precisely aligned with the enterprise's targeted culture. The governance approach that's most appropriate and most effective for a specific enterprise will be based on the enterprise's specific situation. Aligning governance with the enterprise's needs demands a clear-eyed assessment of issues like the nature of the enterprise and its industry, the complexity of its organizational structures, the regulatory environment it operates in, and the importance of its brand reputation.

This evaluation of the enterprise's unique situation will make it possible to establish an operating structure that enables effective security risk oversight. This is essentially a cultural assessment, which takes a panoramic view of the enterprise: how it operates, who makes what decisions, what those decisions are based on, and who's accountable for them. And that means different approaches for different situations. For example, a fast-moving enterprise with an essentially improvisational management style, like a tech startup, may need an operating structure that's smaller and more nimble, so that it can execute quick decisions. On the other hand, a well-established enterprise, especially one working in a highly regulated environment, must make more nuanced and studied decisions, so as not to disrupt the trust it has developed with its many stakeholders.

So where does alignment or creation of an enterprise risk governance strategy begin? Governance begins at the top (see Figure 3-1 for an example). What this means is that the enterprise's most senior leadership—the board of directors, the CEO, and the entire C-suite—must make a serious commitment to the governance process. And they must communicate commitment, clearly and authoritatively, down through the entire organizational structure. Senior-level buy-in sets the tone for the enterprise's governance strategy and its application. It ensures that the right people are making the right commitments for the right reasons. And, just as important, it ensures that the right resources—people, processes, and technology—are made available to execute the governance strategy.

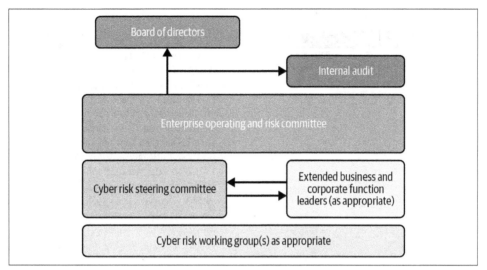

Figure 3-1. Illustrative cyber risk governance model

These are high-level decisions that must necessarily be made above and outside the security organization. Senior decision makers must be responsible and accountable for them, but security still has a critical role to play. To take just the most obvious example, the security organization has the deepest understanding of the threat environment, and can communicate that understanding to the governance body to inform its decisions. And security can use its knowledge of the threat environment to convey the critical message that governance is a must-have for the enterprise.

To implement Agile governance, risk decision makers will need to ensure that their program aligns with their enterprise-specific requirements and capabilities. To help with this process, we've designed the CRMP framework described in Chapter 2, which identifies the key underlying principles and sets of practices based on authoritative guidance. This framework serves as a guide for operationalizing the program and evolving cyber risk strategies and practices. The principles are intended to be flexible, adaptable, and scalable. For more detail on the comprehensive framework itself, see the Appendix. See Table 3-1 for the principles related to Agile governance specifically.

Table 3-1. CRMP framework—Agile governance

CRMP component	Principles	Informative references
Agile governance	See "Seven Principles of Agile Governance" on page 49.	• SEC Final Cyber Rule (*https://oreil.ly/o2TGU*) • NIST CSF 2.0 (*https://oreil.ly/xngbU*) • 2023 NACD Director's Handbook (*https://oreil.ly/8enA4*) • ISO 27001:2022 (*https://oreil.ly/0ID28*) • NIST 8286 (*https://oreil.ly/WOC5f*) • IIA Three Lines Model (*https://oreil.ly/00AQ6*) • SEC 2018 Guidance (*https://oreil.ly/SVwOx*) • ISO 31000:2018 (*https://oreil.ly/vuqzY*) • AICPA CRMP (*https://oreil.ly/d5n8o*)
Risk-informed system	See "Five Principles of a Risk-Informed System" on page 66.	• SEC Final Cyber Rule (*https://oreil.ly/o2TGU*) • NIST CSF 2.0 (*https://oreil.ly/xngbU*) • 2023 NACD Director's Handbook (*https://oreil.ly/8enA4*) • ISO 27001:2022 (*https://oreil.ly/0ID28*) • IIA Three Lines Model (*https://oreil.ly/00AQ6*) • ISO 31000:2018 (*https://oreil.ly/vuqzY*) • AICPA CRMP (*https://oreil.ly/d5n8o*)
Risk-based strategy and execution	See "Six Principles of Risk-Based Strategy and Execution" on page 88.	• SEC Final Cyber Rule (*https://oreil.ly/o2TGU*) • NIST CSF 2.0 (*https://oreil.ly/xngbU*) • 2023 NACD Director's Handbook (*https://oreil.ly/8enA4*) • IIA Three Lines Model (*https://oreil.ly/00AQ6*) • ISO 31000:2018 (*https://oreil.ly/vuqzY*) • AICPA CRMP (*https://oreil.ly/d5n8o*)
Risk escalation and disclosure	See "Five Principles of Risk Escalation and Disclosure" on page 114.	• SEC Final Cyber Rule (*https://oreil.ly/o2TGU*) • NIST CSF 2.0 (*https://oreil.ly/xngbU*) • 2023 NACD Director's Handbook (*https://oreil.ly/8enA4*) • IIA Three Lines Model (*https://oreil.ly/00AQ6*) • SEC 2018 Guidance (*https://oreil.ly/SVwOx*) • AICPA CRMP (*https://oreil.ly/d5n8o*)

An Agile governance framework is critical, but designing it, establishing it, and making certain it's appropriate for your enterprise is not easy. The governance framework must be comprehensive enough to manage the enterprise against foreseeable risks, but unnecessary complexity will make it unwieldy and potentially make individuals look for ways around it, defeating its purpose.

When developing a governance framework, one size does not fit all. An enterprise in a highly regulated industry, for example, will need more clearly defined standards to meet compliance regulations as well as the requirements of third parties, like partners and customers. What this means in practice is that a multinational investment bank will need a very different set of standards from a tech startup—and for that matter, a tech startup will need a very different set of standards from a well-established tech company, even if both companies are working in the same space.

Seven Principles of Agile Governance

Whatever the enterprise's requirements, its Agile governance framework and practices should follow seven key principles, as outlined in the following sections.

Principle 1: Establish Policies and Processes

Enterprise-wide policies and processes must be in place for establishing a cyber risk management program.

No enterprise policy, for risk governance or anything else, can be effective unless it's clearly defined, formalized, and communicated to everyone who needs to know about it. The governance group, and its executive sponsors, need to ensure that they create the necessary policies and procedures for the formal management of cyber risk—in the form of the CRMP that this book details.

A critical step in this process is the governance body issuing a comprehensive policy statement establishing what the enterprise plans to do, and why, and how it will impact stakeholders across the enterprise. This sends a much-needed message about the importance of the governance effort—and the enterprise's seriousness about it.

The governance policy statement, like any form of business communication, needs to align with the enterprise culture. It will need to be presented in language that's clear and accessible to everyone involved, without unnecessary legal, technical, or business jargon. And it will need to discuss the policy's goals, its anticipated outcomes, and its likely impact on business interactions. Perhaps most importantly, it should establish accountability and leave absolutely no doubt about what is expected of stakeholders. It should explain the basic principles of risk transparency and why they're so important. Employees at all levels and across all functions need to understand the enterprise's degree of risk appetite and the importance of adhering to it. That means recognizing potential risks and reporting them to the appropriate individual or function—not ignoring them or hoping they'll go away or, worse, concealing them.

> Any enterprise's governance practices must be appropriate for its requirements and capabilities.

A wide range of industry standards are available to assist enterprises with these efforts, including:

2023 Draft NIST CSF 2.0 GV.PO-01, 02 (https://oreil.ly/xngbU)
NIST recognizes the importance of policies, processes, and procedures in the context of managing cyber risks and defining a program. By having these in place, an organization can ensure a systematic and consistent approach to managing cyber risk strategically (that is, a CRMP as described in this book).

ISO/IEC 27001:2022 5.2 (https://oreil.ly/0ID28)

ISO emphasizes in Clause 5.2 that top management should establish an information security policy that is aligned with the business and risk context of the organization.

ISO 31000:2018 6.1 (https://oreil.ly/vuqzY)

This ISO guideline describes a risk management process that involves the systematic application of policies, procedures, and practices to the activities of communicating and consulting, establishing the context, and assessing, treating, monitoring, reviewing, recording, and reporting risk.

2018 SEC Commission Statement and Guidance on Public Company Cybersecurity Disclosures (https://oreil.ly/SVwOx)

"We believe disclosures regarding a company's cybersecurity risk management program and how the board of directors engages with management on cybersecurity issues allow investors to assess how a board of directors is discharging its risk oversight responsibility in this increasingly important area" (page 18, paragraph 2).

"Cybersecurity risk management policies and procedures are key elements of enterprise-wide risk management, including as it relates to compliance with the federal securities laws" (page 18, paragraph 3).

Principle 2: Establish Governance and Roles and Responsibilities Across the "Three Lines Model"

Cyber risk governance must be established with clearly defined roles, responsibilities, and outputs across the "Three Lines Model."

Governance can't be conducted independently or in isolation. As we've already stressed, a formal program is essential for effective risk management, and any enterprise's governance practices must be a part of such a program. But governance practices won't be the same for every enterprise. A manufacturer with operations all over the world will almost certainly need an extensive formal governance body—with representation from the C-suite and other senior executives—that meets regularly and has exacting requirements for reporting to the board of directors. A small tech startup, by contrast, may find it adequate to simply designate a small group with risk-related responsibilities and task them with establishing and enforcing governance standards and practices and escalating issues that may arise. And many enterprises—perhaps most—will elect to do something in between these two opposites, perhaps with a committee that meets regularly or semiregularly and advises senior leadership on problems or concerns.

Whatever approach to governance the enterprise chooses, it must clearly establish and communicate the expected outputs (that is, the risk outcomes), roles, and governance responsibilities. One highly useful and widely used approach to establishing outputs, roles, and responsibilities is the Institute of Internal Auditors (IIA) Three Lines of Defense.

One useful framework for designing risk governance comes from the IIA, a professional association that establishes standards and certification for corporate auditors worldwide (see Figure 3-2). The IIA's Three Lines Model (an update of the original "Three Lines of Defense") can be broadly applied to most types and sizes of enterprises, and not only to auditing. In its simplest terms, this framework comprises three sets of roles responsible for different aspects of risk governance:

First line
> These are management personnel responsible for ensuring that the enterprise achieves its organizational objectives, including providing products and services to customers and meeting defined risk management objectives.

Second line
> The second line is made up of specialists with risk management expertise who monitor the first line's practices, offering guidance and support and—crucially—challenging practices that may not meet the enterprise's risk standards.

Third line
> This is the internal audit organization, which provides independent and objective guidance and assurance on all matters related to the achievement of the enterprise's objectives—including risk.

It's important to note that only the third line operates independently. The first and second lines communicate and collaborate to create the risk framework, the second line monitors and challenges the risk output of the first line on an ongoing basis, while the third line will provide independent audits. All three lines manage on behalf of the governing body responsible for delegating authority, establishing accountability, and ensuring integrity. Internal audit may also be augmented by external providers—outside independent auditors or consultants—that can provide additional assurance.

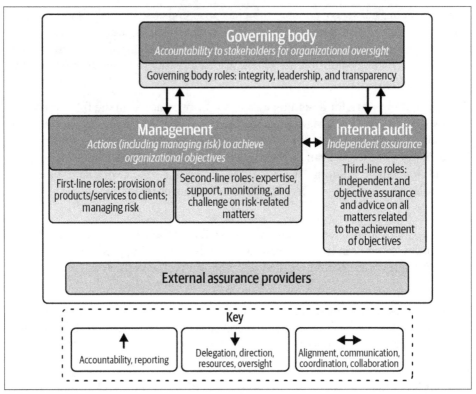

Figure 3-2. The IIA's Three Lines Model (https://oreil.ly/0OAQ6)[2]

Let's take a look at some of the specific authorities that provide guidance and perspective as it relates to this principle:

2023 SEC Regulation S–K Item 106(c)—Governance and Form 20-F (https://oreil.ly/o2TGU)

> This item emphasizes a multilayered approach to cyber risk governance. The SEC recognizes the importance of both a high-level (board) and operational (management) oversight for cybersecurity, reinforcing that governance must be robust and spread across different levels of an organization with clearly defined roles and responsibilities.

---

2 The Institute of Internal Auditors, "The IIA's Three Lines Model: An update of the Three Lines of Defense," (*https://oreil.ly/0OAQ6*) July 2020.

2023 Draft NIST CSF 2.0 GV.RR-01–04 (https://oreil.ly/xngbU)
> NIST's CSF requires the establishment of cybersecurity roles and responsibilities for the entire workforce and that these roles and responsibilities be coordinated and aligned with all these stakeholders.

ISO 31000:2018 5.2, 5.4.3 (https://oreil.ly/vuqzY)
> This key risk management framework, recognized by industry organizations worldwide, requires that risk management be recognized as a core responsibility, and that specific organizational roles—risk owners—authorities, responsibilities, and accountabilities be assigned. And it goes further, saying that senior management and oversight bodies, where applicable, should ensure that these factors must be communicated across all levels of the enterprise.

2020 IIA Three Lines Model Principle 2–4 (https://oreil.ly/0OAQ6)
> All of IIA's Three Lines Model emphasizes the spirit of this principle, especially IIA Principles 2 through 4 in this case of defined roles underscoring the requirement to have appropriate structures and processes in place.

Principle 3: Align Governance Practices with Existing Risk Frameworks

Cyber risk governance practices should be aligned with any existing enterprise or organizational risk frameworks.

To ensure Agile governance, senior leadership must establish governance practices that are clearly aligned with the enterprise's strategic business priorities and objectives. The cyber risk management framework should align with any other risk frameworks that may already be in place across the enterprise, like enterprise risk management, supply chain, third party, and IT/OT risk management frameworks. This alignment is important because it allows for better risk coordination and risk communication using similar risk tools, like a similar risk taxonomy. Not all enterprises have risk management programs, of course, but the CRMP should fully align with whatever risk functions and components are in place. A broad range of standards and protocols underscore the importance and give additional guidance for this principle, including:

2023 NACD Director's Handbook on Cyber-Risk Oversight Principles 1, 4 (https://oreil.ly/wTGwV)
> The NACD stresses the importance of managing cyber risk not just as a technical problem unique and separate from other business risks but rather as part of a comprehensive enterprise risk management (ERM) program (i.e., alignment with existing risk frameworks such as ERM).

2023 Draft NIST CSF 2.0 GV.RM-03 (https://oreil.ly/xngbU)
> NIST recognizes that cyber risk management should not operate in isolation but rather as an integral part of the broader ERM. This holistic approach enables a

comprehensive understanding of the organization's overall risk landscape, leading to more informed decision making. It ensures consistency and avoids potential gaps or overlaps in risk management efforts.

NISTIR 8286 (https://oreil.ly/WOC5f)
NISTIR 8286 advocates for an integrated approach toward understanding and managing cybersecurity risk as a part of the broader enterprise risk landscape. Facilitating a seamless alignment between the cyber risk governance practices and existing enterprise frameworks ensures that organizations can create a harmonized, well-coordinated understanding and strategy that embeds cybersecurity considerations into the overall organizational risk management processes, thereby enhancing the resilience and security posture of the enterprise.

The alignment we're talking about is largely a question of ensuring that cyber risk management governance practices are working appropriately with any risk practice or governance model that's already in place. The enterprise's cyber governance practice must never stand on its own. For example, if an enterprise has an ERM program reporting to a board audit committee, the cybersecurity governance practice should align with and report using those higher-level governance structures. This makes it possible for the business and the governance body to make decisions based on a common understanding of risks, the likelihood/impact scales of those risks, reports from the enterprise risk register, and other factors.

The NIST standard referenced earlier was created to describe how a CRMP and an ERM program should work together. One key factor: the two programs' risk outputs should be similar in format and in their understanding of defined terms. In its simplest terms, this means concepts like "critical risk" should have the same meaning for both. (This is all a function of overall operational resiliency [OpRes], which is discussed in Chapter 8.)

Principle 4: Board of Directors and Senior Executives Define Scope

The scope of an enterprise's cyber risk practices should be defined and approved by its board of directors and senior executives.

The risk areas to be covered by an enterprise may vary widely, depending on many of the factors (including industry, geography, and regulatory environment) that we've already discussed. For some, it will be adequate to address only risks related to IT and other digital assets (including operational assets). Others will need to implement risk practices that address other security functions, physical risks, fraud, business continuity management, and disaster recovery, among others.

What scope means is, in effect, what is and is not to be protected. For effective and Agile governance, it's crucial that the scope of risk practices be defined at the most senior levels, with specific risk decisions within that scope then made by the risk owners, who are responsible for the assets impacted by risk decisions.

A few of the frameworks and standards addressing this concern include:

2023 Draft NIST CSF 2.0 GV.OC-01, GV.RR-01 (https://oreil.ly/xngbU)
> GV.OC-01, under "Organizational Context," emphasizes that it's the executives who have a comprehensive understanding of the organizational mission. They can best define the scope of risk practices that align to the organization's mission and business environment in order to prioritize cyber risks. GV.RR-01, under "Roles and Responsibilities," emphasizes that leadership should be assigned and take responsibility for decisions associated with cyber risks and establish a risk-aware culture. By taking responsibility for risk management decisions, the executives not only validate the defined scope but also champion the embedding of risk-aware culture throughout the organization.

ISO 31000:2018 5.2 (https://oreil.ly/vuqzY)
> This standard holds that top management, and in some cases oversight bodies, should ensure that risk management is integrated into all enterprise activities and should demonstrate leadership of and commitment to those activities.

What this means in effect is that what is and is not to be protected—the enterprise's overall governance posture—should be defined and approved at the highest levels. A CISO might, for example, think that operational technology wasn't part of her job description, and so refuse to take risk responsibility for that area. That might be a defensible position to take—the resulting lack of visibility might be an acceptable risk—but the decision should be made by the enterprise's overall governance body or equivalent, not by the CISO.

Once the scope and roles are established, approved, and communicated, in most cases specific tactical response decisions should be made by the risk owner—that is, the person or persons responsible for protecting the asset. A security vulnerability impacting Microsoft Teams, for example, won't require that engineers or facilities managers be consulted.

Principle 5: Board of Directors and Senior Executives Provide Oversight

> *The board of directors and senior executives should provide proper oversight of the enterprise's cyber risk practices.*

Oversight and accountability are critical to the success of any risk management program, and this is especially true of governance practices. Oversight and accountability must be conducted at very senior levels of the enterprise, senior executives at minimum, the board of directors, or both. The reason is simple: they're the ones who have legal and regulatory liability for the oversight of risk management practices, and they're the ones who'll be held responsible by shareholders and consumer advocacy groups and, most importantly, the courts. As rulings in the series of legal cases outlined in Chapter 2 clearly show, the courts will no longer accept "I didn't know" or "I never saw that as my responsibility" as an excuse for a risk management failure.

The SEC Sets a Baseline for Board-Level Accountability

The SEC has been particularly clear about board-level governance and especially about risk oversight responsibilities: "We believe disclosures regarding a company's *cybersecurity risk management program* and how the board of directors engages with management on cybersecurity issues allow investors to assess how a board of directors is discharging its risk oversight responsibility in this increasingly important area."[3]

The inescapable conclusion is that governance oversight must be a top-down effort, with commitment at the highest levels that a CRMP has been established, implemented, and managed by the business. The importance of this reality is reflected in its appearance in a significant number of industry standards and protocols, including:

SEC Regulation S–K Item 106(c)—Governance and Form 20–F (https://oreil.ly/o2TGU)
This item underscores the critical role of the board in providing direction, oversight, and accountability for cybersecurity risks. This is foundational to the principle, reinforcing the idea that cybersecurity is not just an IT issue but a board-level strategic concern.

2023 Draft NIST CSF 2.0 GV.RR-01 (https://oreil.ly/xngbU)
The NIST Subcategory highlights the central role of senior leadership (the board of directors and/or executives) in managing cyber risks. It underscores that cyber is not merely an IT issue but a strategic business matter that requires accountability and the attention at the highest levels of the organization.

2023 NACD Director's Handbook on Cyber-Risk Oversight Principle 3 (https://oreil.ly/8enA4)
NACD's Principle 3, which advocates for a structured board oversight system, underscores the belief that good governance and effective risk management start from the top. The board of directors and/or senior executives are in a unique position to provide strategic direction, maintain accountability, and ensure the effectiveness of governance practices.

---

3 "Commission Statement and Guidance on Public Company Cybersecurity Disclosures," (*https://oreil.ly/GrB9e*) Securities and Exchange Commission 17, CFR Parts 229 and 249 (Release Nos. 33-10459; 34-82746).

2017 AICPA CRMP Description Criteria DC8 (https://oreil.ly/d5n8o)
The AICPA standard lays out a process for board oversight of an enterprise's cybersecurity risk management program.

Principle 6: Audit Governance Processes

Audit processes should provide appropriate review and assessment of the enterprise's cyber risk governance practices.

Every enterprise's internal audit organization should be actively involved in reviewing its governance practices and assessing their effectiveness on a regular basis, because auditors have a mandated obligation to do so. Here again, this requirement is driven by legal decisions and regulatory requirements. The internal audit organization has important financial responsibilities, of course, but its governance responsibilities don't end there.

Internal audit should review the entirety of the CRMP, with a view to determining whether it has the appropriate scope, has obtained the necessary senior-level sponsorship, is applying accepted best practices, and is capable of producing the needed risk outputs. And because the CRMP is tied to a working governance framework, it should also audit the enterprise's governance practices—both their design and their real-world application—on a regular basis. This principle is driven by several important sets of guidelines and industry standards, including:

2020 IIA Three Lines Model Principle 4 (https://oreil.ly/0OAQ6)
IIA's principles on third-line roles emphasizes the role of internal audit as an independent and objective assurance provider.

2018 SEC Commission Statement and Guidance on Public Company Cybersecurity Disclosures, Page 18, Paragraph 3 (https://oreil.ly/SVwOx)
"We encourage companies to adopt comprehensive policies and procedures related to cybersecurity and to assess their compliance regularly, including the sufficiency of their disclosure controls and procedures as they relate to cybersecurity disclosure."

ISO 31000:2018 5.6 (https://oreil.ly/vuqzY)
This ISO standard calls for periodic evaluation of the effectiveness of the risk management framework and to determine whether it remains suitable to support achieving the objectives of the organization.

Principle 7: Align Resources to the Defined Roles and Responsibilities

Appropriate resources and skill sets should be aligned to the defined roles and responsibilities with ongoing training in place.

No component of a CRMP can be effective unless it's given the necessary commitment, prioritization, resources, and especially governance. It will be essential to determine that individuals with the necessary risk-related skill sets are dedicated to these tasks, not simply add responsibilities to frontline operational personnel who may not have a comprehensive understanding of risk management, nor the time to commit to this practice.

The governance body must also be prepared to evolve and adapt, sometimes very rapidly, to address the enterprise's overall business strategy and objectives. (This is another aspect of the agility we've been discussing throughout this chapter.) Digitalization makes this an especially urgent concern. If the business is, for example, digitalizing its products or services, or its internal process, it needs the right data to support risk decision making. This may, for example, mean determining whether a specific asset represents critical infrastructure, or a key component of a supply chain, so that business-appropriate risk decisions can be made about it—and changed when conditions change.

The drivers of these requirements include:

2023 Draft NIST CSF 2.0 GV.RR-03 (https://oreil.ly/xngbU)
Emphasizes adequate resources be allocated commensurate with cybersecurity risk strategy, roles and responsibilities, and policies.

ISO/IEC 27001:2022 7.1 (https://oreil.ly/0ID28)
Clause 7.1 recommends the organization shall determine and provide the resources needed for the establishment, implementation, maintenance, and continual improvement of the information security management system.

2023 NACD Director's Handbook on Cyber-Risk Oversight Principle 3 (https://oreil.ly/ 8enA4)
NACD's Principle 3 acknowledges in particular the need for the board to have access to expertise in cyber risk management. It suggests that equipping board members with the right skills and resources enhances their ability to provide effective oversight and make informed decisions regarding cybersecurity.

2017 AICPA CRMP Description Criteria DC10 (https://oreil.ly/d5n8o)
The AICPA sets out a process for hiring and developing competent individuals and holding them accountable for their cybersecurity responsibilities.

The Bottom Line

A key point to reiterate as we conclude this chapter is that security is inherently a risk practice, and its role is to guide the business through informed security risk decision-making practices. The role is to ensure that business decisions by business leaders (asset owners and stakeholders) are informed. Senior-level buy-in, through the formalization of an organized Agile governance body, is essential to ensuring that governance itself and risk considerations are taken seriously across the enterprise. Just as important, those high-level decision makers—when they're fully and actively engaged in the effort—set the tone for the overall governance effort. And they take responsibility for establishing and enforcing the oversight and accountability that are central to effective Agile governance.

Agile governance establishes a framework for risk management decisions made by the right people at the right time for the right reasons. But risk decisions are only as good as the information they're based on. It's essential to establish a risk-informed system as a central component of any cyber risk management program—the second core component and the focus of Chapter 4.

Risk-Informed System

At the beginning of this book, we discussed a few unprecedented and increasingly unpredictable risks enterprises face in a world that's intricately interconnected by digital communication and collaboration technologies—and the critical importance of addressing those risks via a formal cyber risk management program (CRMP).

Despite all the attention we've been giving to digitalization and its impacts, it's important to recognize that digitalization isn't the problem that a CRMP is meant to address. In fact, it isn't necessarily even a problem at all. Digitalization definitely presents risks, many of them unimaginable just a few short years ago, but it also presents extraordinary new business opportunities. The fundamental problem this book addresses is that current approaches to security, and the immaturity of current risk management practices, leave an enormous gap in enterprises' ability to protect themselves against emerging risks while at the same time taking advantage of new business opportunities rapidly and effectively. That requires a clearly defined CRMP based on four key components. The preceding chapter discussed the first of those components, Agile governance. Now we move on to the second: a risk-informed system.

Threat or Opportunity? The Toyota Shutdown

In early March 2022, Toyota, the world's largest automaker, suspended operations for more than a day in 28 production lines across all 14 of its Japanese plants, after a key third-party supplier of automotive components was hit by a ransomware (*https://oreil.ly/Hr9xE*) attack. The attack—suspected to have been a state-sponsored effort in response to the Japanese government's support for Ukraine following its invasion by Russia—targeted Kojima Industries, a major supplier of electronic components and a key player in Toyota's intricately interconnected nationwide *kanban* just-in-time supply system.

Toyota pioneered just-in-time production, the technique of delivering exactly the right item in exactly the right amount at exactly the right time, minutes or even seconds before it's needed. This delivers financial benefits, with cost savings in areas like warehousing and inventory management, but it also enables rapid, precise delivery of customized orders. Toyota clearly sees this operating model as representing a strategic advantage. That's why it seems logical to view the Kojima ransomware and the resulting Toyota supply chain disruption as a failure. But what if it's actually a success story, a story about a risk-informed system that allowed—and even *encouraged*—Toyota to take risks and gain competitive advantage?

We don't have all the inside details here, but we can make some informed assumptions: Toyota viewed the *kanban* system as a strategic component—in fact, as critical infrastructure—of its business model, and company management would have been informed of the full range of risks it faced, including the growing threat of ransomware and other cyberattacks. There would have been no question that ransomware presented real risks, especially given the enormous number of points of vulnerability in a supply chain with hundreds of separate suppliers. So Toyota would undoubtedly have implemented cyber risk mitigation efforts, through security controls and monitoring and incident response capabilities, and would likely have worked out some aspects of the likelihood and impact of potential threats.

Despite the risks, Toyota went ahead with the just-in-time system, apparently satisfied with the balance of risk and reward. Does the 2022 ransomware mean that was the wrong decision? Maybe, maybe not. If the negative impacts outweighed the benefits, then yes. But there's good reason to believe they didn't. Toyota's factories were shut down for barely 24 hours, delaying the production of barely 13,000 (*https://oreil.ly/-Ne8r*) of the more than 10 million vehicles it makes every year. The rewards of just-in-time production, in terms of both cost savings and customized delivery capabilities, almost certainly far outweigh the damage from the attack. The bottom line: it seems entirely likely that Toyota made a risk-informed decision to determine a risk-reward balance—and the results suggest that it was the right decision.

Risk conditions can and do change, sometimes very abruptly, and changed conditions may call for changed decisions. A company that's taking risks to stay ahead of the competition, whether it's an established multinational like Toyota or a fast-growing startup, needs to be continuously apprised of changes in the risk environment in the context of the potential impacts on their operations and assets. A defined and approved risk-informed system creates a process—with defined scope, cadence, and reporting—to inform the many layers of business stakeholders involved in risk decision making.

We're going to turn to what may be the most important program component of all: the information enterprises use to make risk management decisions. We detail how that information must be acquired, assessed, managed, and communicated in a systematic process that ensures that business leaders can make timely, informed risk decisions.

Why Risk Information Matters—at the Highest Levels

A long series of court decisions—including but by no means limited to the cases we've already discussed—have established that enterprise decision makers at the highest levels are responsible for risk failures and, even more importantly, for the failure to be *informed* about risks. This applies to anyone who is making or should be making risk decisions, and that definitely includes boards of directors, CEOs, and senior executives. The courts have made it clear that "I didn't know" or claiming the information was sporadic are not sufficient excuses when things go wrong. The failure to have an effective system for acquiring, assessing, reporting, and escalating risk information leaves all these roles open to serious legal liability, both civil and (as you saw in the case of Boeing's CSO) criminal. And the problems don't end there. The bottom line: the failure to establish a systematic process for getting risk information to the right individuals in a timely manner introduces its own very serious set of risks: legal, regulatory, financial, and reputational.

A quote from the court judgment in the Boeing case makes it clear that risk responsibility for critical functions, accountability, and liability reside at the very highest levels of enterprise decision making: "for mission-critical safety, discretionary management reports that mention safety as part of the company's overall operations are insufficient to support the inference that the Board expected and received regular reports on product safety. Boeing's Board cannot leave 'compliance with [airplane] safety mandates to management's discretion rather than implementing and then overseeing a more structured compliance system.'"[1]

---

1 *In re* C. A. 2019-0907-MTZ (Del. Ch. Sep. 7, 2021), *https://oreil.ly/R_6fF*.

Risk and Risk Information Defined

Let's begin by defining the terms and talking about what risk information is, and especially what it isn't. The National Cyber Security Centre defines risk information as "any information that can influence a decision."

Most enterprise decision makers with risk management responsibilities believe they know what risk is, but unless they're making their risk judgments using a systematic, approved, and formalized process, their understanding of risk is likely to be incomplete, inconsistent, and in many cases simply wrong. This is especially true of security practitioners—even the most senior and most experienced among them. Let's start there.

A security professional is, understandably, likely to think of risk in terms of threats and vulnerabilities and the controls or capabilities in place to address them: malicious insiders, unpatched software vulnerabilities, and data protection. These issues are all obviously important, and information about them is important, even essential—but it isn't *risk* information. Why? Because it isn't fully properly embedded into the business context.

Before we go deeper into risk information, let's take a step back and define what we mean by *risk* itself. Here's a very straightforward definition, presented as a simple equation:

Risk = Likelihood × Impact

Let's break it down a bit further:

Risk = Likelihood (of a threat exploiting a vulnerability) × Impact (on an enterprise process, asset, or objective)

The likelihood of a threat exploiting a vulnerability matters because the threats facing the enterprise and the resulting residual weaknesses (vulnerabilities) are impossible to count, much less respond to completely. One example of the scale of the cyber threat environment: Microsoft identified 1,212 vulnerabilities (*https://oreil.ly/6zs7F*) in its systems in 2022 alone. Most enterprises run complex, heterogeneous IT environments, and many are finding it increasingly difficult to have a clear understanding of what systems and applications they have in place. But understanding the asset is critical to understanding the potential impact if attacked and if there is a likelihood of a potential threat exploiting a vulnerability (weakness).

Here's a simple example. A zero-day exploit targeting Microsoft SQL Server is a serious problem for an enterprise using that platform to support a critical web application, but it's probably not a matter of concern for a web application that is being decommissioned and not public facing.

A threat alone is not a risk—and threat information itself is not risk information.

Now for the impact. It begins with an inventory of what is of most value to the business in terms of business assets, which might include the enterprise's trade secrets and other intellectual property (IP), sensitive customer data, or the underlying code for its e-commerce platform. From there, the potential downstream effects a threat or vulnerability could have on the enterprise's systems, applications, operations, and processes become clearer. Without a comprehensive understanding of the assets impacted, and the resulting consequences or effects, it's impossible to truly understand the risk the enterprise faces—and, of course, impossible to define and execute the appropriate response.

This process of determining the relationship between threat likelihood and impact is obviously relied on heavily in shaping risk information, and it's an essential step in understanding what comprises risk information. The UK's National Cyber Security Centre (NCSC) offers a simple but useful definition: "Risk information is any information that can influence a decision." The NCSC adds, "Some organisations have a tendency to only accept certain types of information as legitimate risk information. Such limitations increase the chance of something important being missed."[2] The clear message: a comprehensive approach to risk information—rather than, say, a narrow focus on a standalone threat or vulnerability—is essential to real-world risk management.

A risk-informed decision system takes these concepts and applies them systematically, repeatably, and consistently. Using a trusted and approved methodology, the enterprise and its leaders can trust the risk outputs and make informed decisions to find the appropriate balance between risk and reward.

The CRMP framework we've been introducing in this book is used here to identify the key underlying principles that will factor into establishing an effective risk-informed system integrated as a part of the broader CRMP. For more detail on the comprehensive framework itself, see the Appendix. For more information on specific implementation considerations, see Chapter 7. For the specifics related to a risk-informed system, see Table 4-1.

---

2 "Risk Management," (*https://oreil.ly/5Bl8q*) National Cyber Security Centre, accessed October 10, 2023, p. 7.

Table 4-1. CRMP framework—risk-informed system

CRMP component	Principles	Informative references
Agile governance	See "Seven Principles of Agile Governance" on page 49.	• SEC Final Cyber Rule (*https://oreil.ly/o2TGU*) • NIST CSF 2.0 (*https://oreil.ly/xngbU*) • 2023 NACD Director's Handbook (*https://oreil.ly/8enA4*) • ISO 27001:2022 (*https://oreil.ly/0lD28*) • NIST 8286 (*https://oreil.ly/WOC5f*) • IIA Three Lines Model (*https://oreil.ly/00AQ6*) • SEC 2018 Guidance (*https://oreil.ly/SVwOx*) • ISO 31000:2018 (*https://oreil.ly/vuqzY*) • AICPA CRMP (*https://oreil.ly/d5n8o*)
Risk-informed system	See "Five Principles of a Risk-Informed System" on page 66.	• SEC Final Cyber Rule (*https://oreil.ly/o2TGU*) • NIST CSF 2.0 (*https://oreil.ly/xngbU*) • 2023 NACD Director's Handbook (*https://oreil.ly/8enA4*) • ISO 27001:2022 (*https://oreil.ly/0lD28*) • IIA Three Lines Model (*https://oreil.ly/00AQ6*) • ISO 31000:2018 (*https://oreil.ly/vuqzY*) • AICPA CRMP (*https://oreil.ly/d5n8o*)
Risk-based strategy and execution	See "Six Principles of Risk-Based Strategy and Execution" on page 88.	• SEC Final Cyber Rule (*https://oreil.ly/o2TGU*) • NIST CSF 2.0 (*https://oreil.ly/xngbU*) • 2023 NACD Director's Handbook (*https://oreil.ly/8enA4*) • IIA Three Lines Model (*https://oreil.ly/00AQ6*) • ISO 31000:2018 (*https://oreil.ly/vuqzY*) • AICPA CRMP (*https://oreil.ly/d5n8o*)
Risk escalation and disclosure	See "Five Principles of Risk Escalation and Disclosure" on page 114.	• SEC Final Cyber Rule (*https://oreil.ly/o2TGU*) • NIST CSF 2.0 (*https://oreil.ly/xngbU*) • 2023 NACD Director's Handbook (*https://oreil.ly/8enA4*) • IIA Three Lines Model (*https://oreil.ly/00AQ6*) • SEC 2018 Guidance (*https://oreil.ly/SVwOx*) • AICPA CRMP (*https://oreil.ly/d5n8o*)

Five Principles of a Risk-Informed System

This book lays out a CRMP, which is a formal, systematic, *cyber-specific* set of practices for addressing the challenges and opportunities of a rapidly changing risk environment aligned with the demands of the authoritative sources we've been discussing. We describe best practices for ensuring that that program is informed by timely, appropriate risk information. There are five key principles that must be in place for any risk-informed decision-making process to be effective and appropriate to an enterprise's specific needs.

Principle 1: Define a Risk Assessment Framework and Methodology

A risk framework and methodology must be defined and executed on to identify, assess, and measure cyber risk within the organizational context.

A systematic approach to identifying, assessing, and measuring cyber risk is critical, because it provides the governance body we discussed in the last chapter with the trusted and repeatable information it needs to make appropriate risk-informed decisions. The security organization is central to this effort, providing the governance body and the enterprise as a whole with the information it needs to make risk decisions, but it doesn't make the decisions, and it's neither responsible nor accountable for them.

> The security organization's role isn't to make risk decisions—it's to guide the enterprise through a risk-informed decision-making process.

The information the security organization provides in collaboration with other parts of the organization should all be considered as part of a cyber risk-informed system that educates and guides the governance body and business stakeholders. This information may include enterprise risk information, identification of IT, operational technology (OT), Internet of Things (IoT) assets, threat intelligence, defined enterprise risk appetite, business priorities, future business strategies, existing mitigation efforts, and lessons learned.

But why does a framework and methodology need to be in place? Many enterprises—and security organizations—already have practices and processes for identifying risk, but these tend to be ad hoc, done as siloed efforts, or conducted only at long intervals and then more or less forgotten. They also tend to be derived from past incidents, like data breaches and virus outbreaks, or control failures. (And if the hyperspeed changes of the digital age have taught us anything, it's that the past alone is never an adequate guide to the future.) Risk information and identification practices must be conducted in a regular cadence that's defined and approved by the decision makers, because the failure to receive ongoing risk information is itself a risk.

An approved framework and methodology replace this essentially ad hoc or reactive approach with a systematic means of gathering data to inform acceptable risk levels, identifying emerging and potential risks and managing or mitigating risks that actually occur. It's important to note that while metrics play an important role in this process, they must be the right metrics—not operational or compliance metrics, but *risk* metrics that provide accessible, actionable information that's appropriate to the business context.

One of the most common challenges enterprises face in implementing and executing on risk-informed processes is that they have too much data—or the wrong kind of data—and they struggle to contextualize that data so that it's actionable and relevant to their risk decisions. Another challenge is to translate the data into terms and language that will be clearly understood by the intended audience and with the intended purpose. The board of directors and senior executives, for example, will be looking for a high-level set of insights into the most urgent risks or related business concerns, the enterprise's risk appetite, budget impacts, and other business concerns. A chief information officer (CIO) or business leader may be better-served by more granular data appropriate to their decision-making needs. The granularity of this risk-informed system is part of defining the risk-informed framework that needs to be discussed, developed, and approved by the business. This will necessarily be an ongoing process, and it will require ongoing monitoring and reporting against baseline results, so that it's possible to identify and respond to emerging trends. (The reporting should align with the established process for budgeting and prioritization, which is discussed in the next chapter.) And all these measures have a single overarching purpose: to ensure the effective integration of cybersecurity as part of an overarching enterprise-wide risk management system.

The following industry guidance is especially important here:

SEC Regulation S–K Item 106(b)—Risk Management and Strategy (https://oreil.ly/o2TGU)
> The essence of this item is ensuring companies have systematic processes to assess and identify material risks from cybersecurity threats. It reinforces the principle that organizations need an established framework to navigate the complexities of cyber risk, especially in the context of its broader business strategy and financial implications.

2023 NACD Director's Handbook on Cyber-Risk Oversight Principle 1, 4, 5 (https://oreil.ly/8enA4)
> For cybersecurity to be viewed as a "strategic risk" as the NACD states, cyber risks must be viewed through the enterprise context, not just through an IT lens. This underscores the importance of the previous component as well, "Agile Governance," and the need to work with the business to understand their concerns to be able to identify, assess, and measure risk within the enterprise context.

2023 Draft NIST CSF 2.0 GV.RM, ID.RA (https://oreil.ly/xngbU)
> NIST provides perspective across these categories, providing guidance and underscoring the need for an established framework and methodology.

ISO/IEC 27001:2022 6.1.2, 6.1.3 (https://oreil.ly/0ID28)
> ISO/IEC 27001 adopts a risk-based approach. Top management is responsible for ensuring the organization's risks are identified, assessed, and treated appropriately, which includes defining the risk assessment methodology that fits the

organizational context. Clauses 6.1.2 and 6.1.3 call for risk assessment and risk treatment processes. Additionally, ISO/IEC 27005 provides more detailed guidance on information security risk management.

2017 AICPA CRMP Description Criteria DC11 (https://oreil.ly/d5n8o)
This accountancy standard calls for a process for identifying cybersecurity risks and environmental, technological, organizational, and other changes that could have a significant effect on the entity's cybersecurity risk management program and assessing the related risks to the achievement of the entity's cybersecurity objectives.

Principle 2: Establish a Methodology for Risk Thresholds

An approved and repeatable methodology for acceptable risk thresholds—both appetite and tolerance—must be established.

Several methodologies exist for establishing acceptable risk levels, but we'll discuss three here. Whatever methodology you're utilizing should find acceptable levels of risk appetite and risk tolerance for specific enterprise environments and, crucially, ensure that those risk levels are approved by the risk owners and any other senior decision makers. The methodology that is adopted or developed may vary widely, but whatever methodology is used, it should address five functions:

Defining current-state risk levels
This means evaluating the risks the enterprise currently faces and the effectiveness of the risk mitigation measures that are currently in place.

Defining and agreeing on desired future-state risk levels
A definition of acceptable future risks—developed in collaboration with the governance body—makes it possible for the enterprise to prioritize its risk management endeavors to deal with changing and emerging risks.

Using the accepted future-state risk levels to develop an overarching risk strategy and execution model
This is crucial, not only because it aligns the enterprise's risk appetite and tolerance levels with its overall business strategy, but also because it makes it possible to develop and defend appropriate budget allocations. (This issue will be covered extensively in the next chapter.)

Monitoring the execution of risk strategy
This must be an ongoing process, overseen by the governance body, to determine its effectiveness and to ensure that the enterprise remains within acceptable risk parameters.

Continuous monitoring based on the agreed-on cadence

An appropriate cadence for reviewing, assessing, and monitoring risk appetite and risk tolerance at set intervals (see "Principle 4: Agree on a Risk Assessment Interval" on page 73) will make it possible to anticipate and adapt to changes in the risk environment.

Risk Appetite and Risk Tolerance: The Crucial Difference

Many enterprise decision-makers—even highly skilled security professionals—are unclear about the terms *risk appetite* and *risk tolerance*, so let's take a moment to clarify the difference. COSO's definitions (*https://oreil.ly/UunvF*) provide a useful overview:

- Risk appetite is the amount of risk, on a broad level, an organization is willing to accept in pursuit of value. Each organization pursues various objectives to add value and should broadly understand the risk it is willing to take in doing so.

- Risk tolerances guide operating units as they implement risk appetite within their sphere of operation. Risk tolerances communicate a degree of flexibility, while risk appetite sets a limit beyond which risk should not be taken.

Different enterprises will unquestionably have different risk appetites and risk tolerance, and there are many different approaches to defining them and establishing the desired balance between them. But whatever approach is taken, it's the business that must make the final decision as to what constitutes acceptable risk to enable better decision making and execution. A repeatable methodology must be in place for informing the business and receiving its approval.

The need for effective, appropriate risk measurement is driven—and supported—by a broad array of standards and protocols, including:

- The NIST Cybersecurity Framework 2.0 (*https://oreil.ly/xngbU*), which emphasizes that risk appetite and risk tolerance should be determined and communicated based on the organization's business environment.

- The NACD Director's Handbook on Cyber-Risk Oversight Principle 1, 5 (*https://oreil.ly/qgV40*). Principle 1 underscores the necessity for cyber risk discussions to align with strategic objectives and business opportunities. To actualize this, a robust methodology is essential—one that fosters business engagement and facilitates risk appetite measurement, as delineated by management and sanctioned by the board. The NACD handbook Principle 5 speaks on how risk appetite statements should be formulated with utmost clarity, objectivity, and measurability, while also considering subjective elements such as the economic backdrop prevalent at the time of initial determination.

Whatever cyber security risk assessment methodology is chosen, it will have certain fundamental common purposes. It will define risk levels, translate them into terms various stakeholders will clearly understand, and align risk levels with different levels of governance—and, if possible, with the enterprise's other risk functions. It will make it possible to communicate to stakeholders the journey the enterprise is undertaking to achieve risk maturity. And it will deliver outputs with governance functions at all levels.

It's important to note that achieving the desired and appropriate level of risk assessment takes time and effort. In effect, it's likely to be a journey, beginning with maturity modeling, then integrating KPI/performance metrics, then moving on to qualitative assessment and finally risk quantification, likely using automated tools.

The ultimate goal of this principle is to ensure that a framework is in place to ensure that the enterprise, and its risk decision makers, use all available data within the selected framework to align on acceptable risk levels and use the output to inform the governance body.

Principle 3: Establish Understanding of Risk-Informed Needs

The governance body should be identified and engaged in establishing a comprehensive understanding of its cyber risk–informed needs.

Cyber security risk management, like all forms of risk management, requires commitment from and engagement by a broad range of enterprise stakeholders, including senior decision makers (we discussed this in detail in the last chapter). This requires effective communication—targeted at different personas and audiences, presented in ways that those stakeholders can readily understand, and aligned with the requirements of the enterprise's governance body.

The needs of different stakeholders will, of course, vary widely. Security practitioners may need highly technical information, business unit leaders will look for information focused on their areas' operational performance, and senior executives and boards of directors will likely want only the most high-level information. It's important to note that this process must be a conversation, not a one-way flow of information from the risk functions to other stakeholders. The ultimate goal is to provide all parties involved with risk information and risk measurements that are appropriate and adequate for them to make risk-based business decisions—and conduct their business activities within defined and established risk tolerances.

NIST has developed a useful cybersecurity-focused methodology for identifying and estimating cyber security risk (see Figure 4-1).

An important element of the development of a risk-informed system is the establishment of a working relationship between the appropriate stakeholders and the desired risk information. This relationship will help define the purpose and structure of the system and ensure that it's established and formally approved by the business leaders, and not simply the result of information being presented.

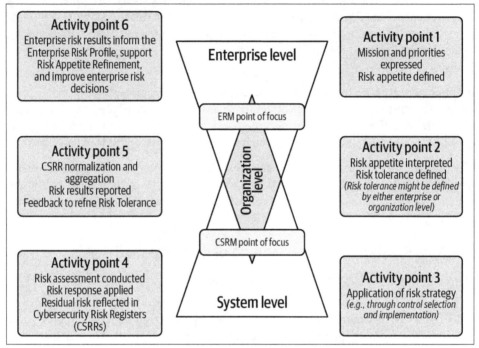

Figure 4-1. NIST illustration of enterprise risk and coordination[3]

These industry standards are additional references supporting this principle:

2023 Draft NIST CSF 2.0 GV.OC-02 (https://oreil.ly/xngbU)
This subcategory highlights the importance of identifying both internal and external stakeholders and understanding their expectations in relation to managing cyber risk.

2017 AICPA CRMP Description Criteria DC13 (https://oreil.ly/d5n8o)
AICPA lays out a process for internally communicating relevant cybersecurity information necessary to support the functioning of the entity's cybersecurity risk management program, including objectives and responsibilities for cyberse-

---

3 Source: "NISTIR 8286A: Identifying and Estimating Cybersecurity Risk for Enterprise Risk Management," NIST, November 2021, *https://oreil.ly/jcUFj.*

curity and thresholds for communicating identified security events and their resolutions.

2020 IIA Three Lines Model Principle 1 (https://oreil.ly/0OAQ6)
IIA's Governance principle emphasizes accountability to stakeholders and the focus on identifying and engaging stakeholders to understand risk-informed needs, promoting transparency and communication.

Principle 4: Agree on a Risk Assessment Interval

The risk assessment process should be performed according to an agreed-on interval with its results regularly evaluated.

Risk is not static—it never was, of course, and digitalization has made that truer than ever—and that means that risk management can't be static, either. For this reason, a risk-informed system must recognize that businesses change and risk changes along with them, and vice versa. This reality requires the establishment of a risk assessment life cycle and cadence steps for assessing risks and the impacts of risk controls on an ongoing basis at set intervals.

Enterprises frequently use risk registers—documents that note various risks and types of risks at a specific point in time—to capture the risks they face. This is a useful tool, and even a necessary one, and in today's high-pressure digitized business environment, it will usually be part of a risk-informed decision-making process because of its utility as a reference document. But it's important to recognize that it's just a tool, and one that must be used consistently and iteratively to reflect the changing nature of enterprise risk. The risk register must be continuously updated as new risks, their likelihood, and their impact are identified, so that new risk responses can be decided on by the governance body and also entered into the risk register. Whenever a new risk response is applied to an item in the risk register, that update represents the new current state in the risk assessment cycle. This allows for timely, regular, and systematic intake, review, and analysis.

Another important point about the cadence of the risk assessment process is that it's likely to be different for every enterprise—and the enterprise needs to establish a cadence it's comfortable with, one that isn't excessively time-consuming or disruptive. Some may find it adequate to conduct a risk assessment refresh on an annual basis, monitoring its KRIs throughout the year for significant change. For others (e.g., enterprises in highly regulated verticals like financial services), it may be helpful to have an automated cyber risk quantification engine that presents updated risk values on an ongoing basis.

The FAIR Institute Risk Model

There are many different models for evaluating risks to determine likelihood and impact. One of the most influential comes from the FAIR (Factor Analysis of Information Risk) Institute , a nonprofit organization dedicated to "[establishing and promoting] risk management best practices that empower risk professionals to collaborate with their business partners on achieving the right balance between protecting the organization and running the business." (That's the balance between risk and reward that we stressed in the first chapter.) In essence, it's a more detailed version of the likelihood-times-impact equation we gave earlier, expressed in terms of annual financial loss expectancy or exposure. The likelihood components are on the left, while the impacts are on the right, and both feed into the overall understanding of risk (see Figure 4-2).

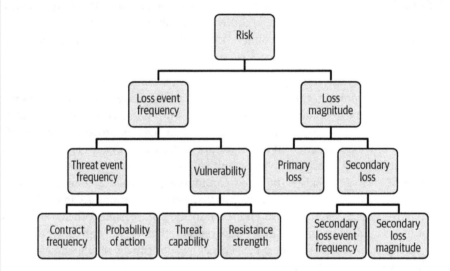

Figure 4-2. *FAIR Institute standard quantitative model for information security and operational risk[4]*

The need for a cadenced risk assessment process is emphasized and necessary to meet guidance by the following standards:

---

4 Source: "The FAIR Model," (*https://oreil.ly/S1Fcq*) FAIR Institute/Risk Lens, 2017.

SEC Regulation S–K Item 106(b)—risk management and strategy (https://oreil.ly/o2TGU)

By focusing on how cyber risks might affect business operations or financial conditions, this item prompts organizations to continually reevaluate their risk posture in the context of evolving threats and business priorities. This enforces the principle's emphasis on an iterative risk assessment process.

2023 NACD Director's Handbook on Cyber-Risk Oversight Principle 5 (https://oreil.ly/qgV40)

NACD's call for consistent cybersecurity measurement and reporting emphasizes the importance of the regular, systematic risk assessment process.

2023 Draft NIST CSF 2.0 ID.RA, ID.IM.01-03 (https://oreil.ly/xngbU)

ID.RA emphasizes the importance of conducting risk assessments, and ID.IM emphasizes regularly reviewing and adjusting the organization's risk management processes to ensure they cover the organization's requirements and adequately address identified risks. Both underscore the need for a proactive approach to cybersecurity, with an emphasis on continual adjustment of strategies based on the evolving risk landscape. Generally, the NIST Draft also aligns with the idea that effective cyber risk management is not a one-time or "check-the-box" effort but should operate as an ongoing program.

Principle 5: Enable Reporting Processes

Reporting processes should equip the governance body with insights on the impact of cyber risks on existing practices and strategic decisions.

A risk-informed system is one with defined policies and established processes, and these processes must include reporting to the governing body and all other relevant stakeholders. The reporting process will alert the governing body, and through it the business, to security events—that is, risks that exceed agreed-on thresholds and require response, acceptance, or other risk treatment. This is especially critical because these alerts will drive levels of reporting and, where required, escalation. (We'll be discussing risk escalation in detail in a later chapter.)

Reporting is communication, and like any form of communication, it must be accessible, actionable, and specific—in both content and style—to the target audience. Board reporting is a good example of the requirements of effective reporting. It may require that you communicate about a complex technical subject with people who don't typically have technical backgrounds or deep technical understanding. The directors' responsibilities are essentially fiduciary—that is, focused on the financial health of the enterprise as a whole. And that means board reporting should communicate cyber risk in business terms that are mapped directly to key business operation processes and metrics. The ultimate goal: to inspire confidence in the board that cyber risk is being managed effectively.

Remember, reporting—whatever the subject, whatever the audience—is essentially storytelling. A fundamental component of effective reporting is crafting a story—a clear, easy-to-follow narrative that makes the target audience feel as well as think. An extensive body of research shows that most audiences—even the most sophisticated—make decisions based at least as much on emotion as on logic. Many of the stakeholders in risk management processes are, however, more accustomed to simply communicating metrics and other data. Technical professionals tend to lead with a mass of data that they understand and know supports the points they want to make but that is likely to be incomprehensible and, worse, unconvincing to a largely nontechnical audience. A far better approach is to begin with a story that has emotional impact—a security flaw that's been successfully mitigated—and then follow up with supporting data.

The industry standards and protocols most relevant to governance reporting practices are:

2023 Draft NIST CSF 2.0 GV.OV-01 through 03 (https://oreil.ly/xngbU)
> These subcategories emphasize that organizational leaders should review and assess the effectiveness and adequacy of the cybersecurity risk management performance and its outcomes, which can only be achieved through systematic and transparent reporting processes. This feedback loop allows leaders to adjust strategies as needed, ensuring the organization's cybersecurity posture remains robust and responsive to the evolving threat landscape.

2023 NACD Director's Handbook on Cyber-Risk Oversight Principle 5 (https://oreil.ly/qgV40)
> NACD Principle 5 highlights the need for regular reporting and measurement of cyber risks, particularly in response to changing business environments. This practice allows organizations to stay updated about their risk posture and make informed decisions, which is a key part of enabling effective Agile governance.

2017 AICPA CRMP Description Criteria DC13, DC16 (https://oreil.ly/d5n8o)
> This accountancy standard calls for a process for internally communicating relevant cybersecurity information necessary to support the functioning of the entity's cybersecurity risk management program. This includes objectives and thresholds for communicating identified security events to the relevant stakeholders, including management and the board, as appropriate.

The Bottom Line

In this chapter, we've underscored the urgency of a systematic approach to shaping a risk-informed system—an approach that's both programmatic and finely tuned to the specific contexts to which it is applied. This approach isn't static. It requires precise outputs like risk reporting and the agility to delineate clear boundaries of appetite and tolerance. As established by legal precedents, anything deemed mission critical—a category that unequivocally includes the cyber domain—demands this level of scrutiny and strategic oversight.

This means a risk-informed system shouldn't operate in isolation. It must be seamlessly integrated into the broader cyber risk management program, fostering collaboration and coordination with its other core components. This not only facilitates informed governance but also paves the way for the formulation and implementation of a risk-based strategy, which will be the focal point of our ensuing chapter.

CHAPTER 5

Risk-Based Strategy and Execution

Throughout this book, we've stressed the need for a cyber risk management program (CRMP) that brings together risk owners, security professionals, and other stakeholders in a formal, systematic set of processes that replace ad hoc, incident-based approaches. It's the only way to ensure the enterprise as a whole addresses the challenges of a fast-moving risk environment and helps protect itself from liability. But developing and implementing a program that meets an enterprise's specific needs is no simple undertaking. It requires a clearly defined strategy and consistent execution against that strategy—and that's the focus of this chapter. We'll detail six key principles of risk-based strategy and execution, and lay out the regulatory frameworks and industry protocols influencing them. We'll identify the roles of key stakeholders—especially the CISO and the rest of the security organization, as well as internal and external auditors—in this highly collaborative process of continuous improvement. And we'll look at it all through the lens of a spectacular recent example of how radically and how rapidly the enterprise risk environment, and its strategic risk management needs, can change: the sudden public introduction of generative artificial intelligence (AI).

Cyber risk management—the art of balancing risk and reward in a digital world—is more challenging than ever. The stakes are high and getting higher all the time, and both the business environment and the risk landscape are constantly changing. But the reality is, most enterprises simply aren't approaching their cyber risk management practices in the systematic way that today's highly volatile risk environment so urgently requires. This leaves them open to unapproved levels of risk, but it can also lead them to *avoid* risks they should be prepared to take. This almost always leads to enterprises misallocating their risk budgets and other resources, frequently spending more or less than they should, or spending in the wrong places and often without business-defined direction. That makes a formal CRMP essential.

Most enterprises do have at least some risk management practices or processes in place, and many have implemented some enabling technologies as well. But few have approached management in the formalized, systematic, enterprise-wide manner this book calls for and legal and regulatory authorities increasingly demand. Risk management efforts tend to be siloed, with the security organization, the risk management team, the risk owners, and other important stakeholders communicating only occasionally and collaborating even less. Security can often feel like a compliance exercise or a set of ad hoc reactions after damaging risk events have occurred. That means enterprises likely aren't making proactive, risk-based decisions—and they're certainly not executing against a risk-based strategy that considers acceptable levels of risk and the costs associated with reaching those levels.

The security organization's role in risk-based strategy and execution is to work closely with risk owners and other stakeholders to help them. This can be accomplished using the risk-informed system to establish their risk appetites and tolerances. Then the organization can determine whether those appetites and tolerances can be reached using existing budgets, personnel, and tools. If that second goal is impossible to achieve, security needs to go back to the risk owner and explain that the risk appetite and tolerance will have to be changed or a new budget allocated.

Let's look at a hypothetical example. The senior executive responsible for a business-critical system, like an ecommerce platform, may tell the CISO that nothing less than "five-nines" (99.999%) reliability is acceptable, and that the system must be completely protected against ransomware and other cyberattacks that could cause system downtime. The CISO should then evaluate the security processes and technologies that are already in place to assess whether they're capable of achieving those risk tolerances. In some cases, they won't be, and either additional budget will be required or the asset owner will need to accept a higher risk tolerance.

In this case, the CISO will have to go back to the asset owner and have an ongoing and iterative discussion about the balance of risk and reward. (In the previous hypothetical example, it may be necessary to make it clear that five-nines uptime is simply unachievable.) The asset owner—who, to be clear, is also the risk owner—will need to make difficult decisions based on the formula we introduced in the last chapter: *Risk = Likelihood (of a threat exploiting a vulnerability) × Impact (on an enterprise process, asset, or objective)*. It's entirely possible that, having considered all known risk factors, the asset owner may decide that a lower level of protection, one that requires less spending, is acceptable. Or the decision may be made that the system is simply too important to take chances with and new security investments are appropriate.

It's important to recognize that risk discussions shouldn't rest on any one person's shoulders, or be based on personal relationships or occasional event-driven interactions. People and roles change constantly, and risk-related events occur randomly and suddenly, so both these realities require a systematic approach that defines everyone's roles and responsibilities before an event occurs. This approach—the CRMP that we're laying out throughout this book—should rely on the risk-informed system and Agile governance practices we discussed in the previous two chapters. This is crucial, because it means that no individual, and certainly not the CISO or other security leader, will have the responsibility for risk decisions. And it also means that the appropriate individuals will make budget and resource decisions on a context-informed basis. New IT spending can be difficult to justify: there's never enough money to go around, and every dollar spent in one area is a dollar *not* spent in another. This is especially true in cybersecurity, where new threats and vulnerabilities are constantly emerging and the associated risks to the enterprise are at best poorly understood. The asset owner, the CISO, and in most cases a number of other stakeholders will need to develop a use case for any new resources. And even if they reach the opposite conclusion that a higher level of risk is acceptable, that decision, too, must be based on the complete enterprise context. Trade-offs should be taken into consideration.

The Differences Between an Asset Owner and a Stakeholder

An *asset owner* and a *stakeholder* represent two distinct roles, each with its own specific responsibilities and interests. An asset owner is an individual or entity with the ultimate responsibility for a particular asset's well-being and functioning—ensuring that the asset is properly maintained, safeguarded, and operated. This person or group is directly accountable for any risk associated with that asset. A stakeholder, by contrast, is any individual, group, or organization that might be affected by, have an interest in, or have the power to influence a decision or outcome related to a particular cyber risk or asset. Stakeholders don't necessarily have direct control over an asset, but they have a vested interest in its security. In a cyber scenario, for example, consider a company's customer database. The IT director who maintains and ensures the security of the database would be the asset owner. Meanwhile, the company's clients, employees, shareholders, and even regulatory bodies would be stakeholders, since a data breach could directly or indirectly affect them.

Security's role in risk-based strategy and execution is to guide risk owners in making informed risk decisions.

It's important to recognize that these are business decisions, not technology decisions. Security's role in this process is to guide risk owners—and potentially many other stakeholders, including the enterprise's governance body—in making informed risk decisions. A collaborative approach to decisions like these, using both input from all impacted stakeholders and actionable risk information, will make it possible to define acceptable risk levels aligned with the enterprise context. A CISO may, for example, have to explain to a risk owner that the rigorous security technologies they want to put in place could slow their systems to a crawl, so that business is impacted and potential opportunities for innovation are missed.

These factors make designing a risk-based strategy and executing on it critically important. It should be a central focus of any true CRMP. That's always been the case, and never more so than right now, when changes in the way the world works—and the risks those changes bring—are coming at us so hard and so fast, it's almost impossible to keep up with them. The reality is, even the most experienced risk management professional can be blindsided by a new technological development. That happened to us while we were writing this book, when we ran headfirst into a spectacular example of high-impact, high-risk—and potentially high-reward—digital change.

ChatGPT Shakes the Business World

The constant changes in the enterprise business environment that need to be considered may include major shifts in business models, new competitive challenges from unexpected or unconventional competitors, disruptive new technologies—or all three at once. That's what happened in November 2022, when OpenAI introduced the AI tool ChatGPT 3.5 and made it available to the public on a trial basis.

ChatGPT is an AI tool that uses large language models, open and proprietary information services, and both supervised and reinforcement learning techniques to respond to requests in highly accessible ways. What that means in practice is that users can ask ChatGPT questions or give it prompts, in simple, straightforward English, and get responses back in the same way. ChatGPT can tell a joke, write a haiku, translate dozens of languages, output lines of computer code, and more.

The public reaction was stunning. ChatGPT was embraced more rapidly and more enthusiastically than perhaps any new technology since the mobile phone. OpenAI reported more than 100 million ChatGPT users within its *first two months*, and by early 2023 it had 100 million users visiting it *every day*. (By comparison, it took Instagram two and a half years to acquire 100 million *total* users.) Many people were simply using it as a toy, of course, but many others saw its potential for use as a serious tool, and business applications began emerging almost immediately.

It was obvious from the first that ChatGPT was going to have a highly disruptive and highly unpredictable impact on the way the world works, including the business world. Business users immediately saw ChatGPT as a means of simplifying the process of creating business reports and other enterprise communications materials. Programmers began using it as a time-saving way to produce code. (Some of that code was wrong (*https://oreil.ly/J7I7I*), as it turned out.) And it soon became clear that basic functions like these barely scratched the surface. As end users became more familiar and more comfortable with ChatGPT, more and more use cases for the tool emerged, and it became clear that many more would emerge over time. It now seems all but certain that in the future, AI tools like ChatGPT can and will be used to automate mundane tasks—customer service and data entry, to name just a couple of obvious examples. This will free workers to focus on more value-added projects—and help to enhance human decision-making processes by providing detailed analysis of large datasets and making informed predictions about outcomes.

AI Risks: Two Tech Giants Choose Two Paths

If the potential benefits of AI tools like ChatGPT are both real and wildly unpredictable, so, too, are the risks they present. We'll be detailing some of them a little later in this chapter, but for now, we want to consider risk-informed decision making by some of OpenAI's competitors. ChatGPT was the first major AI initiative to go public, but it wasn't by any means the only one in the works. Let's look at two of them, from Microsoft and Google, and the decisions those two digital powerhouses made about them. It's clear that both companies, and many others, saw ChatGPT as an immediate opportunity or a very serious competitive threat—or both—and began taking steps to approach it as such. But they did it in very different ways, making strategic decisions that were almost certainly risk-informed and risk-based.

Microsoft was already an investor in OpenAI, and after ChatGPT's launch it added billions of dollars more in funding. Then in February 2023—less than two months after ChatGPT's introduction—it added AI capabilities to its Bing search engine on a trial basis. The launch didn't go smoothly. Bing with ChatGPT made basic mathematical errors (*https://oreil.ly/A7Ahi*), including errors in reporting about companies' financials. It insisted to some users that the year was 2022, not 2023, and got basic geography wrong. And it got worse. Some users reported being subjected to insults, including racial and ethnic slurs (*https://oreil.ly/biV8R*), when they used the AI-enhanced Bing. (Microsoft says it has corrected this problem, but it has since reportedly encountered new ones.)

It's interesting, and highly relevant to the issues we're discussing in this chapter (i.e., the balancing of risk and reward) that Google didn't immediately make its own AI search offering available to the public. That clearly wasn't because ChatGPT wasn't seen as a threat. Alphabet, Google's parent company, reportedly took it so seriously that Google founders Larry Page and Sergey Brin were brought in to take charge of its AI project DeepMind. But even though it had an AI-driven search engine in production, called Bard with LaMDA, and even though many industry observers believed Google had the technical lead in AI, it chose not to make it available to the public immediately. (Google did do a public demonstration, and like Microsoft's, it didn't go well: Google's AI got basic financials wrong, too, and it seemingly made up "facts.") Instead, Google decided to make LaMDA available only to a small number of "trusted testers" and waited to release Bard to the public.

So what might have driven these two global tech providers to make completely different decisions in the face of opportunities and a perceived competitive threat? Both companies have deep pockets, seemingly limitless technical resources, and an obvious interest in driving users to their search engines. But they're very different types of companies, and they have very different positions in the search field. Google is, of course, the world's leading search engine by a very large margin, with almost an 85% share of the search market. That makes search, and the advertising revenue it brings in, central to its business model. Microsoft comes in second in the search market, but it's an extremely distant second, with Bing having a share of less than 9%. That means search is not a significant component of Microsoft's business. And we believe those two facts were central to Google's and Microsoft's very different decisions in response to the introduction of ChatGPT. These decisions were likely based on an informed view of the enterprise opportunities and risks involved, with the ultimate goal of balancing risk and reward.

NIST AI Risk Management Framework

Governments worldwide clearly recognize the urgent need for a formal approach to the new and unpredictable risks AI represents. The US government's concern is reflected in NIST's January 2023 release of its AI Risk Framework RMF 1.0 (*https://oreil.ly/H3NRm*) and related materials. Though the functions defined in the framework—Govern, Map, Measure, and Manage—use different terminology, they align very closely with the four core concepts of the cyber risk management program outlined in this book.

Here's how we came to this conclusion. Google's search capabilities, which have actually used AI and machine learning techniques for years, are widely perceived as the best available, and the company's business model depends heavily on its not losing that reputation. If Google had introduced a deeply flawed AI project, the resulting reputational damage could have cost the company market share, and with it critical advertising revenue. Microsoft, by contrast, makes most of its revenue in areas completely unrelated to search, and it may have decided that any traffic driven to Bing by the introduction of AI could only be helpful—and likely wouldn't do the company significant harm.

Both companies likely made their AI strategic decisions based on enterprise risk context, with clearly defined risk strategy and execution in place.

Wall Street: Move Fast—or Be Replaced

There's one business-critical risk that deserves special attention. It isn't new by any means but is radically accelerated by digitalization and especially by AI: *substitution risk*. In its simplest terms, this means the possibility that an enterprise's business model, or the enterprise itself, may actually be replaced by a new, aggressive, entirely unexpected competitor, or that its products or services are simply obsolete. A long-term study (*https://oreil.ly/NA4e0*) shows that the lifespan of a company listed on the Standard & Poor's (S&P) 500—which has long been one of the key market indexes—will drop to 15–20 years this decade, because companies have merged or been acquired or gone out of business altogether. In some cases, this will have happened because an enterprise has taken on too much risk, or the wrong kind of risk. But it's important to recognize that some enterprises will disappear because they failed to take on risks that were necessary to remain competitive.

> In the digital age, an enterprise can go out of business because it took on risks it shouldn't have—or because it failed to take risks it should have.

The result of this never-ending process of the destruction of old enterprises and the creation of new ones will inevitably be an accelerating and expanding set of cyber and other risks, most of which are impossible to predict with any degree of certainty. That uncertainty is precisely the reason enterprises need formal CRMPs that are based on clearly defined strategies and executed in line with clearly established principles.

The ability to execute a mature cyber risk program, and any risk program for that matter, is a strategic advantage. If the security team can inform the executives of risks lurking around the corner, provide insight and communicate through its execution capabilities on how fast it can identify those risks and hit the brakes, while knowing the latency of those breaks, a company can move faster than its competitors by executing to the right balance of risk and reward. The programmatic approach allows for this thoroughness and trust in the framework and risk outputs.

The Digital Game Changers Just Keep Coming

ChatGPT and the dozens of other AI initiatives that are coming on the market are getting all the attention at the moment, but AI isn't the only transformative and disruptive technology introducing new and unexpected risks. McKinsey predicts that more technological progress will be experienced in the next 10 years than in the preceding *century*, and has identified the top 10 technological trends (*https://oreil.ly/Xn6IV*) that will be most important in the coming decade:

Process automation and virtualization
> Robots, automation, 3D printing, the Industrial Internet of Things (IIoT), and other technologies will radically transform the nature of work.

The future of connectivity
> Faster digital connections and greater network availability, made possible by 5G and the IoT, will increase the digitalization and decentralization of economic activity.

Distributed infrastructure
> Cloud computing—especially hybrid and multicloud—will make enterprise operations faster, more agile, and less expensive.

Next-generation computing
> This trend builds on a broad array of technologies, including quantum computing and autonomous vehicles, to dramatically increase enterprises' digital capabilities.

Applied AI
> McKinsey believes that AI—which, let's not forget, is still in its nascent phase—will be used in vast numbers of practical applications. For example, the consulting firm predicts that by 2024, more than 50% of people's interactions with computers will involve AI-generated speech.

The future of programming
> Techniques like neural networks and machine learning will increasingly automate the process of writing code, which will make creating software faster, less expensive, and far more scalable.

Trust architecture
> Trust architectures—for example, the use of distributed ledgers like blockchains—will be used to improve the security of sensitive information.

The "bio revolution"
> Advances in life sciences, including DNA sequencing and gene therapies, will have a significant impact on industries including agriculture and healthcare.

Next-generation materials

New developments in materials science are resulting in new materials that are stronger, are lighter, and conduct electricity better than anything previously known. The result will be radical transformation in many areas, including energy, semiconductors, transportation, and manufacturing.

Clean technology

The cost of clean technologies—renewable energy, energy-efficient buildings, and electric vehicles, to name just a few—are falling dramatically, driving more widespread use and more widespread disruption of traditional tech models.

Defining Risk-Based Strategy and Execution

Security has a unique and critical role to play in addressing the rapidly evolving attack surfaces and emerging risks presented by AI and other digital technologies, and a formal CRMP is essential to enabling the security organization to fulfill this role. By guiding risk owners through a risk-informed decision-making process and helping them understand the new cyber risks that are emerging from these new technologies, the program drives the development and execution of a strategy based on agreed-on risk thresholds. Just as importantly, it makes it possible to define an agreed-on and defendable budget that provides purpose, direction, and prioritization for headcount and budget resources, tools, third-party interactions, and other issues.

Security threats and vulnerabilities aren't the only concerns enterprises and their security organizations will need to address via risk-based execution. Changes in the business (and technical) environment can take many other forms, and they don't necessarily mean increases in risk factors. The opposite may in fact be true. The availability of a new security tool, for example, might drive down residual risk levels, while an unpatched vulnerability could threaten a business asset or operational process and add to risk exposure. Risk, like the overall enterprise environment, is constantly changing, and this is especially true of cyber risk. And that makes risk-based strategy and execution, in the form of a CRMP, absolutely critical to an enterprise's survival.

Refer to Table 5-1 for a summary of the CRMP framework components, principles, and references. The Appendix gives a detailed look at the CRMP framework. In the next section, we discuss the principles necessary to establishing an effective risk-based strategy and execution model as part of the broader CRMP.

For more detail on the comprehensive CRMP framework itself, see the Appendix. For more information on specific implementation considerations, see Chapter 7.

Table 5-1. CRMP framework—risk-based strategy and execution

CRMP component	Principles	Informative references
Agile governance	See "Seven Principles of Agile Governance" on page 49.	• SEC Final Cyber Rule (*https://oreil.ly/o2TGU*) • NIST CSF 2.0 (*https://oreil.ly/xngbU*) • 2023 NACD Director's Handbook (*https://oreil.ly/8enA4*) • ISO 27001:2022 (*https://oreil.ly/0lD28*) • NIST 8286 (*https://oreil.ly/WOC5f*) • IIA Three Lines Model (*https://oreil.ly/00AQ6*) • SEC 2018 Guidance (*https://oreil.ly/SVwOx*) • ISO 31000:2018 (*https://oreil.ly/vuqzY*) • AICPA CRMP (*https://oreil.ly/d5n8o*)
Risk-informed system	See "Five Principles of a Risk-Informed System" on page 66.	• SEC Final Cyber Rule (*https://oreil.ly/o2TGU*) • NIST CSF 2.0 (*https://oreil.ly/xngbU*) • 2023 NACD Director's Handbook (*https://oreil.ly/8enA4*) • ISO 27001:2022 (*https://oreil.ly/0lD28*) • IIA Three Lines Model (*https://oreil.ly/00AQ6*) • ISO 31000:2018 (*https://oreil.ly/vuqzY*) • AICPA CRMP (*https://oreil.ly/d5n8o*)
Risk-based strategy and execution	See "Six Principles of Risk-Based Strategy and Execution" on page 88.	• SEC Final Cyber Rule (*https://oreil.ly/o2TGU*) • NIST CSF 2.0 (*https://oreil.ly/xngbU*) • 2023 NACD Director's Handbook (*https://oreil.ly/8enA4*) • IIA Three Lines Model (*https://oreil.ly/00AQ6*) • ISO 31000:2018 (*https://oreil.ly/vuqzY*) • AICPA CRMP (*https://oreil.ly/d5n8o*)
Risk escalation and disclosure	See "Five Principles of Risk Escalation and Disclosure" on page 114.	• SEC Final Cyber Rule (*https://oreil.ly/o2TGU*) • NIST CSF 2.0 (*https://oreil.ly/xngbU*) • 2023 NACD Director's Handbook (*https://oreil.ly/8enA4*) • IIA Three Lines Model (*https://oreil.ly/00AQ6*) • SEC 2018 Guidance (*https://oreil.ly/SVwOx*) • AICPA CRMP (*https://oreil.ly/d5n8o*)

Six Principles of Risk-Based Strategy and Execution

The rapid, and rapidly accelerating, changes in the enterprise risk environment demand an entirely new approach to risk management, and especially to cyber risk management. Ad hoc or reactive efforts, or initiatives driven fundamentally by regulatory or corporate compliance requirements, are no longer remotely adequate to today's—and tomorrow's—highly volatile economic, social, political, and technological environment.

The security organization has an important, even critical, role to play in addressing enterprises' urgent need for risk-based strategy and execution, but it must evolve to deliver greater real-world business value. This will mean providing the governance body with risk information that provides context around the enterprise's risk appetite and tolerance, and then creating a strategic risk treatment plan—and an associated budget—that makes it possible to develop policies to execute to that appetite and tolerance.

There are, of course, many different ways of designing and implementing risk-based strategy and execution, but certain key principles must always be followed. Let's look at those next.

Principle 1: Define Acceptable Risk Thresholds

Acceptable cyber risk thresholds must be clearly understood, established, and approved by the risk owners based on the risk framework and methodology.

In the previous chapter, we discussed the critical importance of establishing a methodology for defining acceptable risk levels, in terms of both risk appetite and risk tolerance. A definition of acceptable future risks—developed in collaboration with the governance body—makes it possible for the enterprise to prioritize its risk management endeavors to deal with changing and emerging risks. But effective risk-based strategy and execution—ensuring that risk management is actually working to meet the enterprise's strategic goals—requires that the owners of a specific risk in question play a clear role in this process. And the place to start is by working with the risk owners to establish an understanding of the current state. It's only when all the impacted stakeholders understand their current state, in terms of risk and measures being taken to address it, that they can begin to outline a realistic future state.

The risk owners may be the individuals responsible for a specific enterprise asset, line-of-business leaders, senior executives, or even the board of directors. Whatever their role, they must clearly understand what's at stake in a given risk decision so that the appropriate balance of risk and reward can be determined. For example, risk owners might have to decide on the potential cost of a work stoppage caused by a cyberattack and the cost of the measures needed to prevent such an attack. Security's role here is to provide guidance, ensuring that the risk owners have the necessary information to make informed decisions when establishing the appropriate tolerance.

These standards all have the clear implication that because, as we've established, it's impossible to completely eliminate risk, it's critical to establish the right balance between risk and reward—and only the risk owners can make this determination. They can do this, guided by the security organization, using an appetite and tolerance methodology framework with repeatable and accurate outputs. And the outputs should be translated into terms that are granular enough to enable strategic execution.

Once risk appetite and tolerance are clearly understood and established by the risk owners, they should be approved at the appropriate governance level (most commonly by executive leadership). This will make it possible to move on to establishing capability models that define both current- and future-state tolerance levels and justify the necessary budget and other resources.

Budgets are, as always, an overriding concern. There's only so much money available to spend, and in most cases, money that goes toward cyber risk will have to be taken away from something else, whether marketing, research and development, or security. But it's important to recognize that the process of establishing a desired future state for cyber risk won't necessarily mean spending more money, whether on new security measures or new technologies. It may, in fact, mean that the enterprise decides that a higher level of risk is acceptable and that scarce budget resources can be spent elsewhere.

Risk-based budgeting is strategic and cannot be separated from the idea of helping the enterprise find its risk and reward balance. Enterprises often establish a risk budget first, and use it to determine the head count and tools needed—a classic case of "putting the cart before the horse." Sometimes the budget is based on a percentage of the overall IT budget, or it represents a set percentage over the previous year or even the cost of yet another tool to address yet another threat. All of these decisions are done without an understanding of the enterprise's defined tolerance.

This principle is driven and supported by several cyber-specific standards and protocols, including:

2023 NACD Director's Handbook on Cyber-Risk Oversight Principle 1 (https://oreil.ly/ 8enA4)
> For cybersecurity to be viewed as a "strategic risk," there must be a clear framework (as defined in "Risk-Informed System," Principle 1) with business-approved risk thresholds for managing it. In other words, the strategic decision making regarding what level of risk is acceptable lies in the hands of the risk owners. This approach ensures that cybersecurity risk is not just treated as a technical problem but rather a strategic one that can have significant impacts on the organization's operations and objectives.

2023 Draft NIST CSF 2.0 GV.RM-02 (https://oreil.ly/xngbU)
> This subcategory refers to determining and communicating the organization's risk appetite and risk tolerance, which could be the measures of the organization's acceptable risk thresholds, based on the specific context of its business environment.

Principle 2: Align Strategy and Budget with Approved Risk Thresholds

The cyber risk treatment plan and budget should be aligned with the approved risk thresholds.

When risk appetite and tolerance are clearly established and approved, a strategy for reaching the desired future state must be developed. The need to balance risk and reward makes managing and maximizing finite risk resources a critical concern. The security organization plays a central role here, evaluating, designing, implementing, and controlling risk management strategies, including not only mitigation, transfer, and acceptance, but also prerisk acceptance processes and postrisk analysis. This is especially important because it makes it possible to develop and defend appropriate budget allocations.

> Every risk decision almost always has financial impacts—and that means major risk decisions should always involve the CFO or some other high-level financial decision maker.

Once again, budgets will be an overriding factor, and this means the security organization's leadership will need to work closely with the executives or the governance body to align the enterprise's business objectives with the risk strategy, the overall portfolio of security practices and available resources, and ultimately the enterprise's business needs. Alignment with business strategy can be difficult, given the complexity of modern enterprises. Several major companies have, for example, suffered highly damaging cyberattacks because they failed to perform their due diligence following a merger or acquisition, which inevitably changes an enterprise's risk profile.

Security will also need to coordinate with other risk-related operational functions to consider issues like business continuity and disaster recovery, the capabilities of the security operations center (SOC) and the overall IT organization, and third-party competencies. Risk prioritization and mitigation responses should be considered and weighted throughout this process. A key factor in making this determination will be time: the enterprise may settle on a long-term strategy (for example, the decision to reduce risk by x millions of dollars over a period over x years), but it might be facing an urgent threat that requires immediate remediation. These are all decisions that can only be made in complete alignment with the approved risk levels, and they all have financial consequences. The enterprise should certainly be conducting at least an annual review to determine what changes to both operating and capital expenditures will need to be made. But the dynamic nature of cyber risk will almost certainly require more immediate responses requiring adjustments.

A number of standards—some but not all cyber-specific—relate to this principle, including:

2023 Draft NIST CSF 2.0 GV.RM-04 (https://oreil.ly/xngbU)
> NIST emphasizes establishing and communicating a strategic direction that includes appropriate risk response options. These options could include risk transfer mechanisms like insurance, investment in mitigation measures, risk avoidance, and risk acceptance, all of which should align with the allocated

budget for cybersecurity. See Table 5-2 for response types for cybersecurity risks and Figure 5-1 for a sample risk response workflow.

2023 NACD Director's Handbook on Cyber-Risk Oversight Principle 1 (https://oreil.ly/wTGwV)

As with Risk-Based Strategy and Execution Principle 1, the NACD Principle 1 underscores the need for a strategic understanding of acceptable risk thresholds and aligning cybersecurity procedures accordingly. The entire cybersecurity strategy of the organization is shaped by the decisions made about acceptable risk thresholds. This demonstrates the strategic nature of cybersecurity because it acknowledges that the strategic choices and investments an organization makes in cybersecurity need to correspond to the risk they are willing to accept.

ISO 31000 6.5.1, 6.5.2 (https://oreil.ly/vuqzY)

The ISO identifies the purpose of risk treatment as selecting and implementing options for addressing risk, which involves balancing the potential benefits of options against the cost, effort, or disadvantages of implementing them.

2017 AICPA CRMP Description Criteria DC17 (https://oreil.ly/d5n8o)

The accountancy standards call for a process for developing a response to assessed risks, including the design and implementation of control processes.

Table 5-2. Response types for cybersecurity risks[a]

Type	Description
Accept	Accept cybersecurity risk tolerance levels. No additional risk response action is needed except for monitoring.
Transfer	For cybersecurity risks that fall outside of tolerance levels, reduce them to an acceptable level by sharing a portion of the consequences with another party (e.g., cybersecurity insurance). While some of the financial consequences may be transferrable, there are often consequences that cannot be transferred, like the loss of customer trust. (Sometimes referenced as Sharing.)
Mitigate	Apply actions (e.g., security controls discussed in Section 3.5.1) that reduce the threats, vulnerabilities, and impacts of a given risk to an acceptable level. Responses could include those that help prevent a loss (i.e., reducing the probability of occurrence or the likelihood that a threat event materializes or succeeds) or that help limit such a loss by decreasing damage and liability.
Avoid	Take actions to eliminate the activities or conditions that give rise to risk. Avoiding risk may be the best option if there is no cost-effective method for reducing the cybersecurity risk to an acceptable level. The cost of the lost opportunity associated with such a decision should be considered as well.

[a] Source: Kevin Stine, Stephen Quinn, Greg Witte, R. K. Gardner, "Integrating Cybersecurity and Enterprise Risk Management (ERM)," (*https://oreil.ly/RISYP*) NISTIR 8286, October 2020.

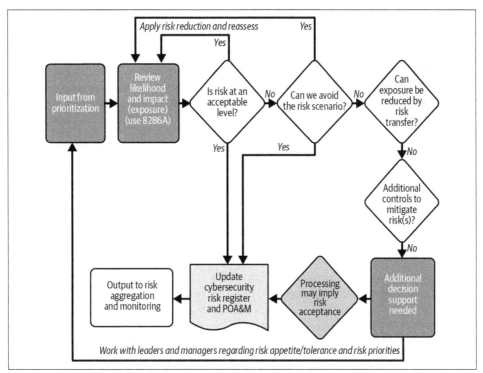

Figure 5-1. Risk response workflow[1]

Principle 3: Execute to Meet Approved Risk Thresholds

The cyber risk treatment plan should be executed to meet the approved risk thresholds.

The execution of the defined strategic risk treatment plan—the day-to-day management of the processes, mechanisms, techniques, and tools used—needs to be as formal and systematic as the process of creating and approving the plan aimed at meeting the business-defined tolerance. This will enable risk treatment to remain current and aligned with the established risk and control framework, and risk assessments and audits to remain proactive and aligned with current risks and gaps. This means reaching the desired tolerance, within the desired time frame and budget.

---

1 Source: Stine, Quinn, Witte, Gardner, "Integrating Cybersecurity and Enterprise Risk Management (ERM)."

Cyber Risk and Insurance

One highly specialized industry is looking closely at cyber risk, and it's not liking what it sees. That's the insurance industry, which has centuries of experience in making risk-based decisions. Cyber insurance policies—compensating for the cost of system outages caused by ransomware and other cyberattacks, for example—carry extremely high premiums, with significant coverage exemptions, simply because insurers don't have the data they need to determine the true extent of the organization's risk exposure. (By contrast, a life insurance premium can be calculated based on millions of data points.) The result is that many enterprises are deciding that cyber insurance is simply too expensive, and they're choosing to spend their finite resources elsewhere to achieve their risk management objectives.

The process components associated with execution include the prevention, detection of and response to security events, and recovery activities and capacity management during disruptive events (for example, disaster recovery). But they also extend to identification of high-priority assets and significant changes in enterprise operations, as well as the applicability of laws, regulations, and other obligations to risk treatment activities. And as always, execution must form part of an integrated operational risk framework or overarching security risk management framework (for example, an operational risk or ERM framework).

This requires agility, because—as we've noted repeatedly—both business needs and risks change, sometimes rapidly and dramatically. A budget may seem to be a fixed entity, and managing the annual budget is certainly an important goal. But in reality, a budget is and should be a snapshot of a moment in time, and with a risk-based execution model, it needs to be agile.

The standards and protocols relevant to strategic risk execution include:

2023 Draft NIST CSF 2.0 GV.RR-03 (https://oreil.ly/xngbU)
This subcategory emphasizes allocating adequate resources commensurate with cybersecurity risk strategy, roles and responsibilities, and policies.

ISO 31000 6.5.3 (https://oreil.ly/vuqzY)
This segment of the ISO standard delineates the rationale behind the formulation and execution of risk treatment plans. The aim is to clearly articulate the chosen treatment strategies to ensure a unified understanding among stakeholders. It facilitates progress monitoring and clearly demarcates the sequence of implementing risk treatment and fostering clarity and alignment in execution.

Principle 4: Monitor on an Ongoing Basis

The execution of the cyber risk treatment plan should be monitored on an ongoing basis with established performance indicators and operational metrics.

A continuous review of risk mitigation performance with defined risk and performance indicators and operational metrics, balancing business objectives against identified risks, is essential to successful risk-based strategy and execution. This monitoring process is overseen by the governance body and conducted at a defined cadence using meaningful metrics like approved and accepted KPIs and KRIs. The process ensures effective operational execution of people, processes, and technology within acceptable risk parameters. It makes anticipating and adapting to changes in the risk environment possible via appropriate and flexible resource allocation based on a moving risk portfolio.

Ongoing monitoring makes it possible to identify and respond to changes in the overall environment, including changes in laws, regulations, and industry standards as well as the emergence of new business operations and objectives, new risks, new technologies, and new mitigation strategies. It also enables the security program to continuously adapt to the monitored and changing risk profile—potentially triggering changes needed in risk tolerances levels, which should then be appropriately communicated to the enterprise's governance body and all stakeholders.

The industry standards that are specifically relevant to this principle include:

2023 NACD Director's Handbook on Cyber-Risk Oversight Principle 5 (https://oreil.ly/ 8enA4)
> The NACD principle stresses the need for an ongoing, structured approach to tracking cybersecurity performance, enabling organizations to make informed decisions, adapt strategies as needed, and ensure that risk treatment plans are executed effectively. This alignment underscores the critical role of measurement and reporting in managing cybersecurity risks and maintaining a robust, resilient defense posture.

2023 Draft NIST CSF 2.0 GV.OV-01 through 03 (https://oreil.ly/xngbU)
> These subcategories involve assessing and reviewing the effectiveness and adequacy of the cybersecurity risk management strategy and its results. This assessment and review process is an integral part of monitoring and adjusting the strategy's execution.

2017 AICPA CRMP Description Criteria DC15, DC16 (https://oreil.ly/d5n8o)
> These accounting-focused standards describe processes for conducting ongoing and periodic evaluations of the operating effectiveness of key controls and other components related to cybersecurity. These standards also evaluate and communicate security threats, vulnerabilities, and control deficiencies to the parties responsible for taking corrective action.

Principle 5: Audit Against Risk Thresholds

The audit function should review and assess proper execution of the cyber risk treatment plan based on the approved risk thresholds.

The audit function—the third line of defense we identified in Chapter 3—is critical to ensuring that the enterprise's cyber risk strategy is aligned with its overall business strategy, and especially that its risk treatment plan is aligned with established risk appetite and tolerance. Ongoing and periodical auditing of the risk treatment plan and its execution ensures the proper functioning of the CRMP and its execution against the established risk framework.

Audit does not simply measure an enterprise's risk treatment plan against established best practices and governance standards to ensure that it's compliant. The audit function also needs to determine whether the enterprise's overall risk management program is providing stakeholders with the information they need—at an appropriately granular level—to make risk-informed strategic decisions. This function also ensures that the right balance between risk and reward is both established and accepted at the appropriate levels. In terms of execution, auditing must also confirm that both the security organization and the risk owners are remaining within defined tolerances, that execution against tolerances is both timely and flexible, and that the risk budget is based on identified risk factors.

Two key sets of industry standards are particularly relevant to the audit function:

2017 AICPA CRMP Description Criteria (https://oreil.ly/d5n8o)
AICPA, which has an obvious interest in auditing-related activities, outlines a framework that can be used to review, assess, and describe the CRMP.

2020 IIA Three Lines Model Principle 4 (https://oreil.ly/OOAQ6)
This principle highlights internal audit's role in continuous improvement through systematic processes, with an emphasis on monitoring the proper execution of risk treatment plans and promoting consistent and effective risk management.

Principle 6: Include Third Parties in Risk Treatment Plan

The cyber risk treatment plan should consider third parties including partners, suppliers, and supply chain participants.

In today's business environment, an enterprise will have complex working relationships with a broad range of third-party entities, including partners, suppliers, logistics providers, and other supply chain participants and sometimes even competitors. This demands a risk treatment strategy that extends well beyond the enterprise. The enterprise's relationships with these third parties expose it to a broad array of risks, ranging from supply chain failures to the exposure of IP to reputational damage from a partner's unethical practices. In fact, many enterprises' single greatest source of risk comes from third parties, because of their extremely limited visibility in third parties' operations. These risks must be managed through a comprehensive risk treatment strategy that spans the entire ecosystem.

A spectacular example of third-party cybersecurity risk came in early 2020, when a massive cyberattack, thought to be sponsored by the Russian government, penetrated thousands of public- and private-sector entities worldwide. Hackers broke into the systems of SolarWinds (*https://oreil.ly/ncbXM*), an important US-based provider of IT management software, and inserted malicious code into its Orion platform that spread to the company's tens of thousands of customers through regular software updates. The code created a backdoor into the customers' systems, enabling the hackers to extract sensitive information from an astonishing range of entities, including Boeing, Microsoft, VMWare, the North Atlantic Treaty Organization (NATO), the US Centers for Disease Control, and the European Parliament. The full extent of the damage caused by the attack remains unclear—in part because of government and corporate secrecy—but SolarWinds has stated that approximately 18,000 of its customers downloaded the compromised software.

That last statistic alone should be enough to make anyone involved with cyber risk management sit up and take notice. When an attack on a single enterprise can result in potential damage to thousands and thousands of other enterprises, it's clear that essential third-party risk must be recognized as a critical concern by the enterprise and its governance bodies, and addressed by its CRMP.

Many enterprises' single greatest source of risk is their engagement with third parties.

A set of standards addresses the unique problem of managing third-party/supply chain risks:

2023 Draft NIST CSF 2.0 GV.SC, ID.IM-02 (https://oreil.ly/xngbU)
The entire NIST "Cybersecurity Supply Chain Risk Management" Category and also the "Improvement" Subcategory 02 underscore the importance of establishing, managing, and continually monitoring third parties as a part of risk treatment strategies.

SEC Regulation S–K Item 106(b)—Risk Management and Strategy (https://oreil.ly/o2TGU)
This principle is supported by the SEC Regulation S–K Item 106(b), which underscores the need for a disclosure of a registrant's cybersecurity risk management and strategy. Particularly, it mentions a point of focus on the ability of the registrant to oversee and identify significant risks stemming from cybersecurity threats, notably those related to the involvement of third-party service providers,

as they may be material to the business. Subsequently, leading practice would suggest an organization's risk treatment plan is taking management of third-party security risks into account.

The Bottom Line

Every security team has a strategy and execution model. The key difference here is that a risk-based strategy and execution model is driving the business by using the risk-informed system to define its tolerance supported by budget, headcount, and skill sets. The alignment of resources and execution priorities within accepted appetites and tolerances is an ongoing balancing act—a dynamic process integrated into an enterprise's strategic vision, facilitated by the core components of a cyber risk management program working in unison.

One crucial component of a risk-based system and its execution is establishing what specific stakeholders should do when there are changes in the risk environment—when risks fall outside of a tolerance: what decisions and actions need to be taken and by whom; and who, inside and outside the enterprise, needs to be informed. This critical function is risk escalation and disclosure—and it's the focus of the next chapter.

CHAPTER 6

Risk Escalation and Disclosure

In the preceding chapters, we've been laying out the foundational building blocks of a cyber risk management program (CRMP) with the capabilities needed to protect the enterprise and its stakeholders against the broad array of known and unknown risks that digitalization introduces. We established the necessity of Agile governance, with the right people making and being held accountable for risk decisions. We showed the importance of having a risk-informed system in place to ensure that appropriate, actionable risk information is delivered to the appropriate parties, including risk owners and the governance body. And we laid out the basis for risk strategy and execution: the process of making risk decisions and acting on them. Now it's time to look at the last core component of a CRMP—risk escalation and disclosure—and the reasons it's so critical to the program's success.

> Risk escalation and disclosure—ensuring that the right people and entities are informed of risk issues at the right time and in the right way—can help to prevent a problem from becoming a disaster, and can retain or restore the trust of the public and regulators.

The need for cyber risk escalation and disclosure is driven by the reality that an enterprise's risk environment will inevitably be especially rapid and unpredictable. Those changes, if not addressed formally and proactively, can cause serious, sometimes even irreparable, harm to the enterprise and its most senior decision makers. This may take the form of reputational damage to the enterprise or its brand, or loss of trust by customers, investors, or partners. (These factors may carry greater or lesser weight depending on the specific enterprise or industry.) But by far the most important reason a CRMP must integrate effective risk escalation and disclosure practices is intense pressure from the courts and regulatory bodies. A seemingly endless series of legal decisions has made it clear that the courts are not satisfied with standard enterprise cyber risk practices. It's also clear that the courts believe enterprises, and especially publicly traded companies, aren't being transparent or timely enough in their public disclosures of security incidents and other cyber risk issues. Regulators, notably the SEC, are building on these decisions with increasingly stringent mandates that enterprises can't afford not to comply with fully. And both the courts and regulators are expressing their seriousness about risk escalation and especially disclosure with awards, fines, and other settlements running to hundreds of millions, and even billions, of dollars.

Risk Escalation and Disclosure Defined

Risk escalation and disclosure are closely related concepts, but they're also entirely different concepts, so let's begin by clarifying what we mean by them.

Risk escalation is the process of bringing a risk or risk event to the attention of appropriate and accountable internal stakeholders (for example, an enterprise risk governance body or even its board of directors). It's important to recognize that this is not the same as incident response. An incident will almost always trigger a response of some kind, but a far broader range of risks will require escalation of some kind. The decision about the level of escalation is based on whether the instance exceeds a certain threshold defined by the enterprise's risk classification and risk tolerance levels.

Risk disclosure means informing certain individuals and entities that a risk has been identified or an event has occurred. This process, too, is based on predefined risk thresholds. There are two key facts that must be understood about risk disclosure. The first is that, as we've already noted, in many cases it's required by laws or regulatory compliance mandates, making the failure to disclose a risk event a very serious matter. The second is that, unlike risk escalation, risk disclosure in most cases means informing parties both inside and outside the enterprise. These parties may include the board of directors, the enterprise's governance body, stockholders, customers and clients, and—critically—regulators. In some cases, even the courts are involved. There are four main reasons risks need to be disclosed:

- Public companies' obligation to disclose material risks (a concept we'll be discussing in detail later in this chapter)
- Regulatory compliance obligations
- Legal requirements (for example, the data privacy obligations of the European Union [EU] General Data Protection Regulation [GDPR])
- The need to maintain public trust

The SEC and Risk Disclosure

As you'll see, there are a great many regulatory bodies worldwide that are concerned with cyber risk oversight and risk disclosure. In this chapter, we focus primarily on the SEC and its specific requirements. That's because the SEC has authority over all publicly traded companies in the US, and that makes it the most important regulatory body for enterprises, including some operating beyond the US. As you'll see later in this chapter, there are many other regulatory bodies worldwide whose requirements enterprises must understand and address. Their compliance requirements may overlap and in some cases supersede and even contradict one another. For example, foreign-owned companies listed on US exchanges, like the New York Stock Exchange (NYSE) and the Nasdaq, will need to meet both SEC requirements and those of their home countries' regulators, which may be quite different. It's clear that cyber risk disclosure represents an increasingly serious focus of interest and action for the SEC. Following the lead of the courts, the SEC plainly believes enterprises aren't disclosing risks in an adequately transparent and timely fashion, and that this limits current and prospective investors' abilities to trust they're making informed investment decisions. Ensuring investor trust is the SEC's most important function, which is why its concern about disclosure is driving new and increasingly rigorous regulatory compliance requirements.

As we've mentioned, in July 2023 the SEC introduced a new set of rules that require public companies to report cyber incidents and to periodically report on their cyber risk management, strategy, and governance practices. (The SEC's cyber rules, and the reasoning that underlies them, align closely with the purpose and intent of this book.)

The inescapable conclusion to be drawn from this move by the SEC, and many other regulatory bodies, is that enterprises everywhere have no choice but to dramatically improve their cyber risk disclosure and escalation practices. And the only way for enterprises to meet their legal and regulatory obligations and disclose risks with accuracy and timeliness is for all components of a CRMP to work together seamlessly.

Regulatory Bodies Worldwide Require Risk Disclosure

The SEC is the most important financial regulator in the US, but it isn't the only one in the world—or even in the US. Enterprises with operations in different regions and jurisdictions will need to meet the requirements of a broad range of regulatory bodies regarding risk disclosure, including:

- Australian Securities and Investments Commission (ASIC): an independent Australian government body responsible for regulating the country's corporations

- Autorité des Marchés Financiers (AMF—Financial Markets Authority): the primary regulator of financial markets in France

- Bundesanstalt für Finanzdienstleistungsaufsicht (BaFin—Federal Financial Supervisory Authority): the supervisory authority responsible for regulating Germany's financial services industry

- Canadian Securities Administrators (CSA): an organization that brings together the securities regulators for Canada's provinces and territories to harmonize the regulation of the country's capital markets

- China Securities Regulatory Commission (CSRC): the principal securities regulator in the People's Republic of China (PRC)

- European Securities and Markets (ESMA): an independent authority that works to protect the stability of the EU financial systems

- Financial Conduct Authority (FCA): the regulator for financial services companies and financial markets in the UK

- Financial Industry Regulatory Authority (FINRA): the body that writes and enforces rules for brokers and broker-dealers in the US

- International Organization of Securities Commissions (IOSCO): the international body that brings together the world's securities regulators

- Japan Financial Services Agency (JFSA): the government agency responsible for supervising the Japanese financial services industry

- Securities and Exchange Board of India (SEBI): the regulator responsible for the Indian securities market

- Swiss Financial Market Supervisory Authority (FINMA): the regulatory body responsible for Switzerland's banking industry and other financial institutions

These regulatory bodies, and others, understandably function in different ways to address their unique national or regional environments. Nonetheless, they have all established consistent obligations, which we've covered in this book and which must be addressed by a CRMP. In the simplest terms, these obligations are to ensure that the right people are responsible for oversight through a proper governance model, that they're regularly apprised of cyber risk through risk-informed systems, that effective risk-based strategy and execution are in place, and that risks are escalated—and, where applicable, disclosed—in a timely and accurate manner.

Risk Factors and Material Risk: Two Key Concepts

Two concepts are central to any discussion of risk escalation and risk disclosure, and they deserve an in-depth look. The SEC has recently updated its rules and guidance on both these concepts—risk factors and material risk—and the subject's importance to the SEC makes those updates an excellent starting point for understanding them.

Risk factors: In 2020, the SEC updated its rules and guidance on risk factor modernization and disclosure, with the underlying objective of improving the quality of risk factor disclosures with more relevant and specific information about risks. The update made it clear that risk factors should be concise, understandable, and transparent. They should also be organized under relevant headings and focused on the most significant risks that investors would find useful in assessing a company. The SEC divided risk factors into three categories:

- Company-specific risks
- Industry risks
- Risks related to specific securities (that is, specific investments)

Material risk: Financial markets depend heavily on transparency. In its simplest terms, this means that anyone considering investing in a company has the right to know any information that would be likely to have an impact on that decision. According to the SEC, building on an influential 1972 Supreme Court decision, materiality relates to "those matters to which there is a substantial likelihood that a reasonable investor would attach importance in determining whether to purchase the security registered." This is what we mean by "materially relevant" (or simply "material") risk information, and it unquestionably applies to cyber risk. Now, not all risk information is material. A small data breach that's resolved quickly probably wouldn't be materially relevant, and neither would an isolated instance of fraud. But a large-scale hack impacting millions of consumers is clearly material, and so is a long-term pattern of fraud. And materially relevant risks and incidents must be reported to the relevant regulators, which in the case of a publicly traded company in the US means, first and foremost, the SEC.

Risk Escalation

Risk escalation, as we've already noted, is the process of using a risk-informed system to identify, assess, and prioritize risks that may have increased—in likelihood, in impact, or both—and bring them to the attention of designated persons or entities so that they can take appropriate action. It's absolutely essential to recognize that when we use the term *risk* in this context, we're not simply referring to incidents that have already happened and require a response, like data breaches or malware attacks. And it's equally essential to recognize that risk escalation is not the same as responding to an incident. A risk event may be triggered by many factors, such as a change in the enterprise's operating environment. These factors may require a reassessment of risk thresholds, but not a specific response to an actual loss event that has already occurred.

Risk escalation is not the same as incident response. An incident will almost always require some type of response, but it may or may not change a risk level that triggers strategic risk escalation for decision-making purposes or disclosure.

Senior enterprise decision makers have a wealth of experience and expertise in determining whether risk events reach or exceed thresholds that require escalation or disclosure—that is, whether they're materially relevant. But a seemingly endless series of cyber risk management failures indicates that, despite their expertise, decision makers lack the necessary understanding of the impacts or have chosen to disregard those digitalization risks we've been discussing. Meanwhile, legislators, regulators, and courts are now making it clear that this is unacceptable and that enterprises require cyber expertise, as well as cyber accountability, at the highest levels.

Formal cyber risk escalation processes offer enterprises important operational improvements. One example is early detection, which makes it possible to identify potential issues early and enables timely and effective responses to prevent or mitigate damaging outcomes. Early detection significantly improves risk decision making, so that risk owners, governance bodies, and other key stakeholders can make informed decisions on emerging risks and other changes in the risk environment— decisions that align with the enterprise's established risk thresholds. Risk escalation helps to establish a culture of open and expected communication and collaboration, where employees feel free, and in fact obligated, to share concerns about risks. (It also makes it possible for security professionals and other risk practitioners to prioritize escalations, so they don't lose credibility by drawing senior decision makers' attention to issues that don't really require it.) This is especially important, because defining decision making and accountability takes internal "political" pressures off employees, by allowing them to point to executive-approved policies that require escalation, even if that escalation places an influential person or internal organization in a bad light.

These factors all contribute to the key benefits of a CRMP that we've been discussing. They enhance the enterprise's reputation, showing its commitment to risk management and increasing the confidence of a broad range of stakeholders, from customers to investors to partners. Effective cyber risk escalation practices have other financial benefits, of course: escalating a risk so that it can be addressed immediately can save enterprises huge costs resulting from risks that are not addressed in a timely and effective fashion.

Most importantly, risk escalation is central to the enterprise's critical efforts to meet their legal and regulatory compliance responsibilities to manage security as a risk function. The courts and regulatory bodies are entirely willing to punish risk decision makers—all the way up to the board level—for their failure to be informed and address risk issues. In other words, "I wasn't informed" is not an acceptable defense when things go wrong.

Cyber risk escalation is the formal practice of ensuring the right people have the right information at the right time. But this isn't a simple undertaking. Risks—and cyber risks in particular—are complex, fast-moving, and difficult to identify and prioritize. One essential mechanism that every enterprise should be using in its risk escalation efforts is the assessment process enabled by the risk-informed system we detailed in Chapter 4.

Cyber Risk Classification

In Chapter 4, we stressed the need for the potential impact of a cyber event to be communicated in business terms that risk owners and other stakeholders can clearly understand. This use of clearly recognizable business terminology—aligned as much as possible with the overall enterprise risk management (ERM) approach—makes it possible for a nontechnical audience to understand risk and make informed decisions about it.

The risk assessment and the classification of the residual risk (Critical, High, Medium, Low) are necessary parts of the risk escalation and disclosure component of the CRMP. There are two other considerations that stakeholders must clearly understand and determine as a risk is evaluated: whether an identified risk is material, and whether it is beyond the enterprise's defined appetite or tolerance:

Material risk
> This is a risk that (as we've already explained) could impact investment decisions and investor trust, and that from a cyber perspective would be incorporated into the already established enterprise process for determining materiality.

Risks beyond appetite or tolerance
> These are risks that could cause serious damage (for example, loss of life) to the enterprise or its employees or other stakeholders beyond the organization's risk appetite or tolerance. (This would be determined by the risk-based strategy and execution component of the CRMP.) For some enterprises, risk appetite or tolerance may be determined at the overall risk classification level (that is, all critical risks that are beyond the defined appetite or tolerance). Others may determine tolerance specifically at the impact category level (for example, the enterprise might determine that a High impact to the Operational risk category is tolerable but only a Low impact to the Environmental category is tolerable).

Once the appropriate context has been established, the information can be escalated—programmatically, based on the risk level—through the governance body or a defined hierarchy of stakeholders (see Figure 6-1). Depending on the risk level and the appropriate level of governance, responsibilities may be assigned as follows:

Recommend

A given group or committee is responsible for providing cyber risk recommendations to the next level of governance.

Decide

A group or committee is responsible for making cyber risk decisions based on the analysis and provided recommendations.

Inform

The group or committee is informed of any decisions made regarding the cyber risk response.

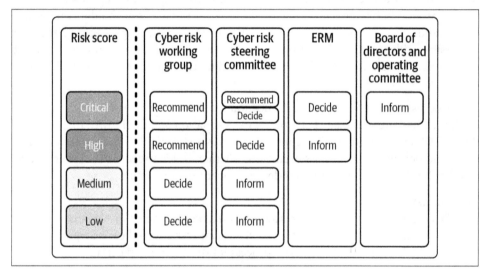

Figure 6-1. A sample risk escalation hierarchy

Yahoo!'s Massive Data Breach

Beginning sometime in 2013, the internet services provider Yahoo! experienced a series of what was believed to be state-sponsored attacks based in Russia, which together represent what likely remains to this day the largest data breach in history. One breach occurred in late 2014 and impacted more than 500 million Yahoo! user accounts, but it wasn't disclosed until the second half of 2016. Yahoo! eventually acknowledged that that breach—initially believed to have impacted an already staggering one *billion* user accounts—had actually compromised all *three* billion of its accounts. The consequences for the company's users were shocking. Sensitive personal information on hundreds of millions of Yahoo! users was offered for sale on the dark web, and the company eventually reported that the attackers probably had the capability to falsify login credentials, making it possible for them to access any account without a password.

In its Making Findings Order against Yahoo!, the SEC noted that "despite its knowledge of the 2014 data breach, Yahoo! did not disclose the data breach in its public filings for nearly two years. To the contrary, Yahoo!'s risk factor disclosures in its annual and quarterly reports from 2014 through 2016 were materially misleading in that they claimed the company only faced the risk of potential future data breaches that might expose the company to loss of its users' personal information stored in its information systems, as well as potential future litigation, remediation, increased costs for security measures, loss of revenue, damage to its reputation, and liability, without disclosing that a massive data breach had in fact already occurred."[1]

The company paid a heavy price for that series of failures. Before the breaches were announced, Yahoo! was negotiating for Verizon Communications to purchase a large portion of its operations for $4.83 billion. Verizon, which was informed of the breaches only two days before the public became aware of it, considered taking legal action to stop the acquisition, but finally went through with the deal—at a price $350 million less than was initially agreed on. The company's CEO, unsurprisingly, did not keep her job. Neither did its chief lawyer.

The financial damage didn't end there. Yahoo! paid a $35 million penalty to the SEC for misleading investors by failing to disclose the data breaches. The SEC stated that Yahoo! first became aware of one of the data breaches within days but failed to disclose it until more than two years later, when the company was in the process of closing its acquisition deal with Verizon. Yahoo! also settled a class action lawsuit on behalf of Yahoo! users for more than $117 million.

This is a spectacular example of what we mean by materially relevant risk information. Millions of parties—individual users, current and prospective shareholders, and companies like Verizon—had a right to know that Yahoo! had experienced a massive security failure. Because Yahoo! failed to disclose in a timely manner information that was clearly material, none of these parties was in a position to make informed decisions about whether to use the company's services, invest in its stock, or—in Verizon's case—acquire a large portion of its assets. It was a new crisis, added to an existing crisis, that was self-inflicted and avoidable.

Escalation and Disclosure: Not Just Security Incidents

It's important to recognize that when we talk about cyber risks requiring escalation and disclosure, we don't simply mean cyber incidents, like malware, data breaches, identity thefts, or ransomware attacks. A broad and endlessly growing range of

---

1 Altaba Inc., f/d/b/a Yahoo! Inc., April 24, 2018, *https://oreil.ly/cVzfG*.

factors can impact an enterprise's risk posture, both positively and negatively. The implementation of a new technology, like cloud computing or automation, could, for example, introduce a new attack surface and new security vulnerabilities. A change in the enterprise's operating model or even the regions where it does business may carry with it new regulatory compliance requirements. Even the decision to introduce a new product or service could introduce the risk of reputational damage that needs new consideration. Like all the other factors that are considered by an effective CRMP, the risk environment can be continuously monitored and aligned with an ERM program, if there is one in place. NIST 8286 provides an excellent framework for integrating cyber risk with enterprise risk.

A key premise underlying the need for risk escalation and disclosure is the principle that it is impossible to eliminate all risk. Enterprises need to take on appropriate risk in order to remain competitive, and their risk decisions need to be made and approved by the appropriate parties. When risk factors change, they need to be brought to the attention of the right authorities.

Disclosure: A Mandatory Concern for Enterprises

Cyber risk disclosure—essentially, extending escalation to persons and bodies outside the enterprise—is arguably even more important than escalation, because the consequences of failing to disclose risks can result in serious, even existential, damage.

The sets of interested parties to whom risk information must be disclosed can be divided into three basic categories:

Shareholders and other investors (both current and prospective)
> As we've seen, a broad range of financial regulators worldwide have authority over the disclosure requirements of publicly traded companies. Their mandates vary widely, but they all share a common goal: to promote public trust in the markets by ensuring that investors receive transparent and accurate information. And many of these regulatory bodies, if not most of them, are making it increasingly clear that they are prepared to take serious action against companies that don't comply with their disclosure requirements.

Regulatory bodies
> A broad range of regulatory compliance requirements that extend far beyond financial disclosure apply to enterprises across many industries and for many reasons. The security of confidential and otherwise sensitive information is one of the most important issues they address. Privacy regulations in many regions, notably the EU General Data Protection Regulation (GDPR), clearly specify where and how sensitive data can be stored, and they prescribe serious punishments for violations of the rules—and for failure to disclose violations. In 2021, Amazon was fined (*https://oreil.ly/ZeYo3*) an astonishing 746 million euros

(approximately US\$877 million) for violating GDPR data collection rules. EU member France separately fined Amazon 35 million euros (approximately \$38 million) for a related offense, showing that enterprises must be prepared to deal with multiple, and sometimes even contradictory, regulatory requirements. Distinct industry regulators have also developed specific criteria and thresholds for risk and incident reporting requirements, tailored to the unique circumstances and settings of individual enterprises.

The public

Few assets are more important to an enterprise than the trust of its many stakeholders, including its customers, its investors, its partners, and its employees. Trust, as a valued commodity, can be an issue even for individuals who don't have a direct stake in the enterprise's operations, by influencing the actions of governmental and regulatory entities and public (for example, consumer) advocacy groups. The cyber risk environment, with its endless series of well-publicized security failures, has inevitably made the public highly likely to distrust enterprises, especially when it comes to protecting their personal information and their digitalized products. Complete and transparent disclosure of enterprise risk practices—including but not limited to their responses to security incidents—is critical to maintaining or restoring the public trust.

The Equifax Scandal

A recent case involving Equifax, one of the world's most important credit reporting agencies, offers a spectacular example of what can go wrong when appropriate risk disclosure practices *aren't* in place—or, if they are in place, aren't followed. Between May and July 2017, the Atlanta-based Equifax experienced what to this day remains one of the worst data breaches in history. The private information of more than 160 million people in the US, the UK, and Canada was compromised in what the US government has alleged was a massive identity and data theft committed by state-sponsored actors in the People's Republic of China. The hackers exploited Equifax's failure to implement a critical server security update, and were able to scan the companies' databases undetected for more than two months.

Equifax's lax security practices were obviously a matter of deep concern for the company's customers, shareholders, and regulators in at least three countries. But it was something else Equifax failed to do that proved especially damaging to the company, and it's something that's especially relevant to this chapter. The company discovered the breach in July 2017 but didn't report it until September, and even then it didn't accurately report the full extent of the breach. (The company's senior executives can't be accused of not acting rapidly when it was in their personal interest. Three of them, including the CFO, sold almost \$1.8 million in Equifax stock shortly after the breach was discovered but long before it was disclosed and the stock price fell.) As late as March 2018, Equifax was revising upward its estimates of the number of individuals whose information had been compromised, and was also changing its account of what types of information had been stolen. And that failure to escalate and disclose the breach in the timely, accurate fashion required by court precedent and regulatory bodies, especially the SEC in the US, made the data breach far more damaging than it would otherwise have been.

The damage from the breach followed a pattern that by now will be familiar to the readers of this book. Within days of Equifax's initial disclosure, the company's stock value had fallen by a staggering $4 billion. Needless to say, Equifax suffered severe reputational damage—an especially acute concern in financial services, an industry in which trust is perhaps the single most important asset a company has. There were lawsuits, of course, including a massive class action suit that was settled in 2021 for approximately $425 million. Actions taken by the Federal Trade Commission (FTC), other regulators, and many state governments resulted in Equifax paying $300 million to a victim compensation fund, $175 million to US states and territories, and $100 million in federal fines.

There's no question that a data breach on this scale would have been extremely damaging to Equifax or any other enterprise, but it was the company's failure to fulfill its clearly established obligation to disclose the breach that turned a disaster into a catastrophe. As a publicly traded company operating in the US, Equifax was required to disclose any risks that were determined to be "materially relevant"—that's a concept that's central to this chapter—in a timely manner. By failing to do so by any reasonable standard, the company exposed itself to the most serious legal and regulatory liability imaginable. A materially relevant risk, in its simplest terms, is one that could have an influence on the decision as to whether or not to invest in a company. The SEC has established a clear and precise standard for determining whether a risk is materially relevant: "whether there is a substantial likelihood that a reasonable investor would consider the information important in decision-making and whether a reasonable investor would view the information to significantly alter the 'total mix' of information available."[2]

It was precisely the failure to disclose what were clearly materially relevant issues that proved so damaging to Equifax. It's impossible to calculate the total damage—financial, reputational, and otherwise—that Equifax suffered as a result of its multiple disclosure failures. But the monetary cost alone must run to the billions of dollars, and it almost certainly would have been far less if the company had followed the SEC rules and other regulatory guidance.

---

2 Cydney Posner, "SEC Proposal to Modernize Reg S-K," Harvard Law School Forum on Corporate Governance, August 20, 2019, *https://oreil.ly/zDtZt*.

When Multiple Risks Combine to Become a Material Risk

Beginning in late 2016, Wells Fargo, one of the largest and most important US-based financial institutions, was caught up in a huge scandal involving the creation of millions of fraudulent bank accounts for clients without their consent. Representatives of Wells Fargo's US banking operation added new accounts to clients' existing ones—creating credit card accounts for clients who had only checking or savings accounts—without their consent or even their knowledge, with the result that these customers incurred additional fees and charges.

Regulatory agencies, including the US. Consumer Financial Protection Bureau (CFPB), fined Wells Fargo a total of $185 million for what it clearly established was widespread fraud. Lawsuits—many of them still ongoing—requested damages of almost $3 billion. The bank's CEO was forced to resign, and the company suffered severe reputational damage that continues to this day.

The Wells Fargo scandal is an excellent example of what we mean when we say that risks become material in the aggregate. The creation of each of the fraudulent accounts represented only a comparatively minor infraction. (To be clear, each was still almost certainly a criminal fraud, but its cost to each individual client was, in most cases, fairly small.) If the practice had, for example, been limited to a single bank branch, or even a single operating region, it would likely not have represented a materially relevant risk—that is, it would likely not have needed to be disclosed to the SEC and other regulators. But the investigations into the case clearly established that the fraud was far-reaching and resulted from intense corporate pressure for branch representatives to engage in a practice called "cross-selling." Investigations also established that Wells Fargo's most senior management knew or should have known that widespread fraud was taking place. That made all those small fraudulent transactions "material in the aggregate" and therefore subject to the disclosure rules of the SEC and other regulatory bodies. This also turned a series of small issues into a massive problem that's still causing Wells Fargo, and of course its shareholders, serious damage.

Here's an example of how this would work in relation to cyber incidents: a series of several small breaches—the digital equivalent of all those small frauds—could be material in aggregate. That could obviously be relevant to an investor who's considering buying or selling shares in the enterprise—and that's what potentially makes it a material incident. The SEC specifically made mention in its latest cyber rule stating that the definition of a "cybersecurity incident" (*https://oreil.ly/o2TGU*) would extend to a "series of related unauthorized occurrences." Examples include the same malicious actor engaging in a number of smaller but continuous cyberattacks related in time and form, or a series of related attacks from multiple actors exploiting the same vulnerability and collectively impeding the company's business materiality.

SEC Materiality Considerations

The SEC has presented a list (*https://oreil.ly/GrB9e*)—which, to be clear, is not complete—of issues that public companies should consider in determining whether to disclose cybersecurity risks. The materiality determination should be made on the collective analysis or, as the SEC puts it, the "total mix" of these considerations:

- Previous cybersecurity incidents, including their severity and frequency
- The probability of the occurrence of cybersecurity incidents and their potential magnitude
- The adequacy of preventative actions taken to reduce cybersecurity risks, and their associated costs, potentially including a discussion of any limits to the company's ability to prevent or mitigate certain cybersecurity risks
- The aspects of the company's business and operations that give rise to material cybersecurity risks and the potential costs and consequences of such risks, including industry-specific risks and third-party supplier and service provider risks
- The costs associated with maintaining cybersecurity protections, including any insurance coverage relating to cybersecurity incidents or payments to service providers
- The potential for reputational damage
- Current or proposed pending laws and regulations that could affect a company's cybersecurity requirements and their associated costs
- Litigation, regulatory investigation, and remediation costs associated with cybersecurity incidents.

Enterprise risk management and cyber risk management practices must be fully aligned to ensure that risk decisions are made based on common information and common understanding.

Ensuring That a Crisis Doesn't Become a Catastrophe

The 2021 ransomware attack on Colonial Pipeline isn't just an example of how dangerous the cyber risk environment has become. It also clearly shows the benefits—to the enterprise under attack, to its shareholders, and to the public—of rapid, appropriate escalation and disclosure. Unlike Equifax, and many other enterprises that have faced serious cyber threats, Colonial escalated its issues swiftly, and was open and forthcoming about the situation, its potential impacts, and the actions it was taking. Let's take a look at the 2021 timeline of events:

- May 6: Hackers attack Colonial's systems, stealing data, locking computers, and demanding a ransom payment.
- May 7: Colonial pays $4.4 million in ransom.
- May 8–9: The company publicly announces that it's been attacked and shuts off some pipelines and other systems, then details its plans for restarting systems.
- May 10–11: The FBI confirms the specific ransomware (DarkSide) used in the attack and issues an advisory for enterprises dealing with it.
- May 12: Colonial resumes operations and announces fuel delivery timelines to reduce panic buying.

In barely a week, Colonial went from suffering a crippling cyberattack that shut down most of its operations to being well on its way to complete recovery. The company limited its potential reputational damage—because it had clearly done everything it should have done—and received little or no significant criticism from regulators or legislators. In fact, the attack resulted in important action in the public interest, including the reintroduction of the Pipeline Security Act, a bill to clarify security responsibilities for oil and gas pipelines, and a Department of Homeland Security directive outlining new pipeline cybersecurity requirements.

It's tempting to point to Colonial's response as an extraordinary achievement—and it's certainly not commonplace—but the reality is, this is simply the way enterprises should be expected to respond to cyber risk events. And this is increasingly the way the courts and regulators expect them to respond. They should escalate issues to the appropriate and accountable level, and then disclose them to the appropriate stakeholders and authorities. And the only way enterprises can expect to do that on a consistent, actionable basis is to have a formal cyber risk management program in place.

Cyber Risk Management Program and ERM Alignment

ERM and cyber risk management are both essential to protecting enterprises and their personnel and ensuring business continuity, and they're both driven by legal and regulatory requirements and industry frameworks. They both require the close collaboration of multiple enterprise stakeholders, including boards of directors, senior executives, and departments including legal, compliance, and auditing—and they both require input from IT. But there are important differences. ERM covers all types of risk. In contrast, cyber risk management focuses specifically on malicious risks introduced by enterprises' growing reliance on intricately interconnected digital technologies, and it also requires more technical expertise and specialized tools and technologies. It's extremely important to make this distinction clear, because many enterprises are essentially "burying" cyber risk in enterprise risk, making it far more difficult to identify specifically cyber-related risks and of course to escalate and disclose them.

Nonetheless, cyber risk *is* an enterprise risk, and the courts and regulators have made it clear that it must be considered as such. For this reason, cyber risk decisions must align with, and be informed by, whatever overall risk management framework is in place (which may or may not be a formal ERM program). This is not a question of organizational alignment—that raises too many "political" issues—but rather of aligning programs and program objectives, coordinating information gathering, and reporting and agreeing on the appropriate balance of risk and reward. This has been a common theme in the principles defining the other three components of a CRMP (Chapters 3–5).

Five Principles of Risk Escalation and Disclosure

The framework we introduced throughout the book can be used to identify the key underlying principles that will factor into the development, consideration, and implementation of an organization's risk escalation and disclosure processes (see Table 6-1).

Table 6-1. CRMP—risk escalation and disclosure

CRMP component	Principles	Informative references
Agile governance	See "Seven Principles of Agile Governance" on page 49.	• SEC Final Cyber Rule (*https://oreil.ly/o2TGU*) • NIST CSF 2.0 (*https://oreil.ly/xngbU*) • 2023 NACD Director's Handbook (*https://oreil.ly/8enA4*) • ISO 27001:2022 (*https://oreil.ly/0ID28*) • NIST 8286 (*https://oreil.ly/WOC5f*) • IIA Three Lines Model (*https://oreil.ly/0OAQ6*) • SEC 2018 Guidance (*https://oreil.ly/SVwOx*) • ISO 31000:2018 (*https://oreil.ly/vuqzY*) • AICPA CRMP (*https://oreil.ly/d5n8o*)
Risk-informed system	See "Five Principles of a Risk-Informed System" on page 66.	• SEC Final Cyber Rule (*https://oreil.ly/o2TGU*) • NIST CSF 2.0 (*https://oreil.ly/xngbU*) • 2023 NACD Director's Handbook (*https://oreil.ly/8enA4*) • ISO 27001:2022 (*https://oreil.ly/0ID28*) • IIA Three Lines Model (*https://oreil.ly/0OAQ6*) • ISO 31000:2018 (*https://oreil.ly/vuqzY*) • AICPA CRMP (*https://oreil.ly/d5n8o*)

CRMP component	Principles	Informative references
Risk-based strategy and execution	See "Six Principles of Risk-Based Strategy and Execution" on page 88.	• SEC Final Cyber Rule (*https://oreil.ly/o2TGU*) • NIST CSF 2.0 (*https://oreil.ly/xngbU*) • 2023 NACD Director's Handbook (*https://oreil.ly/8enA4*) • IIA Three Lines Model (*https://oreil.ly/00AQ6*) • ISO 31000:2018 (*https://oreil.ly/vuqzY*) • AICPA CRMP (*https://oreil.ly/d5n8o*)
Risk escalation and disclosure	See "Five Principles of Risk Escalation and Disclosure" on page 114.	• SEC Final Cyber Rule (*https://oreil.ly/o2TGU*) • NIST CSF 2.0 (*https://oreil.ly/xngbU*) • 2023 NACD Director's Handbook (*https://oreil.ly/8enA4*) • IIA Three Lines Model (*https://oreil.ly/00AQ6*) • SEC 2018 Guidance (*https://oreil.ly/SVwOx*) • AICPA CRMP (*https://oreil.ly/d5n8o*)

For more detail on the comprehensive framework itself, see the Appendix.

Cyber risk escalation and disclosure, like the other components of a CRMP, is not a one-size-fits-all proposition. Enterprises face different cyber risk environments, informed and influenced by all the factors we've been discussing. They also have different capabilities to address risk and, crucially, operate under different legal standards and regulatory compliance requirements. That said, all effective cyber risk escalation and disclosure practices have certain key principles in common.

Principle 1: Establish Escalation Processes

Formal cyber risk escalation processes must be established.

Throughout this book, we've stressed the importance of formalized processes, with defined roles, functions, responsibilities, and accountability—and nowhere is this more important than in risk escalation practices. These practices, like many other aspects of cyber risk management, are frequently conducted on an informal, ad hoc, or relationship-based basis. And even when escalation processes are in place, they're often not adequately defined, with risk classification mechanisms that clearly define responsibilities for informing the appropriate stakeholders of risks and escalating risks to the appropriate levels of governance. Another weakness is escalating control failures or vulnerabilities without the business context needed to indicate the real-world risk level. It's important to remember the formula for defining risk: *Likelihood (of a threat exploiting a vulnerability) x Impact (on an enterprise process, asset, or objective).* But control failure or vulnerability represents only half of that equation.

Risk classifications—based on enterprise-specific criteria and approved by the governance body—lie at the center of a CRMP. They're used to define levels of severity and urgency, so that appropriate prioritization decisions can be made and appropriate actions can be taken when mitigating or managing risks. Defining clear criteria for each classification allows organizations to prioritize the escalation and disclosure process, define individuals' or organizations' responsibilities for escalation and disclosure, and ensure that risk decision making, information, and escalation are conducted at the appropriate levels of governance.

The need for risk escalation processes aligned with defined risk classifications and appropriate governance levels is driven by a broad range of standards and protocols, including:

SEC Regulation S–K Item 106(c)—Governance (https://oreil.ly/o2TGU)
Formalized escalation processes are required to guide a board, which has oversight of risks from cybersecurity threats, and management, which assesses and manages material risks from cybersecurity threats and proper transparency of risk information. Companies must be able to communicate significant cyber threats and risks through the governance body, underscoring the importance of established pathways for escalation.

2018 SEC Commission Statement and Guidance on Public Company Cybersecurity Disclosures (https://oreil.ly/SVwOx)
The SEC emphasized in its 2018 guidance the importance of establishing formal risk escalation procedures to manage cyber risks effectively and ensure that enterprises can rapidly identify, assess, and respond to potential cyber threats. In so doing, a company could minimize the threats and potential impact on their operations, clients, and overall market stability. Three components of the SEC statement and guidance are especially relevant to the issue of disclosure:

- "Crucial to a public company's ability to make any required disclosure of cybersecurity risks and incidents in the appropriate time frame are disclosure controls and procedures that provide an appropriate method of discerning the impact that such matters may have on the company and its business, financial condition, and results of operations, as well as a protocol to determine the potential materiality of such risks and incidents" (page 1, paragraph 1).

- "Companies should assess whether they have sufficient disclosure controls and procedures in place to ensure that relevant information about cybersecurity risks and incidents is processed and reported to the appropriate personnel, including up the corporate ladder, to enable senior management to make disclosure decisions" (page 18, paragraph 3).

- "Controls and procedures should enable companies to identify cybersecurity risks and incidents, assess and analyze their impact on a company's business, evaluate the significance associated with such risks and incidents, provide for open communications between technical experts and disclosure advisors, and make timely disclosures regarding such risks and incidents" (page 20, paragraph 1).

2017 AICPA CRMP Description Criteria DC13, DC16 (https://oreil.ly/d5n8o)

These two accounting industry standards call for established processes for internally communicating relevant cyber risk information, including objectives and responsibilities and, critically, thresholds for communicating and identifying security events and the responses to them. AICPA also requires a process for the timely evaluation and communication of identified security threats, vulnerabilities, and deficiencies to the appropriate parties—including the board of directors, when necessary.

2023 NACD Director's Handbook on Cyber-Risk Oversight Principle 2 (https://oreil.ly/8enA4)

NACD's Principle 2 emphasizes the need for formal processes for escalating risks. In the context of cybersecurity, this means recognizing when a cyber risk reaches a level that requires legal action or disclosure. Ineffective risk escalation can lead to legal implications if not handled correctly, hence the relevance to Principle 2 of the NACD.

Principle 2: Establish Disclosure Processes—All Enterprises

The enterprise's cyber disclosure processes should address its specific risk factors, organizational context, and requirements.

The wide variances between different enterprises' risk environments means that their disclosure processes and procedures must be tailored to the risk factors, environment, and requirements specific to each enterprise. Formal risk management processes must be in place to identify and analyze the complete range of enterprise-specific risks—not just a threat or an incident that's already occurred, but also changes in the overall risk environment—and document how they're managed, including via risk acceptance, mitigation, and transfer.

> Risk disclosure is about more than threats and incident response.

An enterprise's responsible parties—risk owners, governance body or bodies, senior executives, and the board of directors—must have a clear understanding of its risk environment and their responsibilities in addressing it. Several of the concepts we discussed earlier in this chapter are especially relevant here. One is, of course, the question of materiality: risk disclosure procedures must be grounded in the recognition of what does and does not represent a material risk, and what measures must be taken in response to such a risk. Regulatory compliance is another critical consideration, and compliance requirements will vary widely depending on the enterprise's industry, the regions where it operates, its size, and even its organizational structure. All these factors and more will determine what risks and risk issues must be disclosed, to whom, and, crucially, how rapidly.

Disclosure is another area where cyber risk must be clearly differentiated from overall enterprise risk. Regulatory bodies including the SEC have made it clear that the widespread practice of generalizing about different types of risk is unacceptable. The result is that cyber risk gets buried in enterprise risk, so that its specific requirements are likely not to be adequately recognized and addressed. The SEC in particular has stated that publicly traded companies' cyber risk disclosure practices aren't specific, clear, or timely enough. And it has noted that it sometimes actually learns about a cyber risk issue in the media before a company has disclosed it—if the issue is disclosed at all. For this reason—and recognizing that cyber risks are uniquely fast-moving—the SEC and other regulators are increasingly demanding that cyber risk be identified and reported separately from overall enterprise risk.

The need for enterprise-specific disclosure procedures is guided by standards and protocols, including:

2023 NACD Director's Handbook on Cyber-Risk Oversight Principle 2 (https://oreil.ly/8enA4)
> Public companies must disclose material risks, risk factors, and incidents related to cybersecurity. Disclosure of such material information often has legal implications and is frequently mandated by regulations, hence the emphasis from the NACD.

2017 AICPA CRMP Description Criteria DC6 and DC14 (https://oreil.ly/d5n8o)
> The accountancy-related standards, unsurprisingly, are especially rigorous where cyber risk disclosure procedures are concerned. DC6 suggests disclosure of security incidents identified in the previous 12 months that significantly impaired the enterprise's achievement of its cybersecurity objectives, as well as information on the nature, timing, and extent or effect of the incidents and their disposition. DC14 defines a process for communicating with external parties regarding matters affecting the functioning of the entity's CRMP.

2023 Draft NIST CSF 2.0 GV.OC-03 (https://oreil.ly/xngbU)
> This subcategory emphasizes understanding and managing legal, regulatory, and contractual requirements regarding cybersecurity, including obligations related to privacy and civil liberties. These requirements often include specific provisions for disclosure, thus making the understanding and management of these requirements critical for proper disclosure procedures.

Principle 3: Establish Disclosure Processes—Public Companies

Public companies must disclose their material risks, risk factors, cyber risk management processes, governance, and material incident reporting.

Publicly traded companies, both domestic and international, because of their urgent need to maintain the trust of current and prospective investors, have especially rigorous risk disclosure responsibilities. Investors have the right, clearly established by legal precedent and regulatory compliance requirements, to make informed investment decisions, evaluate a company's performance, and hold its management—including its board of directors—accountable. These rights definitely extend to public companies' cyber risk management practices, including their overall strategy, their governance practices, and their incident responses. All these aspects of cyber risk management require complete transparency, in terms of accurate and timely disclosure.

The need for clearly defined disclosure practices is driven by a broad range of factors, including the need to protect the company's brand image, avoid reputational damage, and maintain shareholder confidence. But the most important driver of disclosure for public companies is unquestionably the large and fast-growing body of regulatory compliance requirements, notably by the SEC in the US. A long series of court decisions, some of which we've already discussed, make it clear that the SEC has the authority to hold public companies accountable for the failure to disclose cyber risks—including but certainly not limited to security incidents. And the SEC has made it equally clear that it will take action when public companies don't live up to their responsibilities.

The only way for public companies to meet these obligations is to have clearly defined procedures in place for cybersecurity risk management, including strategy, governance, and accountability, and especially for the timely and accurate disclosure of cybersecurity events and other materially relevant cyber risk issues. The key authorities and standards defining these disclosure responsibilities and offering procedures for addressing them are:

2023 SEC Final Rule Cybersecurity Risk Management, Strategy, Governance, Incident Disclosure Rule (https://oreil.ly/o2TGU)
> Each of the items included in the rule (risk management, strategy, governance, incident disclosure) reiterates the paramount importance of transparency in disclosing significant cyber risks and incidents to shareholders and the public. They align with the principle that public companies, in particular, bear a responsibility to communicate their cyber risk posture and significant events transparently.

2023 Draft NIST CSF 2.0 GV.OC-03 (https://oreil.ly/xngbU)

This principle specifically pertains to public companies, which have certain legal and regulatory obligations to disclose their cybersecurity risk management practices. GV.OC-03 is relevant as it focuses on understanding and managing legal, regulatory, and contractual requirements regarding cybersecurity, which for public companies will include specific disclosure requirements.

2018 SEC Commission Statement and Guidance on Public Company Cybersecurity Disclosures (https://oreil.ly/SVwOx)

A broad range of SEC regulations make it clear that a material risk is by definition an enterprise risk, and they hold public companies' cyber risk responsibilities to the same standard as their enterprise risks:

- "The Commission believes that it is critical that public companies take all required actions to inform investors about material cybersecurity risks and incidents in a timely fashion, including those companies that are subject to material cybersecurity risks but may not yet have been the target of a cyberattack" (page 4, paragraph 1).

- "Companies are required to establish and maintain appropriate and effective disclosure controls and procedures that enable them to make accurate and timely disclosures of material events, including those related to cybersecurity. Such robust disclosure controls and procedures assist companies in satisfying their disclosure obligations under the federal securities laws" (pages 6 and 7, paragraph 2).

- "Companies should consider the materiality of cybersecurity risks and incidents when preparing the disclosure that is required in registration statements under the Securities Act of 1933 ('Securities Act') and the Securities Exchange Act of 1934 ('Exchange Act'), and periodic and current reports under the Exchange Act" (page 7, paragraph 3).

- "The materiality of cybersecurity risks and incidents also depends on the range of harm that such incidents could cause. This includes harm to a company's reputation, financial performance, and customer and vendor relationships, as well as the possibility of litigation or regulatory investigations or actions, including regulatory actions by state and federal governmental authorities and non-US authorities" (page 11, paragraph 1).

Under the SEC's new cyber rules, public companies will need to disclose cyber incidents, as well as detailed information about their cyber risk governance, strategy, and risk management (see the SEC's cyber rules in Chapter 2). A defined and implemented CRMP will meet the SEC's intentions, and if the necessary information is properly submitted, it will satisfy these mandatory disclosure requirements. The following sections detail what the SEC rules cover.

Material incident reporting

The rule mandates public companies to disclose material cybersecurity incidents within four business days after determining that a material incident has occurred. This requirement aims to provide timely, relevant, and standardized disclosure to investors and market participants, enabling them to assess the potential effects of material cybersecurity incidents on the registrant's financial and operational status.

Materiality assessment should be a thorough, objective evaluation of the total mix of information, considering all relevant facts and circumstances surrounding the cybersecurity incident, including both quantitative and qualitative factors. Registrants must carefully assess whether an incident is material, based on a well-reasoned, objective approach from a reasonable investor's perspective and considering the total mix of information. The disclosure of cybersecurity incidents that have become material in the aggregate is also required. Registrants must analyze related cybersecurity incidents for materiality, both individually and collectively. If such incidents are material in the aggregate, registrants must disclose relevant information. This requirement ensures transparency and disclosure of continuous or related cyberattacks that collectively have a material impact on the registrant.

Risk management and strategy

The rule addresses the disclosure of a public company's risk management and strategy regarding cybersecurity risks. This requirement aims to provide investors with more consistent and informative disclosures about how registrants identify, assess, and manage cybersecurity risks, as well as the impact of these risks on their business strategy, financial outlook, and financial planning. The requirement for such disclosure gives investors greater transparency into the registrant's strategies and actions for managing cybersecurity risks, allowing them to make better-informed investment decisions.

Governance

The rule addresses the disclosure of a registrant's cybersecurity governance practices, focusing on the board's oversight of cybersecurity risk and management's role in assessing and managing these risks. These disclosure requirements will also help investors gain a better understanding of the public company's approach to managing cybersecurity risks, which can inform their decisions to invest in a company.

Principle 4: Test Escalation and Disclosure Processes

Cyber risk escalation and disclosure processes should be challenged, tested, and updated on an ongoing basis to incorporate lessons learned.

Cyber risk management is an ongoing practice that must constantly be informed by and respond to changing circumstances, and especially changes in the risk environment. (This is true of all risk management, of course, but it's made far more urgent for cyber risk management by the speed of digital-driven change.) And that means escalation and disclosure processes and procedures—as a core component of a CRMP—must be continuously challenged, tested, and updated so that the enterprise as a whole can learn from the lessons of both successes and failures.

Security and risk practitioners, risk owners, governance bodies, and other stakeholders must all be prepared to question their escalation and disclosure processes and procedures. There should be a continuous, interactive process for challenging the program's assumptions about its cyber risk escalation and disclosure requirements, based on identified changes on the complete range of risk factors, including but not limited to emerging threats and vulnerabilities, changes in the industry environment, and operating models. The "second-line" roles we discussed in Chapter 3—the specialists with risk management expertise—should conduct exercises to determine whether risks are being escalated in a timely and accurate fashion and to the designated level. A core focus of an exercise like this should be to determine the criticality and especially the materiality of a risk, to determine whether it falls outside the enterprise's established risk tolerance and creates a situation where there could be heightened liability. And it should also inform the strategy and execution we discussed in the last chapter, to help risk owners and other stakeholders determine whether the established risk tolerance needs to be adjusted and, if so, the adjustments approved.

The need for ongoing testing and updating of escalation and disclosure is provided by the following guidance:

2023 SEC Final Rule Cybersecurity Risk Management, Strategy, Governance, Incident Disclosure Rule (https://oreil.ly/o2TGU)
> The requirements resonate with the principle for a dynamic and evolving approach to disclosure. By ensuring practices are updated to incorporate new learnings and to provide a comprehensive picture of risk management, governance, strategy, and incident disclosure, companies can better maintain stakeholder trust.

2023 Draft NIST CSF 2.0 ID.IM-01–04 (https://oreil.ly/xngbU)
> These subcategories align with this principle as it speaks to reviewing, adjusting, and improving the risk management processes to ensure they cover organizational requirements and risks. As escalation and disclosure practices are a part of

the overall risk management strategy, their regular review and adjustment are necessary based on lessons learned for maintaining effective risk management.

Principle 5: Audit Escalation and Disclosure Processes

Audit should review and assess the enterprise's cyber risk escalation and disclosure processes to ensure their effectiveness, consistency, and compliance with relevant regulations and policies.

The audit function plays a vital role in ensuring the effectiveness and compliance of an enterprise's risk escalation and disclosure processes and procedures. By evaluating the design and implementation of these processes and procedures, identifying gaps and weaknesses, and recommending improvements, auditors help enterprises manage cyber risks more effectively and maintain the trust of stakeholders, including investors, customers, and regulators. Auditors' key responsibilities related to risk escalation and disclosure processes and procedures include:

Assessing the design
Auditors evaluate the design of the enterprise's risk escalation and disclosure processes and procedures to ensure that they're clear, comprehensive, and aligned with its overall risk management objectives and regulatory requirements. This includes reviewing structure, roles and responsibilities, communication channels, and documentation practices.

Testing the implementation
Auditors perform tests to verify that the risk escalation and disclosure processes and procedures are being implemented consistently and effectively enterprise-wide. This may involve reviewing specific incidents, interviewing employees, and examining documentation to assess compliance with established procedures.

Identifying gaps and weaknesses
Through their assessments and tests, auditors identify any gaps or weaknesses in the enterprise's risk escalation and disclosure processes and procedures. These may include inconsistencies in implementation, lack of training or awareness among employees, and insufficient communication and documentation practices.

Recommending improvements
Based on their findings, auditors provide recommendations for enhancing the enterprise's risk escalation and disclosure processes and procedures. These recommendations may address areas like training and awareness, communication channels, documentation, and the overall structure and design of the processes and procedures.

These audit-specific requirements are driven and supported by IIA's Three Lines Model (*https://oreil.ly/0OAQ6*), which emphasizes the third line's role and the critical importance of its independence for objectivity and credibility mapping to the focus on proactive monitoring and assessment of risk escalation and disclosure, reinforcing the need for unbiased evaluation.

The Bottom Line

In closing out this chapter, we want to stress again the regulatory focus and associated liability with risk escalation and disclosure. These aren't "nice-to-have" considerations. They're essential, and they need to be formalized as part of an overall cyber risk management program—with all four core components coordinating together—for escalation and disclosure to be effective. Governments, regulators, and courts, along with industry organizations and the general public, are making that clear through regulatory action, by assessing serious and even crippling fines for violation of the established rules, and by narrowing in on personal liability for executives and board members. And they're not alone: the public are making it clear that they're willing to walk away from companies they feel they can't trust.

Ensuring that risk escalation and disclosure practices are in place isn't simple, and it will require full integration with the other components of the cyber risk management program. Now that we've defined what a cyber risk management program is—pointing to authoritative sources—in the next chapter we'll dive into some implementation strategies and considerations.

CHAPTER 7

Implementing the Cyber Risk Management Program

Throughout this book, we've stressed the critical importance of a formal cyber risk management program (CRMP) that builds on four key components: Agile governance, a risk-informed system, risk-based strategy and execution, and risk escalation and disclosure. All those components must work together seamlessly, and must—crucially—also work together with many other enterprise functions and internal and external stakeholders. And it's important to recognize that getting there won't be a simple undertaking: it's a journey and a living process. Throughout this chapter we'll focus on implementation considerations and notable challenges to help you with your individual journey. Table 7-1 summarizes the principles and references relevant to each of the four components.

Effective CRMP requires senior-level commitment, new roles and responsibilities, potential changes to budget and other resources, and, in most cases, fundamental changes to enterprise culture. This isn't a one-and-done exercise, or simply a policy that's written and approved once and followed without questions, changes, or updates. And it definitely isn't something that can be done on an ad hoc or reactive basis. It requires ongoing, consistent contact between the security organization, risk owners, governance bodies, and many other stakeholders. This collaboration makes it possible to build trusting and lasting relationships that clearly establish risk management as an enabler for the business, not simply a cost center or, worse, an obstacle to doing business. And because the risk environment is constantly changing, the program must be adaptable and able to respond to changes in the environment.

Table 7-1. CRMP framework

CRMP component	Principles	Informative references
Agile governance	See "Seven Principles of Agile Governance" on page 49.	• SEC Final Cyber Rule (*https://oreil.ly/o2TGU*) • NIST CSF 2.0 (*https://oreil.ly/xngbU*) • 2023 NACD Director's Handbook (*https://oreil.ly/8enA4*) • ISO 27001:2022 (*https://oreil.ly/0ID28*) • NIST 8286 (*https://oreil.ly/WOC5f*) • IIA Three Lines Model (*https://oreil.ly/00AQ6*) • SEC 2018 Guidance (*https://oreil.ly/SVwOx*) • ISO 31000:2018 (*https://oreil.ly/vuqzY*) • AICPA CRMP (*https://oreil.ly/d5n8o*)
Risk-informed system	See "Five Principles of a Risk-Informed System" on page 66.	• SEC Final Cyber Rule (*https://oreil.ly/o2TGU*) • NIST CSF 2.0 (*https://oreil.ly/xngbU*) • 2023 NACD Director's Handbook (*https://oreil.ly/8enA4*) • ISO 27001:2022 (*https://oreil.ly/0ID28*) • IIA Three Lines Model (*https://oreil.ly/00AQ6*) • ISO 31000:2018 (*https://oreil.ly/vuqzY*) • AICPA CRMP (*https://oreil.ly/d5n8o*)
Risk-based strategy and execution	See "Six Principles of Risk-Based Strategy and Execution" on page 88.	• SEC Final Cyber Rule (*https://oreil.ly/o2TGU*) • NIST CSF 2.0 (*https://oreil.ly/xngbU*) • 2023 NACD Director's Handbook (*https://oreil.ly/8enA4*) • IIA Three Lines Model (*https://oreil.ly/00AQ6*) • ISO 31000:2018 (*https://oreil.ly/vuqzY*) • AICPA CRMP (*https://oreil.ly/d5n8o*)
Risk escalation and disclosure	See "Five Principles of Risk Escalation and Disclosure" on page 114.	• SEC Final Cyber Rule (*https://oreil.ly/o2TGU*) • NIST CSF 2.0 (*https://oreil.ly/xngbU*) • 2023 NACD Director's Handbook (*https://oreil.ly/8enA4*) • IIA Three Lines Model (*https://oreil.ly/00AQ6*) • SEC 2018 Guidance (*https://oreil.ly/SVwOx*) • AICPA CRMP (*https://oreil.ly/d5n8o*)

The Cyber Risk Management Journey

It may be useful to think of cyber risk management as a journey that likely has a different starting point for every enterprise, depending on its size, its industry, its regulatory environment, its current cyber risk maturity level, and many other factors. This is a journey that will never, and *should* never, end. What immediately matters is how it's introduced and communicated to the enterprise. That's why, for each of the four components of a CRMP, we'll offer considerations for what to do in the first 30 days of a new initiative, and then the next 60 days. Note that these are general guidelines, and that timelines can be adjusted to address enterprise-specific requirements, capabilities, and program maturity.

> Security's output, and its core product, is risk information.

The security organization will often lead the implementation of the CRMP, but this won't always be the case, and it isn't necessarily ideal. Security's fundamental role in cyber risk management is to work proactively to guide the enterprise (its risk owners, its governance authorities, and many other stakeholders) through the process of making informed decisions about risks and risk processes. The ultimate goal, for the security organization and for the enterprise as a whole, is to establish the appropriate balance between risk and reward: this is the process that will protect the enterprise and its stakeholders while still enabling it to remain competitive and, ideally, contributing to its competitiveness.

The challenges enterprises and their many stakeholders face at the outset of the cyber risk management journey will vary widely. And yet all will face a common set of issues that they'll have to address. These will inevitably include the need for senior-level buy-in and ongoing commitment to the program, changes in organizational culture (though not necessarily organizational structure), ongoing communication and collaboration between all stakeholders, and, of course, budget, personnel, tools, and other resources.

The reality is that very few enterprises are doing this well at present. Most probably aren't behind in the cyber risk management practices at the moment. But because of the fast-changing risk environment, and rapidly increasing regulatory and legal liability, they soon will be if they don't act. Enterprises—large and small, public and private—need to make fundamental changes to their current approaches and practices.

A good starting point for the cyber risk management journey is for the program leader—often the chief information security officer (CISO), chief risk officer (CRO), or general counsel—to work on a set of deceptively simple questions:

- "Are the board of directors and senior executives aware that they're responsible for implementing and overseeing a cyber risk management program?"
- "Do these senior decision makers know that a cyber risk management program could protect them from liability?"
- "Is the security organization playing a mature risk-management-based role, and do senior executives expect it to do so?"
- "Are the necessary fundamentals in place (for example, a governance body) to build a cyber risk management program?"
- "Who are the stakeholders I'll need to develop a working relationship with, and what's the best way to start that process?"

The program leader, whether in security or elsewhere in the enterprise, won't be able to answer these questions alone. Establishing this baseline of knowledge and understanding will require input from a broad range of stakeholders. And consulting them and taking their input seriously will help in developing the ongoing relationships that will be required to implement and manage the program.

Beginning the Cyber Risk Management Journey

This book presents a vision of the desired future state for the enterprise's cyber risk management practices, as defined by a formal program developed, implemented, approved, and governed by its most senior leadership, working together with risk owners and the security organization. That future state will necessarily vary widely, depending on the enterprise's risk environment and many other factors. But all enterprises will want to achieve a converged, integrated risk practice that presents the business with a balanced risk portfolio. And as we've already noted, the path to achieving that state will necessarily vary widely. But anyone implementing a CRMP will need to take four basic steps:

1. Designate a cyber risk management program "champion."

2. Conduct a comprehensive assessment of the current state of the enterprise's cyber risk practices.

3. Define an agreed-on target state and map processes and time frames.

4. Execute the roadmap, acknowledging that the program's development will be a long-term process.

No major enterprise undertaking can succeed without senior-level buy-in. The implementation of a CRMP requires a sweeping, fundamental, and long-term buy-in. Few enterprises will have the resources to identify and address all areas of cyber risk from the outset, and the program's implementation will inevitably be a long-term process. All these factors require the commitment of a highly influential officer or senior executive—perhaps the CRO or general counsel, both of whom obviously have a deep investment in risk management. Ideally, this person or persons will be objective and independent. It can also be helpful to have the support of audit, privacy personnel, government affairs, or operations. Regardless, it's absolutely essential that there be strong leadership, clarity of purpose, and support from the "champion."

The key to engaging this cyber risk champion will be essentially the same as engaging other stakeholders, across all functions and at all levels: ensuring that they understand the CRMP's contribution to achieving the enterprise's critical business objectives. This individual should have a broad view of the entire range of risks across the enterprise, not just cyber risks. Whoever is chosen will unquestionably recognize the business value of risk-informed decision making aligned with defined and approved risk appetites and tolerances—because they're accustomed to this practice in all their noncyber activities. And, with guidance and information from the security organization, they can begin communicating this value to their peers.

Any security or risk professional developing a CRMP will need to begin with an open and honest assessment of its existing risk practices and capabilities that challenges the concepts currently in place across each of the CRMP's four components and the principles that support them. This will require in-depth input from a broad range of relevant stakeholders, including but not limited to the CISO, the CRO and the head of the ERM program, representatives from the audit organization, and selected members of the board. For smaller enterprises, this process could easily be scaled down to the appropriate number of members to engage. The assessment should include interviews with relevant stakeholders and a review of any existing artifacts, such as policies and processes, governance structures, risk assessments, risk registers, risk reports, risk taxonomies, and any supporting technologies.

An inventory of risk tools or a set of relationship-based processes can be a helpful starting point, especially since it makes use of existing elements, as opposed to starting from scratch. The assessment should also include the enterprise's risk environment, including the regulatory frameworks and standards that impact it. If there's perceived pushback or a lack of independence, it's often helpful to bring in a third-party view, to allow for an outside perspective and share industry-leading best practices with executives and board members. The result of this process will be a preliminary baseline that makes it possible to identify gaps and conduct early-stage prioritization of the enterprise's most urgent needs.

Once the current state has been established, the next step is to work with the executives to define an agreed-on target state and lay out a detailed roadmap for building or maturing the program. This target state and roadmap is based on the findings of the assessment. This will likely result in setting both short- and long-term goals, prioritizing initiatives and allocating resources appropriately, and, crucially, ensuring that the program understands and is aligned with the enterprise's overall business objectives and risk appetite.

It may be tempting to try to do everything at once, but few enterprises will have the resources or the expertise to identify and address all areas of cyber risk from the outset. Instead, the program leader and other stakeholders should prioritize the roadmap, get approval for the necessary resources, and execute the steps toward maturity in a realistic and practical way. It will be critical to be fully transparent in communicating with the governance body throughout this phase, to ensure support for the security organization executing the plan, the application of appropriate resources, and full accountability.

Implementing the Cyber Risk Management Program

The four key components of the CRMP we've been laying out in this book all present their own specific implementation requirements and challenges. Let's take a closer look at each of them, focusing on common implementation challenges and ways to address them.

Agile Governance

Agile cyber risk governance is essential to the enterprise's success. Without clearly defined governance practices, defined roles and responsibilities, and established accountability for risk decisions, enterprises and their decision makers (from the board of directors on down) face potentially disastrous consequences. As we've seen, governance requirements are driven by a long and ongoing series of court decisions establishing enterprise and personal liability more clearly and more precisely, and by a broad range of associated regulatory frameworks and industry standards and protocols. These drivers make agile and responsive governance practices increasingly urgent, and also complex and challenging to implement.

The seven principles of Agile governance that we detailed in Chapter 3 apply throughout the implementation process:

"Principle 1: Establish Policies and Processes"
>   Enterprise-wide policies and processes must be in place for establishing a cyber risk management program.

"Principle 2: Establish Governance and Roles and Responsibilities Across the "Three Lines Model""
>   Cyber risk governance must be established with clearly defined roles, responsibilities, and outputs across the "Three Lines Model."

"Principle 3: Align Governance Practices with Existing Risk Frameworks"
>   Cyber risk governance practices should be aligned with any existing enterprise or organizational risk frameworks.

"Principle 4: Board of Directors and Senior Executives Define Scope"
>   The scope of an enterprise's cyber risk practices should be defined and approved by its board of directors and senior executives.

"Principle 5: Board of Directors and Senior Executives Provide Oversight"
>   The board of directors and senior executives should provide proper oversight of the enterprise's cyber risk practices.

"Principle 6: Audit Governance Processes"
>   Audit processes should provide appropriate review and assessment of the enterprise's cyber risk governance practices.

"Principle 7: Align Resources to the Defined Roles and Responsibilities"
Appropriate resources and skill sets should be aligned to the defined roles and responsibilities with ongoing training in place.

Consider the following in the first 30 days:

- Designate and convene a cyber risk steering committee comprising representatives from various business units, to guide the implementation of Agile governance and the broader CRMP. A mission statement and short- and long-term goals should be established.
- Clearly outline governance roles and responsibilities across the "Three Lines" model detailed in Chapter 3.
- Ensure that the established cyber governance practices align with existing enterprise or organizational risk frameworks.
- Draft a comprehensive set of policies and procedures for the enterprise-wide CRMP.
- Communicate to impacted stakeholders the planned governance measures and the reasons for them.
- Designate the specific individuals and functions responsible for the different aspects of governance, and ensure they fully understand their roles.

Consider the following in the next 60 days:

- The governance body, including the board and senior executives, should define and approve the scope of cyber risk practices.
- Receive approval, finalize, and implement policies and procedures.
- The board or senior executives tasked with providing oversight of the governance practices should be clearly defined.
- Conduct a gap analysis to determine the resources and skills needed to fulfill the defined roles and responsibilities.
- Implement a process of regular internal audits reviewing the governance practices against the defined policies and procedures.
- Create a continuous training program addressing individuals' assigned roles and responsibilities, to keep the team updated and to enhance their skills.
- Communicate the awareness program to the broader enterprise, to share the new practices and the reasons for them, and to ensure everyone understands their role in the new structure.

Common challenges with Agile governance

In this section, we'll seek to address common challenges enterprises face in implementing Agile governance as part of a CRMP.

Establish a starting point. The preliminary assessment discussed earlier will inform the early priorities of the governance program. If the enterprise already has a risk governance body in place but isn't addressing cyber risk management, it may provide a foundation for the governance initiative. In any case, the initiative will need to begin by addressing the most important issue in the enterprise's specific risk environment—which may include its industry, market conditions, regulatory compliance requirements, and existing obligations.

Gain senior-level commitment. Any major initiative requires both initial and ongoing buy-in and support from high-level decision makers, and governance because it touches on so many areas of the enterprise. And yet a third of the cyber leaders surveyed for the World Economic Forum's 2022 Global Security Outlook (*https://oreil.ly/Ki0cS*) reported that "gaining leadership support" was the most challenging aspect of managing cyber resilience. Cyber risk management leaders can work to overcome this problem by presenting the board or senior leaders with the case for Agile governance in terms that align with enterprise business priorities and industry-specific requirements.

This is an area where it will be particularly important to identify and gain the support of a cyber risk management champion who can tell the governance story in a way the business will understand. As we've already established, the governance practice and its implementation should not be led by the security organization. The audit organization can also provide valuable and persuasive input. Outside consultants may also prove useful in providing an independent and objective view.

Whoever presents the case for agile cyber risk governance, it's essential that one fundamental message be clearly communicated: the responsibility for governance lies at a level significantly higher than the security leadership. Senior leaders who don't address the need for governance are implicitly accepting the risk and the liability that come with that decision.

> If the enterprise's leaders fail to address the need for governance, they're implicitly accepting the risk and the liability that comes with that decision.

Obtain necessary budget and other resource limitations. Funding is always a problem for new initiatives. A CRMP doesn't have to be resource-intensive, but it can be if the decision is made to adopt advanced risk reporting capabilities (like cyber risk quantification) that require new tools. The key to convincing senior decision makers to free up funding for people and tools may, once again, make the point that the failure to address cyber risk implies acceptance of that risk. If, however, funding is not available to support the governance program for the reason that it's too expensive or too complicated or burdensome, it will be necessary to simplify the initiative and accept a higher risk tolerance of not having a proper CRMP in place.

Adapt to the specific enterprise's environment. A governance initiative must address the specific requirements of the enterprise, by defining and establishing four essential elements:

Scope
> The areas the cyber governance initiative covers must be clearly established by the governance body. For example, will it cover only IT or also operational technology (OT), the Internet of Things (IoT), and even third parties like external partners?

Independence
> Because some internal stakeholders have enough influence to place pressure on a governance body in the event of a conflict over a risk issue, independence is critical to ensuring effective governance.

Authority
> The governance body must have the power to enforce its decisions, and that authority must be communicated to all stakeholders.

Transparency
> The enterprise's governance practices, their successes and failures, and any governance changes resulting from identified changes in the risk environment must be regularly communicated to the board or other senior leadership. This will require regular monitoring and review.

Governance, Risk, and Compliance (GRC) Program

An enterprise's GRC program can play a valuable role in the implementation of the cyber risk management program, but in many GRC programs, the compliance functions almost completely overshadow the governance and risk elements. This may be the result of several factors:

Narrow focus
> Many GRC programs focus predominantly on fulfilling legal and regulatory obligations, with little or no emphasis on strategically aligning security with business goals and communicating and leveraging risk for competitive advantage.

Siloed and limited engagement with the business
> GRC functions often operate in silos, isolated from other business units and buried under security.

Risk frameworks that aren't aligned
> Different sets of frameworks that aren't fully aligned and coordinated lead to a lack of clarity and to risk management efforts not being taken seriously. If the information is presented with business functions prioritized differently or using different risk matrices, the target audience is likely to be confused. And the cyber risk framework will likely appear to be less engaged with the broader business and therefore less important and less actionable.

Overemphasis on controls
> GRC programs frequently focus on implementing and maintaining controls, often at the expense of understanding the business context and tailoring the controls to support business activities. This can lead to excessive spending, wasted resources, and ineffective controls.

Risk-Informed System

Risk information is not just about security threats and vulnerabilities, but detailed and actionable information about the enterprise cyber risk environment, translated into business terms. It lies at the heart of any successful CRMP. The real-world stories that we detailed in Chapter 4 make it clear that courts and regulatory bodies worldwide are no longer willing to accept an ad hoc approach as an acceptable risk management approach. There is a directive to have an appropriate risk-informed system in place. The courts and regulatory bodies also make it clear that liability for cyber risk failures now extends to boards of directors, corporate officers, and many other responsible parties. Risk information, as a critical component of a CRMP, is also critical to avoiding or mitigating damage to an enterprise's public reputation and brand image. And, crucially, it's essential to maintaining a competitive edge in a constantly changing business environment.

When a risk-informed system is being implemented, the five key principles outlined in Chapter 4 must be kept in mind at all times:

Principle 1: Define a Risk Assessment Framework and Methodology
> A risk framework and methodology must be defined and executed on to identify, assess, and measure cyber risk within the organizational context.

Principle 2: Establish a Methodology for Risk Thresholds
> An approved and repeatable methodology for acceptable risk thresholds—both appetite and tolerance—must be established.

Principle 3: Establish Understanding of Risk-Informed Needs
The governance body should be identified and engaged in establishing a comprehensive understanding of its cyber risk–informed needs.

Principle 4: Agree on a Risk Assessment Interval
The risk assessment process should be performed according to an agreed-on interval with its results regularly evaluated.

Principle 5: Enable Reporting Processes
Reporting processes should equip the governance body with insights on the impact of cyber risks on existing practices and strategic decisions.

Consider the following in the first 30 days:

- Choose a suitable framework for identifying, assessing, and measuring cyber risk that addresses the enterprise's specific business needs, regulatory requirements, and industry context. Receive approval from the governance body.

- Define the scope of assets being assessed based on the business structure, determine the frequency of assessment, and establish the most appropriate approach for engaging key stakeholders.

- Define or coordinate an enterprise risk matrix. Risk criteria and classifications should be established and approved by the appropriate stakeholders.

- Define a framework for establishing risk levels and thresholds. Select an agreed-on methodology for establishing the enterprise's risk appetite and tolerance.

Consider the following in the next 60 days:

- Finalize the methodology for defining the enterprise's risk appetite and tolerance levels, and get it approved by the relevant parties within the governance body.

- Organize meetings or workshops to develop ongoing engagement by stakeholders and better understanding of the enterprise's risk reporting needs.

- Schedule risk assessments. Establish an agreed-on cadence and scope for performing risk assessments (quarterly, semiannual, or annual, depending on the enterprise's risk profile).

- Conduct an initial risk assessment using the new methodology to develop an understanding of the current risk landscape. This may include running a risk assessment pilot for a single business unit. Engage an outside consultant or other third party, if necessary.

- Develop a reporting process for presenting risk insights to the governance body that captures changes in the enterprise environment that could impact risk practices.

- Begin reporting to the governance body about the current state of risks and how changes in the business environment might impact the enterprise's risk profile.

- Beginning with the methodology and identified risks, develop three to five key risk indicators (KRIs) that are properly thresholded to assess and monitor a top risk or set of risks the enterprise may be facing.

Common challenges with a risk-informed system

Here are some typical challenges the enterprise is likely to face in implementing a risk-informed system.

Dealing with too much data—or the wrong kind of data. This may be the single greatest obstacle to implementing an effective risk-informed system. Enterprises are flooded with data, including operational metrics, some of it critical to cyber risk management, some of it essentially irrelevant. (Security information is expansive and wide-ranging, but not all security information is risk information.) It's essential that risk owners, governance bodies, and other stakeholders aren't flooded with information that won't prove useful to them in making risk decisions. When that happens, they're all too likely to ignore future data that they shouldn't. The key to this effort is ensuring the metrics used and reported are meaningful, appropriately granular, and aligned with agreed-on risk principles and tolerances. One place to start may be to use an existing risk assessment process to develop KRIs and key performance indicators (KPIs) that measure key mitigating controls mapped to the top risks. As with many other focus areas, when starting out, sometimes less is more. Overwhelming stakeholders with information as you begin this journey will detract from the purpose and intent behind implementation.

Communicating information in terms specific stakeholders will understand and accept. It's important to keep the target audience for information in mind at all times. Different types of stakeholders won't just want and need very different types of risk information, but they'll want and need it communicated to them in very different ways. The board of directors, for example, will likely want a high-level view of risk that focuses intensely on its business impacts with perhaps three to four KRIs. Meanwhile, the CISO, chief information officer (CIO), or chief technology officer (CTO) will probably look for more technical detail reporting on performance and operational metrics with more granular risk and tactical metrics. As the program matures, the chief financial officer (CFO) and business leaders may want to see the risks presented in a quantitative format. Using language appropriate to the target audience—essentially, telling a story in the way it will be understood most clearly—is key to ensuring that risk information is clearly understood and enables risk-informed decision making.

Getting the right information to the right people at the right time. This challenge is closely related to the previous one. Risk data is only actionable if it reaches the stakeholders (the board, senior executives, asset and risk owners) who need it, and only if they receive it early enough to make risk-informed decisions based on it. A good first step is to build out risk metrics aligned with identified business concerns and work with the business to establish appropriate risk thresholds and targets. There can also be value in showing data trending over time as a means of adding context.

Additional considerations

The purpose of this book has not been to "teach" per se how to do many of the risk management practices commonly discussed in other industry risk management books. Rather, this book has been focused on defining a CRMP to help organizations navigate cyber risks in the ever evolving digital age. With that being said, the "how" behind some of the risk-informed system principles is an area we feel requires some additional attention.

In Chapter 4 we referenced three common methodologies that can be considered when establishing principle 2, "An approved and repeatable methodology for establishing acceptable risk thresholds—both appetite and tolerance—must be established." These suggested three methodologies are:

- Maturity modeling
- Metrics reporting (KPIs and KRIs)
- Risk assessments (qualitative and quantitative)

All three approaches can generate helpful data that can be used by the governance body to align on acceptable risk levels and drive risk decision making. (This was also discussed in Chapter 5.) Let's take a close look at each of them.

Maturity modeling. Maturity modeling is the process of defining the enterprise's current state of maturity—in terms of people, processes, and technology—and its desired future state. This process is required to identify any gaps and determine how to translate the resulting maturity level into actionable risk terms. Many enterprises have their cybersecurity maturity evaluated internally or by an independent third party against an industry framework like the NIST Cybersecurity Framework. This evaluation, typically conducted annually, has two common goals: to determine whether the enterprise has made progress over previous years, and to show how it compares to its industry peers.

The maturity measurement approach has real value. The maturity reports that are generated serve valuable purposes. They can be used to show that programs and specific security practices are maturing. They can also be used as a comparative report to measure maturity against one's peers in a common industry or similar organization of the same scale. But this approach, too, has a number of weaknesses. The most important is probably that maturity modeling in itself doesn't translate into usable risk information that the business can execute against. It doesn't, for example, communicate the priorities of specific risks by business domain, or communicate the impacts that mitigating those risks will have on budgets and other resources.

KPIs Versus KRIs

KPIs and KRIs are both important in enabling an enterprise to assess its security posture over time. But it's important to understand the difference: KPIs measure the effectiveness of a particular program or process, while KRIs measure the impact of risks on an enterprise's ability to meet its objectives. Sometimes, the measurement itself can serve as both a KRI and a KPI, depending on the context it's used in and who needs to understand it.

Benchmarking against industry peers is a useful part of this process, but it's important to recognize that benchmarking alone doesn't translate into usable risk information. Critically, it doesn't consider potential changes in the risk environment unique to that particular company, especially the type of fast-emerging risks that are introduced by digitalization. It would be a serious mistake, for example, for risk owners to decide that a given current or target risk maturity level is acceptable—or will continue to be acceptable—simply because it compares favorably with the industry average. A much more effective approach is to use benchmarking as only an initial step in the risk-awareness process. But it should then be coupled with a detailed risk statement associated with a certain maturity and analysis of how the risk environment will change over time and what impact these changes will have—on not only risk practices but also budgets. The risk owner may want to achieve an extremely high level of risk mitigation maturity but change their mind when they're made aware of how expensive it's likely to be. (This is the risk-versus-reward discussion again.)

The risk statements associated with each maturity level will change over time, often because of new threats or new available tools. Regardless, when the maturity state, with the aligned risk statement, is presented and approved by the governance body, it is at that point an established "tolerance" can be defined.

Capability Maturity Model Integration

The Capability Maturity Model Integration (CMMI) Model, developed in part by the Carnegie Mellon Software Engineering Institute, is one of the most widely used maturity modeling methodologies. It isn't specifically risk-focused, but it can be used to determine risk maturity. The CMMI establishes a path for an enterprise's performance and process improvement, across five maturity levels, as shown in Figure 7-1.

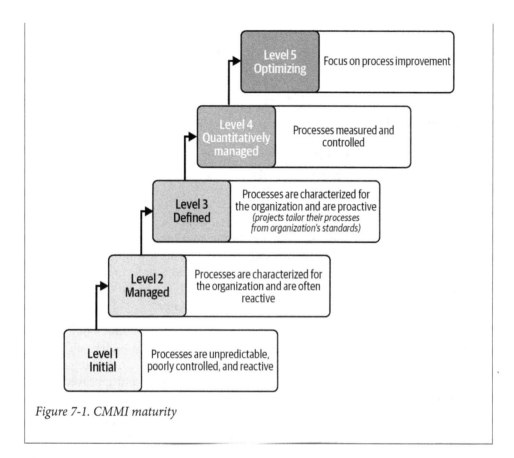

Figure 7-1. CMMI maturity

Metric reporting. The performance measurements/metrics methodology involves using objective data points from the environment to determine the effectiveness and efficiency of existing processes and controls. The methodology identifies gaps between the current and desired future state, and it uses the resulting information to establish, align on, and communicate acceptable risk levels. It's typically based on common KPIs, but the KPI targets are frequently defined haphazardly and, crucially, without approval from the risk owners or the governance body. The result is an essentially bottom-up approach, in which security itself essentially sets a more or less random target and then tracks itself against it. And this fails to establish a true risk threshold agreed upon by the business—the essential element in determining what level of risk is acceptable and appropriate for the business to operate within.

The process of establishing a risk threshold—the amount of risk that the business is prepared to accept—is where the value of performance metrics/measurements lies.

This is a fundamentally subjective approach, driven largely by the security organization and its perception of risk. Here are a couple of examples of KPIs related to vulnerability management:

- The percentage of critical assets to be scanned for software vulnerabilities
- The percentage of software vulnerabilities remediated within the parameters of the defined service-level agreements (SLAs)

The problem here is that the security organization might set a percentage based on experience, general perception of risk, or simply intuition, not on the true risk requirements of the business. Security's view has value, but it will only enable truly effective cybersecurity decision making if that view is used to inform the risk owners who are responsible for establishing risk thresholds based on a broad range of considerations (financial, legal, operational, reputational, and more).

We're not saying performance metrics don't have value. They're a useful tool for monitoring process performance, and they can help an enterprise improve its security and risk practices. But if they need to inform a risk-informed decision-making system, they need to be the right metrics, derived from the right sources, and approved by the right people and roles. So let's talk about metrics that fit this mold.

When high-value performance metrics are defined with input from the business, meaning from the risk owners, they can be used to establish risk thresholds, and that makes them truly meaningful and useful in strategic decision making. A threshold can be thought of as an indicator from a KPI or KRI that shows the point where performance or risk may be going beyond its intended purpose or its acceptable level of risk.

Risk assessments (qualitative and quantitative). Risk assessment systematically evaluates the likelihood and potential impact of a particular risk occurring, and it recommends measures necessary to manage and mitigate that risk. Risk assessment has two basic forms:

Qualitative
   The qualitative approach is the one most enterprises have traditionally used to perform risk assessment, and while it has definite limitations, it also has real value. By their very nature, qualitative assessments are subjective, because they rely on personal or subjective input, which may introduce errors or be influenced by bias. But a qualitative approach isn't necessarily as random as it might seem, especially when it's augmented and cross-referenced with input from multiple in-

person conversations, surveys and other research, and possibly outside experts. In this way, qualitative assessment can help to drive risk decision making and risk-based strategy and execution (a critical subject that we'll be discussing in the next chapter). Figure 7-2 shows how qualitative analysis can be communicated effectively to contribute to risk decision making.

ID	Priority	Risk description	Risk category	Current assessment		
				Likelihood	Impact	Exposure rating
5	TBD	Criminals are able to infiltrate our customers' mobile banking application due to endpoint user validation or an encryption issue, fraudulently causing customer funds to be transferred to an unauthorized location.	System and Information Integrity (SI)/ System and Comms Protection (SC)	H	H	H

Figure 7-2. NISTIR 8286 example of the results of qualitative analysis

Quantitative

This approach is becoming more of a commonplace as enterprises become more aware of the need for precise metrics that translate into dollars-and-cents business value. That's an important goal, but it isn't easy to achieve. A quantitative assessment is a complex, difficult undertaking, because it attempts to assign specific value to risks—reputational damage, for example—that are extremely difficult to quantify with precision. It's also time-consuming and disruptive to enterprise operations because it requires detailed input from many different stakeholders. Trying to quantify the real-world risk of reputational value from a data breach, for example, would require input from, at minimum, the legal, government affairs, and compliance departments, supplemented with data points from other similar attacks that have happened in the past within your industry.

The complexity of quantitative assessment is driving the rapid emergence of a new class of cyber risk quantification (CRQ) software applications that automate the assessment process. These tools take a truly data-driven approach to analyzing risk scenarios pertinent to an enterprise-specific business and technology environment (for example, a ransomware attack causing service disruption to a critical ecommerce website). This makes it possible to communicate cyber risk to the business in dollars-and-cents terms, and identify additional protections that would offer the highest return on investment in terms of risk reduction. This information can be shared with the risk owners so they can make decisions about acceptable risk levels, budgets, and other considerations.

Monte Carlo Simulation

A Monte Carlo simulation is another useful approach to considering complex variables to arrive at more accurate risk assessment by simulating risk outcomes and creating a distribution of results. It's a quantitative methodology that can use computer modeling to quantify the likelihood of a given risk. This enables better analysis and interpretation of potential threats, provides objective data for risk-informed decision making, and also makes it possible to evaluate the appropriateness of specific risk scenarios.

The quantitative approach to risk assessment is clearly valuable, but it does have drawbacks. It may require more time and resources. It may also be difficult for enterprise decision makers to choose the most suitable tool based on the data that they have available. Also, without clear direction on what exactly to quantify and how to use that information within the context of the CRMP, the quantification exercise can be of little value. See Figure 7-3 for an example.

ID	Priority	Risk description	Risk category	Current assessment		
				Likelihood	Impact	Exposure rating
1	TBD	An outsider using an APT breaches the organization's network, remains undetected for months, and exfiltrates much of the organization's critical and proprietary intellectual property by employing a Privilege Escalation attack.	Access control (AC)	0.6	$2,000,000	$1,200,000

Figure 7-3. NISTIR 8286 example of the results of quantitative analysis

Both these approaches have value and should ideally be used in combination to make thresholding decisions—identifying and aligning with acceptable risk levels—possible. Thresholding is what matters most, because it considers purpose, process, and outcome, with a regular cadence, the appropriate level of granularity, and input from the appropriate stakeholders.

Despite their usefulness, it's important to recognize that these approaches, especially when used on an ad hoc or siloed basis, fall short of addressing the enterprise's risk information needs. Only a formal risk-informed system can provide the necessary input for a CRMP and enable the governance body and risk owners to align on risk appetite and tolerance and drive risk-based strategy and execution.

Bayesian Methodology in Cyber Risk Management

Bayesian methodology is a type of probabilistic inference that uses prior knowledge, experience, and evidence to evaluate and update beliefs about the likelihood of a given event happening. This methodology is now widely used in industries as different as medicine and marketing. It can be a valuable tool in supporting enterprise risk decision making due to its ability to provide insight into complex processes while still accounting for uncertainty in an efficient manner.

Here's a simple example of Bayesian decision making. A business owner trying to decide whether or not to invest in a new market doesn't have complete information about the target market, which might include consumer preferences, consumers' disposable incomes, or whatever's needed to make the decision. She might use Bayesian methodology to assess the probability that the project is profitable, based on data collected from similar projects. By combining this with her own prior experience and understanding of the industry, she can make an informed decision.

The same methodology can be applied to cybersecurity risk assessment. Let's say you're a cybersecurity professional who's trying to predict the likelihood of a successful phishing attack targeting your enterprise's employees. A broad range of factors could be taken into account, including the level of security training that's been conducted, the percentage of employees who have failed phishing tests, and even job turnover that might impact employees' security awareness.

Some of the CRQ software tools on the market today use Bayesian techniques, for example, to compute all possible network attack paths, and then deliver an estimate of the likelihood of a breach across multiple scenarios.

Risk-Based Strategy and Execution

Risk management—the art of balancing risk and reward—is never perfect. It's impossible to protect the enterprise against every risk. Any attempt to do so is doomed to failure, and also risks limiting the enterprise's ability to respond quickly to inevitable changes in the risk environment and even to function properly. That's why recognizing and acknowledging that perfection is impossible, and communicating that reality to the enterprise's stakeholders, is the best place to start in implementing risk-based strategy and execution.

This will require ongoing and iterative conversations involving the security organization, risk owners, the governance body, senior executives, and possibly the board of directors. These conversations will make it possible for the risk owners to establish their risk appetites and tolerances, and for the security organization to determine whether those appetites and tolerances are achievable with existing budgets, personnel, and technologies. If it isn't possible—and this will frequently be the case—it will be up to the risk owner to either make the case for more resources or adjust their risk management expectations.

As we explained in Chapter 5, these risk decisions are business decisions, not security decisions. Security's role in the process of balancing risk and reward is to provide the information the risk owners and others need, and then to determine what resources will be required to meet the established expectations. In most cases, there will be an extended back-and-forth as the risk decision makers and security establish an acceptable risk threshold for a given asset or process and then implement the resources needed to achieve it.

The six principles of risk-based strategy and execution that we detailed in Chapter 5 should inform implementation:

Principle 1: Define Acceptable Risk Thresholds
Acceptable cyber risk thresholds must be clearly understood, established, and approved by the risk owners based on the risk framework and methodology.

Principle 2: Align Strategy and Budget with Approved Risk Thresholds
The cyber risk treatment plan and budget should be aligned with the approved risk thresholds.

Principle 3: Execute to Meet Approved Risk Thresholds
The cyber risk treatment plan should be executed to meet the approved risk thresholds.

Principle 4: Monitor on an Ongoing Basis
The execution of the cyber risk treatment plan should be monitored on an ongoing basis with established performance indicators and operational metrics.

Principle 5: Audit Against Risk Thresholds
The audit function should review and assess proper execution of the cyber risk treatment plan based on the approved risk thresholds.

Principle 6: Include Third Parties in Risk Treatment Plan
The cyber risk treatment plan should consider third parties, including partners, suppliers, and supply chain participants.

Consider the following in the first 30 days:

- Begin by defining what constitutes an acceptable level of risk for the enterprise—appetite and tolerance—as approved by risk owners through the governance body.

- Develop a risk treatment strategy that aligns with the defined risk levels. This should involve determining appropriate responses to identified risks, including avoidance, mitigation, transfer, and acceptance.

- Prepare a budget for the risk treatment strategy that's proportionate to the level of acceptable risk and potential impacts of risks materializing.
- Begin developing and defining KPIs and other operational metrics that will help in measuring the effectiveness of the risk treatment strategy.

Consider the following in the next 60 days:

- Implement the enterprise-wide risk treatment strategy, emphasizing the need for communication and cross-departmental coordination.
- Begin continuous monitoring of the risk treatment strategy to ensure its effectiveness, using the KPIs and operational metrics established earlier.
- Start regular reporting to relevant stakeholders on the progress and effectiveness of the risk treatment strategy.
- Initiate the oversight process of the audit function to monitor the proper execution of the risk treatment plan and ensure alignment with acceptable risk levels.

Common challenges with risk-based strategy and execution

The following closely related challenges are common among many security functions seeking to implement a risk-based strategy and execution model.

Inadequate budget and other resources. Balancing risk and reward also means balancing risks, resources, and capability. Risk-based strategy and execution will almost always require investments in new technologies, and sometimes in new skill sets, for either in-house employees or external contractors. A common question often asked is "Where do you start if the budget process is already set (for example, as a percentage of the CIO's budget, or a percentage of the prior year's budget)?" Going forward, the establishment of a budget should be directly tied to the appetite and tolerance levels defined by the business (using the methods outlined in Chapter 5). Whether this is done via risk quantification, maturity modeling, or some other approach, as acceptable risk levels inevitably change with a changing risk environment, there should be a clear understanding of the cost and risk impact associated with the given change.

Compliance-driven strategy. Historically, security programs in organizations have been predominantly compliance focused. At the time, this was an understandable reflection of a business environment where noncompliance was one of the key ways in which enterprises were impacted by cyber events. While important, compliance activities focus on adhering to rules, regulations, and requirements (both regulatory and corporate) versus understanding and communicating to the business the broader impacts of cyber threats. These impacts extend beyond noncompliance to include other categories, like financial, operational, reputational, environmental, and health and safety risks. Cybersecurity is now recognized as a potential material risk for enterprises, and a serious risk for enterprise decision makers from the board down. Operational downtime from a cyberattack, for example, could result in significant financial loss for a manufacturing company. This makes it crucial that their cyber risk strategies aren't fundamentally defined by compliance requirements. Instead, the security strategy should be derived from a comprehensive understanding of the business's risk appetite and tolerance, which may include but will not be limited to compliance considerations. Aligning strategic initiatives and budget proposals with the more broadly defined appetite and tolerance levels will help to address this challenge by establishing a risk-based strategy.

These two challenges—limited resources and a narrow compliance focus—can be addressed in very similar ways, through the implementation of a CRMP. In essence, security should engage the business to understand their concerns, align with their risk appetite and tolerance levels, and then adopt that understanding when shaping and executing the strategy. This is a departure from the traditional "easy way out" of simply aligning the security strategy with a percentage of IT spending or a list of regulatory compliance obligations. Instead, it positions security as a strategic partner with the business, one that makes it possible for the enterprise to achieve its business objectives while effectively managing risks.

Risk Escalation and Disclosure

Risk escalation and disclosure is central to protecting the enterprise and its decision makers. This isn't simply a question of identifying and responding to security incidents or building on established relationships, and it's critical that the responsibility for risk escalation and disclosure not default to the security organization. It must be a formal process, approved by senior leadership and the enterprise's governance body, that clearly designates roles and responsibilities, including who is responsible for making decisions about escalating risks. Risk disclosure extends this process to entities outside the enterprise, including regulatory bodies like the SEC and in some cases even the courts. It also includes procedures that clearly outline the steps to be taken when an appropriate response has been identified. This ensures that all parties are aware of their roles and the process by which risks will be assessed and managed.

The principles of risk escalation and disclosure outlined in Chapter 6 should inform implementation:

Principle 1: Establish Escalation Processes
Formal cyber risk escalation processes must be established.

Principle 2: Establish Disclosure Processes—All Enterprises
The enterprise's cyber disclosure processes should address its specific risk factors, organizational context, and requirements.

Principle 3: Establish Disclosure Processes—Public Companies
Public companies must disclose their material risks, risk factors, cyber risk management processes, governance, and material incident reporting.

Principle 4: Test Escalation and Disclosure Processes
Cyber risk escalation and disclosure processes should be challenged, tested, and updated on an ongoing basis to incorporate lessons learned.

Principle 5: Audit Escalation and Disclosure Processes
Audit should review and assess the enterprise's cyber risk escalation and disclosure processes to ensure their effectiveness, consistency, and compliance with relevant regulations and policies.

Consider the following in the first 30 days:

- Define clear procedures for escalating identified risks. This includes deciding what risks need to be escalated, when, to whom, and what should be in the report.

- For all enterprises, work to ensure that all stakeholders recognize any mandated requirement related to the disclosure of cyber risk management, governance, and material incident reporting. For public companies, define the list of material risk considerations that risks will be applied against in defining whether a risk is material or not.

- Begin formulating or updating procedures for disclosing risks that consider the enterprise's unique risk factors, environment, and requirements.

- Start training key personnel on the new risk escalation and disclosure processes and procedures.

- Begin setting up mechanisms that enable proactive auditing of risk escalation and disclosure processes and procedures.

Consider the following in the next 60 days:

- After thorough development and review—and before implementation—finalize the risk escalation and disclosure procedures and seek approval from the governance body.

- Begin regular monitoring of the implementation and execution of risk escalation and disclosure practices.

- Carry out the first audit of the risk escalation and disclosure processes to ensure their effectiveness and their compliance with relevant policies, procedures, and regulations. Gather findings and feedback and use information received to improve the processes.

Common challenges with risk escalation and disclosure

Here are the common key implementation challenges in this area.

A view of escalation that's largely limited to reacting to an incident.   Risk escalation is the proactive management of potential risks and vulnerabilities that could damage the enterprise. Incident response—the traditional focus of mainstream security organizations and programs—concentrates on reacting effectively to an identified threat or vulnerability. Both are essential to a comprehensive security program, but incident response alone is not enough, especially since it can't satisfy the rigorous legal and regulatory obligations that have been established in this area. As Agile governance practices and a risk-informed system are established (as discussed in Chapter 3 and Chapter 4 respectively), the enterprise will have an increasing capability to identify potential risks, assess their impact, and escalate them based on predefined thresholds. Education and training can also be very useful, by helping to create a culture of risk awareness in which employees understand the importance of escalating potential risks and not just actual incidents.

The failure to identify and focus on enterprise-specific obligations.   Different enterprises have very different risk escalation and disclosure requirements. Public companies must focus especially intensely on materially relevant risks, as required by the SEC and other regulators. And multinational companies will likely have to follow different —and sometimes conflicting—regulations in the different regions they operate in. Enterprises in different industries must also respond to a widely variable set of industry standards and protocols, many of which we detailed in Chapter 6. And enterprises of different sizes and types also face very different sets of obligations. A one-size-fits-all approach to risk management will inevitably overlook enterprise-specific obligations and risk factors. With a risk-informed system of the kind discussed in Chapter 4 in place, the enterprise will make it possible to conduct a comprehensive risk assessment that considers its specific business context and its identified risk profile. This system will also enable a detailed understanding of the unique threats the enterprise faces, as well as its legal and regulatory obligations and how its business operations could be impacted by various risks. The enterprise can leverage that input to tailor its escalation and disclosure requirements accordingly.

Generic, isolated, or excessively broad materiality considerations.   Determining what assets are material, and what risks are material risks, is not a simple or formulaic exercise, but it's frequently undertaken as a generic practice that fails to take in the specifics of the enterprise environment. In many cases, the practice of writing and reporting quarterly risk reports doesn't properly engage with the security organization—or the security organization can't produce the proper risk organization. As we've already discussed in detail, there's increasing scrutiny on this practice, legal and regulatory expectations are changing, and liability is expanding and increasing. This new environment will leave enterprises no choice but to change practices that are no longer adequate. Solving this problem involves refining the criteria used to assess the materiality of risks. This can be achieved by aligning with the risk-informed system outlined in Chapter 4 and setting specific and measurable thresholds for risk escalation based on the potential impact on these objectives.

Selling the Program

Implementing a CRMP will inevitably require serious commitment and support from roles and functions across the enterprise, from the highest levels on down. The ongoing engagement of a broad range of stakeholders—the board of directors, the CEO and CxOs, senior executives, legal and compliance organizations, and of course security—will be critical to the success of the program. But selling the program to all stakeholders, ensuring that they recognize its importance to them and their distinct and sometimes competing agendas, won't be simple or easy.

The security organization obviously has a critical role to play in implementing a CRMP and in contributing to its ongoing success. The CISO and other security practitioners will need to work closely with a broad range of stakeholders at different levels, including the board of directors, corporate officers, and senior executives as well as the legal department and beyond, not to mention many operational roles and external parties like regulators and business partners. And as we've shown, the result will be significantly enhanced personal satisfaction and professional opportunity for the security practitioner. But security's contribution to the program's success will also present enormous benefits for the enterprise as a whole, in a broad range of areas. Let's take a look at some of the benefits and at the value cyber risk practices can deliver in each one.

Enterprise-wide risk-informed decision making
> When security approaches its role as part of an overall risk function, it delivers strategic insights that risk and asset owners, among many other stakeholders, can use to inform their business and operational decisions. This extends far beyond the cyber threats and vulnerabilities that security organizations have traditionally focused on to include the complete risk environment. This comprehensive view, balancing risk and reward, makes it possible for designated, responsible, and accountable decision makers to prepare for and address potential risks while not missing out on promising business opportunities.

The value to the enterprise
> Enterprise-wide risk-informed decision making is a strategic imperative that not only enhances the enterprise's security posture but also drives business growth and operational efficiency. It's a critical enabler for addressing a complex risk environment while also capitalizing on emerging opportunities and

allowing companies to take risks—a competitive advantage over their competition.

Regulatory and legal compliance

Regulators and the courts worldwide are rapidly expanding their requirements of enterprise cybersecurity practices, making them both broader and more stringent. And they're making it clear that they will hold enterprises, and a growing range of enterprise stakeholders, responsible for cyber failures.

The value to the enterprise

A CRMP ensures that the enterprise is fully compliant with all regulatory requirements and legal mandates, mitigating the risk of penalties for noncompliance, reputational damage, and litigation. In essence, a comprehensive CRMP is a critical enabler for maintaining regulatory and legal compliance, safeguarding enterprise integrity, and fostering stakeholder trust.

Public and consumer trust

Consumers have greater expectations of the companies and other enterprises they do business with, and a cyber failure (e.g., a data breach) has been shown to make them take their business to competitors they see as more serious about protecting their sensitive information. The public is also more organized than ever, and pressure from consumer, environmental, and other advocacy groups can do serious damage to an enterprise's reputation and brand image.

The value to the enterprise

A strong cybersecurity posture signals to consumers and the public that the enterprise is serious about protecting their personal data and other sensitive information. A robust cybersecurity strategy is a foundational investment in preserving and enhancing public and consumer trust, protecting the enterprise's reputation, and ensuring its long-term success and sustainability.

Relations with external parties

Enterprises are increasingly operating in complex ecosystems involving a broad range of external partners, technology providers, industry organizations, and even competitors. Trust is critical to these valuable relationships, especially because they involve the sharing of intellectual property and other sensitive data. And an effective CRMP is critical to maintaining and enhancing that trust.

The value to the enterprise

By implementing a robust CRMP, an enterprise can demonstrate its reliability as a trusted partner. This not only strengthens existing relationships but also attracts potential partners, which further expands the enterprise's collaborative network. An effective CRMP is a strategic asset that enhances relations with external parties, fosters a culture of trust, and drives collaborative success in an increasingly interconnected business environment.

Innovation

Effective cyber risk management, informed and guided by the security organization, can help to drive innovation by providing a safe environment to explore and implement new technologies, new operational processes, new products and services, and even entirely new business models. This is especially important because of the breathtaking speed of change in enterprises' risk environments driven by transformational digital technologies like cloud computing, the IoT, and AI, which simultaneously create new and highly damaging risks and important opportunities for business growth.

The value to the enterprise

Effective cyber risk management builds a secure foundation for enterprises' efforts to safely navigate the risks of emerging technologies while still capitalizing on the opportunities they present. This not only mitigates potential threats but also drives innovation and growth. Effective cyber risk management is a strategic enabler of innovation, facilitating the safe exploration and adoption of new technologies and business models, and driving business growth in the digital era.

Operational resilience

Operational resilience—the ability to adapt to and withstand disruptions—is in some respects the end goal of any CRMP. (It's so important, in fact, that the next chapter is dedicated to the subject.) By helping the enterprise to become resilient to its defined and agreed-on risk thresholds and tolerances, security can ensure the continuity of operations even when things go wrong, minimizing disruption and danger.

The value to the enterprise

A robust CRMP equips the enterprise with the necessary tools and strategies to swiftly respond to and recover from disruptions. This resilience safeguards the enterprise's operational integrity and also preserves its public reputation, brand image, and customer trust. In an increasingly volatile and uncertain business environment, operational resilience is no longer a luxury but a necessity. It's a critical determinant of an enterprise's ability to survive and thrive amid disruptions.

When cybersecurity operates as a true risk function and operationalizes a CRMP, it transcends its traditional security-only role. Instead, it becomes a strategic partner that helps the enterprise navigate its digital journey safely and profitably, creating real-world business value.

Managing change can of course be difficult, both for the business and for security. For this reason, the individuals driving the implementation should have regular and ongoing conversations with all the impacted stakeholders to provide guidance on how to establish metrics, to track progress (including successes and failures) as well as mistakes made and lessons learned, and to update the program to adapt to evolving cyber threats and other changes in the risk environment. Once an implementation roadmap has been created and approved, it should be revisited at least annually, so that it can be recalibrated as needed.

A program of the type we've been outlining also offers important benefits to the individual designated to implement and manage the program. Let's take a look at those benefits in Table 7-2, by comparing and contrasting roles of a traditional security leader (CISO or security manager) and one who's working in the framework of a CRMP.

Table 7-2. Cyber risk management versus ad hoc practices

	Cyber risk management program	Ad hoc security risk practices
What is the relationship between security and the business?	Security works in the context of a strategic CRMP, with business-aligned risk appetite and tolerance.	Business engagement is primarily limited to tactical responses to threats and vulnerabilities.
How are budget and other resource decisions made?	Investments in security are optimized to align with business-defined risk tolerance.	Security investment is uncertain, due to disconnect between business and security team.
Who makes the decisions and how?	Risk information is integrated into business decision making, with the CISO or other security leader guiding the business through strategic risk decisions.	Risk decisions default to the security organization and are essentially tactical, often based on threats and vulnerabilities without proper business-defined tolerances.
How does risk escalation work?	Risk escalation is procedural, based on a business-approved risk matrix that mandates timely information flows to proper levels of management. Risks are viewed as a concept broader than incident response.	Risk escalation is typically triggered by an incident and triggers a process-driven response to address the incident, not necessarily the risk. Risks themselves don't programmatically trigger escalation.
What is the CISO job impact?	Job security is more stable as the role of the CISO is to manage risk decisions, not solely to make them.	The CISO is potentially held responsible for any adverse outcomes due to independent risk decisions, potentially leading to job loss.
What is security's impact on business resilience?	The business operates resiliently to an agreed-upon degree, with strategic guidance from the CISO or other security leader.	Business resilience is viewed through the lens of disaster recovery, and not as a core objective of a quality managed risk function.

Throughout this process, security will need to play the fundamental role we've laid out for it throughout this book: supporting risk owners and other stakeholders with information, expertise, and technologies that guide them through an established and approved cyber risk decision-making process. This requires that the security organization and the other stakeholders have a clear understanding of their part in the process, and especially that they recognize the constantly changing nature of cyber risk management. Cyber risks will change over time—as will the technologies, tools, and processes needed to manage and mitigate them—but security's supporting role will not. Security will continue to be an essential partner to the business in helping the enterprise deliver long-term value and embrace new opportunities.

The Bottom Line

There's nothing simple about implementing a cyber risk management program. The complexity of the undertaking, and the constant shifts in the enterprise risk environment, requires an ongoing implementation process, with continuous monitoring and continuous improvement. The individuals responsible for the implementation should think of it as a journey—one that begins with and builds on basic early steps, and one whose route and destination are almost certain to change over time. They should also recognize that it's a journey that requires the ongoing collaboration and cooperation of a broad range of stakeholders. The security organization will provide the information needed to design and implement the program, but the actual decisions will be made by others, including asset and risk owners, governance bodies, the audit organization, senior executives, corporate officers, and the board of directors. The result will be that the enterprise is far better-positioned to address fast-changing risks and keep their operations running effectively.

Mature coordination with other operational risk functions like supply chain, physical security, and business continuity is becoming essential in this fast-moving environment to help the enterprise by achieving appropriate operational resilience, which is the subject of the next chapter.

CHAPTER 8

The CRMP Applied to Operational Risk and Resilience

Throughout this book, we've stressed the fundamental changes—social, political, economic, cultural, and of course technological—that are reshaping the enterprise risk environment in fundamental ways. We've shown examples of the highly damaging, even catastrophic, impacts enterprises face when they fail to manage these emerging and accelerating risks in a formal, programmatic way. And we've detailed some of the many ways effective risk management, and especially cyber risk management, can help enterprises survive and thrive in this new and highly volatile environment, by balancing risk against reward in ways that drive better decision making.

In this chapter, we're going to detail the mission-critical role of a cyber risk management program (CRMP) in operational resilience, and how it coordinates with other operational risk functions to focus on broader operational resilience efforts. Cyber risk management, like every other operational risk management function, has one ultimate objective: achieving operational resilience that balances risk and reward. Cyber risks are unquestionably critical, but they're only one aspect of the risk environment that enterprises need to consider. Senior enterprise decision makers aren't simply thinking about malware and identity theft and data breaches. They're asking far broader questions, which essentially come down to "How resilient are we in the face of an ever-changing risk environment?"

Decision makers are asking that question about supply chain risk, third-party risk, fraud management, business continuity, crisis management, disaster recovery, and IT risk. However, a key problem is that while they're all concerned with essentially the same outcomes, they're approaching their efforts in a fragmented and siloed manner. And that simply doesn't work anymore, if it ever really did. If recent events have taught us anything, it's that all these functions interconnect and lead to the same basic concern with operational resilience.

It's breathtaking to look back on what we've gone through just in the past few years, and to reflect on what we've learned from it. A worldwide pandemic brought with it massive supply chain problems, manufacturing shortages, and fundamental shifts in working models. A war in Europe caused volatility in energy prices and shocking inflation in food prices. There were also natural disasters and extreme weather events linked to global climate change, not to mention evolving political unrest worldwide. Also noticeable, of course, was a huge increase in the frequency and severity of cyber-attacks. These were massive social, economic, and political events—tectonic events—and enterprise leadership needed to address them all, and the risks associated with them, all at once. Some, obviously, were more successful than others, and in most cases the key to their success was a comprehensive, integrated approach to the management of all types of risk, and the impacts of those risks on operational resilience.

Senior decision makers need to consider operational resilience issues from an enterprise-wide perspective. The details matter, of course, but when a leader escalates an operational risk to senior levels, and communicates the associated plans for dealing with the risk going forward, the resolving factor in executives' minds is determining whether the enterprise is resilient to a level they're comfortable with. And that determination must be made in an enterprise-wide context, not through a siloed approach, with each operational risk function bringing its concerns to the executive suite, often in isolation. Digitalization and the interconnectedness it brings with it drives the need for operational risk functions to coordinate their efforts and their risk outputs.

What we're referring to here isn't organizational realignment but rather risk management coordination through common frameworks and coordinated reporting practices. This means coordinated governance that can align priorities and collaborate organically. It requires common risk-informed systems that work off the same risk matrixes and reporting time frames and cadences. It also requires weighting risk factors in a way that recognizes that risks aren't all equal. It calls for thoughtful risk-based strategies that actively manage across functional lines and consider how risks can cross defined responsibilities. And it requires formal escalation and disclosure procedures that are broad in scope and fluently account for multiplying impacts that transcend one department's responsibilities. These are, of course, the fundamentals of the CRMP we've been talking about throughout this book. Each of these other operational risk functions can and should function based on these same fundamental risk elements, which make up their own framework. And with the right approach, these risk ecosystems can and should operate as a coordinated operational risk ecosystem.

Approaching risk management in this systematic manner and providing easily communicated risk information—coordinated and based on the same framework—offers a clearer answer to the essential question, "Are we resilient?" This does not in any way diminish the seriousness of the detailed information provided by the organization doing the reporting. In fact, it stresses and clarifies the seriousness of the organization and its role, by showing that it's meeting its operational objectives and demonstrating mature leadership.

It's not just senior executives and other high-level enterprise decision makers who are asking questions about resilience. Regulators worldwide (*https://oreil.ly/ehivU*) are starting to look at risk management through the lens of operational resilience and the coordination of operational risk functions. They're focusing more intently on best practice, standards, resilience measurements, and prescriptive regulations. The primary reason is that they've come to understand that the real issue isn't the event itself. The issue is whether the enterprise is resilient enough to deal with *all* the impacts of the event, no matter the cause. They've started setting expectations and examining organizations through this lens. The guidance and examinations have been focused on the programmatic practice of risk management.

This broader view moves away from protection best practices and toward the ability to identify critical functions and manage to an operational resilience posture that is appropriate for that enterprise. A key concept that is used increasingly widely—by authorities including the Bank of England and the Basel Committee on Banking Supervision (BCBS)—is the "severe but plausible scenario" (*https://oreil.ly/5fH8n*).

The cybersecurity function must coordinate with all of the enterprise's other risk functions. In fact, if other functions are not focused on operational resilience, it should take the leadership role in this collaborative effort, in large measure because cyber is an extreme risk most enterprises are facing at the moment. Not all of the other risk functions will likely be at the level of maturity necessary for this type of coordination, and that's fine. A mature operational resilience program doesn't have to be achieved overnight, and in most cases it won't be. But viewing risk management from an enterprise-wide operational resilience perspective, and applying systematic program principles throughout the cyber risk management journey, will deliver the necessary maturity.

Operational Resilience Defined

Operational resilience is an enterprise's ability to protect against, withstand, and adapt to disruptions and uncertainties of all kinds, at a defined level and granularity that is approved by the business and executed to.

Operational resilience risk management practices are essentially the glue that holds all these disparate elements together, ensuring that the different roles and responsibilities function, communicate, and collaborate in a formal, defined way that ensures that risks of all kinds—not just cyber—are addressed.

Enterprise Functions That Interact with and Contribute to Operational Resilience

While many of the functions that security professionals and other risk stakeholders routinely carry out are not specific to operational resilience, they have an important role to play in enabling it. Each of these is at its core fundamentally a strategic risk practice, not simply a tactical function. Let's take a close look at some of them, to clarify what they are and how they relate to cyber risk management and especially to operational resilience:

IT risk management
> IT risk management involves the identification and mitigation of risks related to the use, ownership, operation, and adoption of an enterprise's IT assets. This function is critical to operational resilience, and is often closely aligned with cyber risk management.

Physical security
> Physical security focuses on protecting personnel, hardware, software, networks, and data from physical events that could cause severe loss or damage to an enterprise. This role is important for operational resilience as it ensures the continuity of the physical assets that underpin cyber and operational processes, and it also contributes to cyber risk management by preventing unauthorized physical access to digital assets.

Fraud management/loss prevention
> This refers to the efforts taken to prevent and mitigate fraud, including cyber fraud, and prevent the loss of resources, data, or funds. Its contribution to operational resilience is seen in the protection of an organization's assets, while in terms of cyber risk management it involves preventing, detecting, and responding to fraudulent activities in the digital space.

Supply chain/third party
> This function is about managing risks associated with an organization's supply chain and third-party vendors. It's integral to operational resilience as it ensures the continuity and integrity of products, services, or data provided by external parties. From a cyber risk perspective, it also involves managing the cyber risks associated with these external entities.

Business continuity management (BCM)

This is a proactive planning process involving the creation and validation of a practiced logistical plan for the restoration of critical business operations and functions after a disruptive event. It contributes significantly to operational resilience by ensuring that an organization can continue to perform essential functions during a major crisis or disaster. In terms of cyber risk management, it ensures continuity of digital operations even in the face of a significant cyber threat or incident.

Disaster recovery (DR)

DR is the process of restoring the enterprise's IT systems (infrastructure and applications) and data to a state where it can resume normal operations after a disaster. This can be any disruptive event (for example, a cyberattack, data breach, or natural disaster).

Crisis management

This includes the process by which an enterprise handles disruptive and unexpected events that threaten to harm it or its stakeholders. It plays a crucial role in maintaining operational resilience by ensuring a coordinated response to a crisis, thereby limiting damage and reducing recovery time. It also intersects with cyber risk management during cyber-related crises like data breaches and large-scale cyberattacks.

When you look back at the crisis examples we've mentioned in previous chapters, it's easy to see how these operational risk functions are in some ways interconnected both in preparation and in response. It's also easy to see that if each group goes into executives' and other stakeholders' offices to communicate their efforts separately, a true operational resilience picture is hard to piece together.

Cyber Risk Management and Operational Resilience

Why are we taking such a close look at the question of operational resilience in a book about cyber risk management? Let's consider the key reasons:

- Cybersecurity and operational resilience are inextricably interconnected. Cyber threats such as inadvertent data breaches or financially motivated ransomware attacks can severely impact enterprise operations. Cyber risk must be considered holistically, in terms of its contribution to maintaining operational resilience in the face of emerging cyber threats and changes in the overall cyber environment.

- Digitalization, for all the reasons we've discussed in this book, will continue to bring with it enhanced cyber risks, and at increased velocity, throughout every business function in every enterprise.

- The regulators are watching. Regulatory bodies worldwide are making operational resilience a key focus, establishing mandates that require enterprises to both develop and demonstrate preparedness against cyber threats and risks.

- Cyber risks are becoming more complex, sophisticated, and dangerous. Cyber threats and vulnerabilities, like ransomware attacks and data breaches, get most of the media attention and, as we've demonstrated, can have significant business impact. Cyber risk extends far beyond these traditional "security" issues. There are few pure cyber events that would only impact a cyber function and not have a broader impact on other operational areas.

- Cyber risk management is central to delivering enterprise business value. Enterprises that can demonstrate broader operational and risk resilience are more likely to earn the trust of customers, partners, and stakeholders, enhancing their brand reputation and competitive advantage.

A Malware Attack Shuts Down Maersk's Systems Worldwide

Perhaps the best example of the urgent need to achieve comprehensive, enterprise-wide operational resilience is the devastating June 2017 cyberattack known as NotPetya, and especially its impact on the Copenhagen-based multinational Maersk-Møller (commonly known as Maersk). The attack wasn't targeted at Maersk, or any other single enterprise—it was almost certainly a Russian state-sponsored attack meant to bring down systems in Ukraine (*https://oreil.ly/Sn9tH*)—but it spread at astonishing speed, crippling private- and public-sector entities worldwide. Maersk suffered system outages and process failures that impacted every aspect of its enormous range of worldwide operations, as well as hundreds, if not thousands, of other enterprises the company connected with. That's what makes Maersk's experience an object lesson in the importance of ensuring operational resilience through communication and collaboration between all of an enterprise's security and risk management functions. NotPetya began as a cyberattack, but it rapidly became something far more widespread and far more dangerous. And it's clear that Maersk simply wasn't ready for it.

NotPetya Wreaks Havoc Worldwide

The NotPetya attack was probably far more successful, and far more destructive, than its creators ever intended. The hackers likely only meant to damage Ukrainian IT infrastructure, but the malware they created—a worm that masquerades as ransomware but actually destroys operating systems by permanently encrypting their source code—spread at such astonishing speed that it brought down systems far beyond its target. NotPetya was designed to render enterprise computing systems completely inoperable by making their master boot records completely inaccessible. It proved to be astonishingly effective, despite the fact that it exploited a vulnerability in the Windows OS that had already been identified—a vulnerability for which a patch had been available for months. This snapshot of some of the entities that were brought to a standstill by the attack gives a sense of its extraordinary reach:

- The Chernobyl nuclear power plant in Ukraine
- The German postal service
- A major US pharmaceuticals manufacturer
- A chocolate factory in Australia
- A French construction materials supplier
- The world's largest advertising agency

The financial costs of NotPetya are almost impossible to calculate, and many of the impacts of the attack are still being felt. (One important issue that has yet to be resolved is cyber insurance: at least one major insurer has refused to pay on a NotPetya claim because it considers the attack an "act of war.") But some cybersecurity experts estimate that the 2017 attack has had a total cost in excess of $10 billion (*https://oreil.ly/JzjSq*).

Why was Maersk hit so hard? One obvious reason is the company's size and complexity. Maersk is the world's second-largest shipping company by volume, operating more than 700 commercial vessels and carrying tens of millions of tons of cargo—nearly a fifth of the world's entire shipping capacity—to and from almost 200 ports on 5 continents. It's not just a shipping company, either. It's also a major player in industries including logistics, oil drilling, port operations, and supply chain services. When NotPetya shut down the company's IT operations, effectively blocking access to all of its operational data, Maersk had no way of directing the hundreds of its ships at sea, and port facilities were unable to control the highly automated systems that load and unload containers. Maersk's global reach also places it at the center of a huge and intricately interconnected ecosystem of business partners, customers and clients, technology and operations product and service providers, government agencies, and other third parties. (Maersk's digital connections with other enterprises unquestionably helped spread NotPetya far beyond its own IT systems.) And that meant that when NotPetya brought Maersk to a standstill, it brought a huge section of the global economy to a standstill, too. Manufacturers worldwide began running out of essential components almost immediately. As we've stressed previously, that's a fundamental problem with today's digitized just-in-time economy, and retailers' stocks of products began to empty nearly as quickly.

NotPetya's impact on Maersk deserves a closer look, because it demonstrates clearly how far-reaching and how urgent the need for an enterprise-wide operational resilience program really is. It appears that NotPetya crippled virtually every aspect of

Maersk's operations for nearly a week. And the damage extended far beyond the obvious problems with shipping and logistics. For however many days the company's IT systems weren't working, Maersk would have been unable to perform functions as basic as paying its more than 100,000 employees. Hiring and other HR functions would have been on hold. And it would have been unable to provide accurate, up-to-date information to the financial markets or to regulatory bodies. The Maersk episode shows the critical importance of operational resilience—and the essential role that cyber risk management plays in achieving it. Operational resilience goes beyond a standalone CRMP or simply thinking about it as business continuity.

It's necessary to adopt a broader perspective that emphasizes the continuity of the entire operation. It underlines the necessity of the ability of an enterprise to adapt and recover from a variety of incidents, including but not limited to cyberattacks. And that necessity extends well beyond the enterprise itself. A truly effective response to the NotPetya attack would have required extensive communication and collaboration between Maersk's operational risk management functions and those of the many third-party enterprises it works with. A CRMP communicating and collaborating with other security and operational risk functions and leading an enterprise-wide effort would have helped Maersk to identify risks like NotPetya, design protections against them, and build a more coordinated capability in coordination with other operational risk functions in response preparations.

Even though cyberattacks like NotPetya are understandably top of mind these days, it's crucial to think beyond the realm of cybersecurity. Cybersecurity is not an isolated objective; rather, it's a critical component of the overarching goal of ensuring that an organization can withstand and bounce back from all types of disruptions. Cybersecurity acts as a key enabler of operational resilience, safeguarding the continuity of critical business functions against cyber threats.

The development of a functional operational risk and resilience program requires that each operational risk function should rally around core risk management components. The four components in a CRMP—Agile governance, a risk-informed system, risk-based strategy and execution, and risk escalation and disclosure—can also be applied to all other operational risk functions and can work together to coordinate the operational risk functions, address risks, and communicate a broader resilience posture.

Guiding Operational Resilience Using the Four Core Cyber Risk Management Program Components

The four components we've discussed throughout this book can be universally applied to various aspects of business operations, including supply chain, IT risk, fraud management, physical security, business continuity, disaster recovery, and crisis management—all of which are critical to achieving operational resilience. Let's take a look at each one.

Agile Governance

Agile governance is the cornerstone of a CRMP, providing essential oversight and guiding critical decisions. It is the cornerstone of efforts to achieve operational resilience, as well. Agile governance brings together diverse risk operations under a common set of principles and oversight, as detailed in Chapter 3, but adapts its approach to the unique needs of each constituent group. A coordinated governance committee, whether an enterprise risk committee, a developed operational resilience committee, or an integrated risk committee, plays a vital role in coordinating the various operational risk functions. The committee brings together key stakeholders, aligning them around shared expectations and goals for operational risk and resilience (including risk appetite and tolerance). Through regular reporting from the risk-informed system, these stakeholders maintain an informed and up-to-date perspective on the enterprise's risk landscape, allowing them to address risks proactively and to communicate a broader resilience posture.

Driving Coordination Across Risk Functions

Coordinating the various risk functions within an organization is no small task. It requires an entity with a broad overview of the organization's operations, as well as the ability to synthesize information from various sources into actionable insights. So who takes the lead in establishing the group? How should it be organized, and what should it be called?

There are several possible candidates. An operational risk or integrated committee can be effective, especially in enterprises where operational risks are a cause of significant concern in terms of business strategy. An ERM committee takes a broader view, encompassing not just operational risk, but all other forms of risk that the organization faces, including strategic, financial, and reputational risks. While ERM committees do not often have "operational" responsibilities, they are often tasked with the creation of a risk management framework and the definition of the enterprise's risk appetite framework, which is then applied across the various operational risk functions.

Whichever model is chosen, it's essential that the committee be empowered to make decisions and supported by the enterprise's leadership at the highest levels. It also needs to be able to draw on a reliable and comprehensive risk-informed system that provides timely and relevant data to guide its decisions. Ultimately, the goal of any such committee should be to drive the organization toward greater operational resilience and robust risk management. This doesn't require organizational realignment but rather organizational coordination—and that should be its main focus.

Risk-Informed System

A risk-informed system coordinating within other operational risk functions serves as the primary resilience intelligence feed. It should deliver timely, accurate, and comprehensive and coordinated operational risk information, and support executives in understanding and managing the enterprise's overall operational risk profile and ultimately promoting operational resilience. The primary purpose of a risk-informed system is to address a key concern for executives: the extent of the enterprise's resilience. While executives may ask specific risk-related questions in meetings, their overarching concern from an operational point of view is understanding how well the enterprise can absorb and adapt to disruptions. An operational risk-informed system would provide an answer by aggregating and presenting data from across the organization's operational functions, bringing to light its overall resilience through risk information instead of individual siloed risk profiles.

One of the key drivers for operational risk practice of this type is the alignment of information within the risk-informed system. The reporting of inconsistent or misaligned data to executives across risk functions—a common problem in most enterprises—can create confusion and undermine the effectiveness of a system. This makes maintaining consistency and alignment critical, because it ensures that all stakeholders can readily interpret the risk data presented to them and use it to make informed decisions about the enterprise's operational resilience. Clearly, not all risks are equal. Cyber risk may have a significantly higher priority than supply chain risk in financial services, for example, while the opposite may be true for manufacturing. It's important to prioritize risk appropriately, but this must always be done with a focus on alignment with operational risk focus.

Risk-Based Strategy and Execution

Alignment of the risk-based strategy and execution model across operational risk functions provides a unifying framework. With the risk-informed system feeding the governance body, the strategic model establishes the enterprise's risk appetite and tolerance, guiding the prioritization, implementation, and execution of operational risk management activities. The universal application of this model across various aspects of risk operations—IT and supply chain risks, fraud management, physical security, business continuity, disaster recovery, and crisis management—facilitates a harmonized approach to achieving operational resilience. Fundamentally, this is about organizational and risk information coordination and coordinated execution, through prioritization of risks and a clear, coordinated approach to mitigation and response activities. Having a broader operational risk view will help each individual operational risk function better prepare for future strategies and budget justification.

Risk Escalation and Disclosure

Risk escalation and disclosure represents the final pillar to achieve operational resilience. It expands on the capabilities of Agile governance, a risk-informed system, and risk-based strategy and execution. Risk escalation is a systematic process that delivers risk information promptly and in keeping with practices defined by the governance body, so that appropriate action can be taken rapidly. Risk disclosure, on the other hand, is all about communicating risk-related information to the relevant internal and external stakeholders. Internally, effective risk disclosure promotes transparency across the different operational risk functions, contributing to a collective understanding and management of risk. Externally, it demonstrates accountability to regulatory bodies, shareholders, and the public, thereby enhancing the enterprise's credibility and trust.

Here's one important example of the importance of this function: it's almost impossible today to assess and communicate a material risk without also providing information about its potential impact across the entire enterprise. Each operational risk function should contribute to these considerations. If they don't, there will be gaps significant enough to expose the enterprise and its senior decision makers to the regulatory, civil, and even criminal liability we detailed in Chapter 2.

The Bottom Line

In the preceding sections of this chapter, we've laid the groundwork for a comprehensive cyber risk management program. We've highlighted the four fundamental components and how these pieces interconnect to form a robust and resilient strategy. But cyber risk management doesn't stand alone. It's part of a broader fabric, intricately woven with other operational risk functions.

Each of the four components has broader applications that extend well beyond simply managing cyber risks. They form the bedrock to coordinate a more expansive operational resilience strategy that encompasses various aspects of risk operations.

As we move forward, it's important to bear in mind that operational resilience is not a destination but a journey. It's an ongoing process that requires continuous monitoring, evaluation, and refinement. By understanding and integrating these four core components into your organizational practices, cybersecurity and risk management practitioners will be well-equipped to lead the coordination or a needed cohesive approach toward resilience.

In our final chapter, we'll discuss the future, focusing on AI risk management in particular but also more broadly on the unknown risks ahead, and how a cyber risk management program will be a foundation to guide enterprise approaches to them.

CHAPTER 9

AI and Beyond—the Future of Risk Management in a Digitalized World

Throughout this book, we've detailed the positive and negative impacts that established and emerging digital technologies are having and will continue to have at an accelerating pace. Every day seems to bring with it news of some spectacular breakthrough in digital technology that promises—at least theoretically—to completely reshape our daily lives, our working environments, and even entire industries. These developments are creating a new "digital frontier," which is moving so fast that at times it's impossible to know what risks lie ahead. And while in many cases the real-world value of these cutting-edge technologies remains unproven, there's no question that the current wave of digital transformation is bringing with it unparalleled opportunities for improvements in innovation, efficiency, and interconnectivity. But at the same time, they're introducing complex, intricately interconnected, and difficult-to-predict new risks that urgently demand coordination through risk management and the implementation of a comprehensive, mature risk management program.

As we discussed in the previous chapter on the topic of operational resilience, the components of a cyber risk management program (CRMP) and the principles defined can help an organization establish such coordination with new technologies that demand it and deliver on the risk information to enable the business. A risk management program of this type brings consistency and trust in approaching these new technologies, allowing a formalized, coordinated effort across multiple functions, similar to operational resilience.

Terms that were once known only to a handful of highly specialized technologists—blockchain, cryptocurrency, the Internet of Things (IoT), quantum computing, and many more—are now part of everyday conversation, both in the business world and in private life. The public introduction of the generative AI application ChatGPT in late 2022 represented a seismic event in the way the world works, arguably the most significant since the adoption of the internet. And yet, as extraordinarily important as ChatGPT was and is, it was immediately followed by a seemingly endless wave of new AI applications, projects, and use cases, many of which promised to extend AI's capabilities to areas no one had even considered just months before. AI is evolving so fast that some of today's most promising systems and applications could easily be obsolete tomorrow.

It's impossible to have a complete, up-to-the-minute understanding of all the developments in AI, or even the most important ones. We recognize that by the time this book is published, certainly some of the discussion of AI will have advanced from where we are today. There are so many facets to AI, and they're so complex and interconnected with one another and with virtually every aspect of an enterprise's operations. Managing AI risks will require a formal and practical approach, some of the specific practices of which we'll discuss in this chapter. As in the operational resilience conversation, it will be an organization's risk management program and approach that will keep efforts connected across multiple stakeholder involvement when managing AI risks.

AI Defined

There's so much attention being paid to AI today—and so much hype, especially from technology providers looking to sell AI applications—that it's difficult to really understand what AI is and what it can do, much less the risks it introduces. Let's begin our discussion by defining AI and some other, related terms, and detailing some of the ways AI and its components are being used today and may potentially be used in the future:

- NIST defines AI as: "(1) A branch of computer science devoted to developing data processing systems that performs functions normally associated with human intelligence, such as reasoning, learning, and self-improvement; and (2) The capability of a device to perform functions that are normally associated with human intelligence such as reasoning, learning, and self-improvement."[1] This type of "basic" AI has been widely used for years.

- Generative AI—like ChatGPT and competitors like Google's Bard and LaMDA— is where the excitement around AI is largely centered today. This is a subset of "standard" AI that extends its capabilities by creating models and algorithms that can generate new content based on data it's been trained on.

---

1 "Artificial Intelligence," NIST, July 20, 2023, *https://oreil.ly/81irC*.

- Artificial general intelligence (AGI) is a still-hypothetical form of AI, but R&D projects are underway worldwide to make it a reality. AGI (sometimes known as "strong AI") could, at least in theory, be capable of any intellectual task humans are capable of performing and beyond. Some observers believe AGI presents extraordinary, even existential, risks (for example, that an AGI application might decide on its own to do something that's against its creators', or even the human race's, best interests). It's not clear when, or even whether, AGI might come into existence, but its potential needs to be taken very seriously. It may just be science fiction today, but it's important to remember that in many ways yesterday's science fiction can be tomorrow's reality.

To fully understand AI, and to accurately assess its potential opportunities and risks, it's necessary to understand some of its underlying technologies and subcomponents. Let's take a look at the most important:

Machine learning (ML)

There's probably more confusion around ML than any other AI-related term. In fact, the two terms are often used interchangeably, and that's a mistake. ML is a fundamental and critical subcomponent of AI that focuses on developing algorithms and statistical models that make it possible for computers to learn from data without being explicitly programmed for a specific task. Netflix, for example, uses it to recommend films and TV shows based on the viewing patterns of subscribers and, crucially, subscribers with similar tastes.

Deep learning

This is a subset of ML that uses artificial neural networks to learn from data. Neural networks are trained on large datasets, and they can be used to classify images, translate languages, and, most importantly, make predictions and decisions. An example of deep learning is ReCAPTCHA, the tool that many websites use to determine that a user is human by asking them to identify roads, buildings, or other landscape features. Nearly every internet user has encountered ReCAPTCHA, but few realize that their input is used to improve the accuracy of online mapping services and other databases.

Large language models (LLMs)

LLMs are central to generative AI applications like ChatGPT and Bard. An LLM is a type of AI that's trained on a massive dataset—including text, images, and code—that makes it possible for it to understand its meaning. This huge source of data, and the LLM's ability to make sense of it, is what enables generative AI to answer questions, summarize subjects, and translate languages.

Recurrent neural networks (RNNs)

An RNN is a type of artificial neural network—essentially a form of computer programming imitating the way the human brain works—that's designed to process sequential data. In its simplest terms, this means it can learn from input it's received and use it to make predictions about future inputs. RNNs are central to some of the most advanced emerging AI use cases. One important example: they can be used for natural language processing (NLP), so that a computer application can not only recognize an individual's speech—and identify that person—but in some cases even identify and respond to that person's emotional state.

Even AI experts are struggling to keep pace with the never-ending stream of new developments in the field. But it's important that an enterprise's risk management program have a broad and constantly updated understanding of AI and the potential opportunities and challenges it presents. As we discussed in Chapter 2, specifically when it comes to cyber risk management, legislators and regulators are increasingly requiring enterprises—especially publicly traded companies covered by the new SEC rules (*https://oreil.ly/0rvF2*)—to have documented cybersecurity expertise readily available to them, sometimes even at the board level. And for the foreseeable future, cybersecurity expertise will require at least some level of understanding of AI, and especially the emerging risks associated with it as a "new" attack surface. It's the only way enterprises, their risk management and governance bodies, and their risk-impacted stakeholders will be able to perform the most fundamental task of risk management: balancing AI's risks against its rewards.

AI: A Whole New World of Risk

Even if no one knows all the risks AI introduces, or what their impact on a specific enterprise or industry will be, there are some that are already becoming clear. Let's take a look at some of the most important that risk programs should soon begin to manage if they aren't already:

Data and algorithm bias
    AI applications are only as good as the data that informs them and the algorithms that interpret and apply that data—and both are subject to bias. AI has repeatedly been determined to display bias based on age, race, gender, and class, among other factors. For example, a 2015 study (*https://oreil.ly/kmbce*) showed that Google's facial recognition software was more likely to misidentify Black people than white, likely due to having been trained on a dataset that disproportionately used white people.

Security and privacy concerns
    AI systems, like any technology, can be hacked, and the huge datasets present a highly attractive target for bad actors. Not only that, but AI itself can be used in security breaches, with generative AI programs like ChatGPT able to write sophisticated, targeted malware. (We'll be discussing this threat in detail later in this chapter.) That significantly increases cyber risk, because it means hackers

require less technical skills to launch attacks. AI systems like voice assistants also collect huge amounts of data and may not have structures in place to protect confidential information.

Loss of intellectual property (IP) and other sensitive information

This is an issue that's closely related to security and privacy. The use of enormous datasets, with the associated difficulty of determining what levels of protection specific pieces of data require, dramatically increases the already high risk of losing sensitive data. This could mean everything from IP like patents and other trade secrets to sales figures and market plans to personal information about customers and employees.

Fraud

Criminals are always among the first to recognize the potential of new technologies, and AI has been no exception. For example, AI's voice recognition capabilities are already so powerful that specific individuals' voices have been flawlessly duplicated and used in highly targeted "spear phishing" attacks to convince users to allow access to enterprise systems. There's so much concern around this issue that many banks and other financial institutions have stopped using voice recognition as a form of authentication.

Lack of transparency

The lack of transparency with AI obscures decision-making processes, potentially leading to unaccountable outcomes and diminished trust in the technology that may not have the ability to be properly explained.

Loss of enterprise control

There is real concern among researchers and industry observers that AI systems may become so complex, powerful, so autonomous that they begin to make unauthorized decisions and act on them—without any humans' intervention and possibly even without their knowledge.

Workforce volatility

The most immediate and widespread reaction to the introduction of ChatGPT in late 2022 was predictions that millions, even hundreds of millions, of jobs would be lost, with a broad range of functions replaced by AI. By 2030, activities that account for up to 30% of hours (*https://oreil.ly/tkVWF*) currently worked across the US economy could be automated—a trend accelerated by generative AI. Some of that concern is unquestionably well-founded: AI-powered virtual assistants and chatbots are already taking over from human call-center workers, and a significant amount of online content—both text and images—is now created by automation, with only the most minimal human intervention. Many industry observers are predicting that AI will result in the creation of millions of new jobs. But whoever turns out to have been correct, there's no question that the AI era will be a period of extraordinary uncertainty in the job market. Enterprises will have very difficult decisions to make. Do they replace workers with untested technology and risk losing valuable employees at a time when the job market, especially for skilled workers (e.g., workers with advanced cybersecurity and AI skills) remains very tight? Or do they resist adopting AI and risk losing opportunities to more aggressive competitors?

These and many other specific risks all lead up to and influence the high-level enterprise risks we've been discussing throughout this book. The improper use of AI could lead to legal and regulatory liability; reputational damage, loss of confidence by customers, employees, and business partners; and many other serious, even existential, problems. But it's important to recognize that the risks associated with AI don't just arise from its potential for misuse, or from the failure to implement it or monitor its use responsibly. AI represents a fundamental change in the way the world works, and that makes the work of risk management—balancing risk and reward—more difficult than it's ever been.

Enterprises face serious risks if they use AI—and if they don't.

AI isn't something that can be ignored. It presents enterprises with serious risks if they use it—and if they don't. And it makes the need for a comprehensive, robust risk management program more urgent than ever. Managing AI risk effectively, much like achieving operational resiliency, will require coordination and collaboration across multiple business functions and multiple operational risk functions. In the next section, although we won't get into the one-to-one alignment of a CRMP, we will discuss AI risk management concepts and associated frameworks and practices that are tied to risk management efforts and should be tied together in the program. But first, let's take a look at some of the AI terminology that cybersecurity and risk management professionals will need to know, and some of the most urgent threats they may need to address.

Adversarial Machine Learning: NIST Taxonomy and Terminology

In March 2023, NIST released the initial public draft of a report (*https://oreil.ly/UscR7*) aimed at creating a structured taxonomy and terminology of adversarial machine learning (AML), the techniques used to aid in securing the ML technologies that protect many AI applications against potential threats. AML involves securing all components of an AI system, which at a minimum includes the ML data, the ML models used, and the processes for training, testing, and deploying those models, as well as the infrastructure required for their use. The report aligns with the basic concepts of system security, resilience, and robustness detailed in the NIST AI Risk Management Framework.

The NIST report focuses on three types of potential attacks that are of particular concern. (It doesn't primarily consider unintentional factors such as design flaws, data, or algorithm biases that an adversary could exploit, though these are also serious concerns.) The three types of attacks explained in the initial public draft:

Evasion attacks

The goal of evasion attacks have gained interest in AML, where the adversary's goal is to generate adversarial examples that can change the classification of ML testing samples at deployment time. While the ML model can be tricked, humans still recognize it as part of the original class. There is an ongoing cycle of stronger adversarial attacks breaking existing defenses. Mitigating these adversarial examples is challenging. There's also an ongoing cycle of defenses evaluated under weak adversarial models being broken by stronger attacks. Mitigating these attacks presents significant challenges. Methods including adversarial training, randomized smoothing, and formal verification techniques have been proposed to counter evasion attacks, but each comes with limitations. There exists an inherent trade-off between robustness and accuracy, as well as between a model's robustness and fairness guarantees.

Poisoning attacks and mitigations

Poisoning attacks, which are adversarial attacks during the training stage of an ML algorithm, are another threat against ML systems. These attacks can cause either an availability violation or an integrity violation, resulting in the degradation of the ML model on all samples, or harder-to-detect stealthier violations on a small subset of target samples. Several mitigation approaches exist for each type of poisoning attack, though their effectiveness varies depending on the adversarial scenario.

Privacy attacks

Privacy attacks, which involve the reconstruction of private information from aggregate statistical information or the memorization of training data, are becoming increasingly prevalent. Two common types of privacy attack are membership inference attacks, in which an adversary can determine whether a particular record was included in the training dataset, and model extraction attacks, designed to extract information about an ML model. Mitigating these attacks remains a significant challenge in the field of AML researchers and practitioners.

It's important to remember that it's impossible to manage risk in isolation, and this has never been more true than where AI is concerned. The complexity and decision-making autonomy of AI and its underlying technologies—and the increasingly sophisticated nature of the attacks on them—make threats and vulnerabilities more difficult to predict, detect, and mitigate than ever. The intrinsically interconnected nature of our digital ecosystem means that the consequences of one system's vulnerabilities can have highly unpredictable ripple effects across countless others.

Management of AI risk and specific cyber risks must be coordinated with other risk management functions across the organization. The interconnected nature of digital systems means that a vulnerability AI introduces in one area could impact the enterprise's entire network and beyond. A holistic approach to defense, bringing together expertise from different domains, is absolutely essential. Similarly, the increasingly sophisticated nature of adversarial attacks requires an equally sophisticated, holistic approach to defense, combining expertise from different domains.

Risk Management Frameworks with AI Implications

AI risk management is, of course, in its nascent stage, because AI itself is. There are, however, risk management frameworks—both established and under development—designed to help enterprises address the specific risks associated with AI.

NIST AI Risk Management Framework

The NIST AI Risk Management Framework (*https://oreil.ly/_M_Ix*), released in January 2023, represents the most up-to-date and detailed risk-based guidance to AI implementation guidance on AI risk as of this writing. The NIST framework is a risk-based guide to AI implementation that is broadly applicable to most enterprises, which can opt into using the framework voluntarily. US government regulators will most likely use this as a standard for responsible implementation moving forward, particularly with respect to critical infrastructure and publicly traded companies.

The NIST framework focuses on four key functions:

Govern
> The govern function addresses the overall management of AI risk, with a view to establishing an enterprise-wide culture of risk management aligned with many of the principles discussed in Chapter 3 as part of a CRMP. This includes creating accountability structures, developing internal organizations committed to the responsible use of AI, and ensuring that AI systems and their use align with the enterprise's established values.

Map
> In this context, mapping means identifying and assessing the risks associated with the development, deployment, and use of AI systems. It includes identifying all AI-related systems, the data and algorithms they use, and the potential consequences of a successful attack involving them.

Measure

Measuring the effectiveness of AI risk management controls includes monitoring the system for compliance, conducting penetration testing, and reviewing incident reports.

Manage

This function ensures that the AI risk management controls are effective and that they are being implemented correctly, via activities like reviewing and updating the AI risk management plan and policy as well as conducting user training.

Model risk management (MRM) and the Federal Reserve Board's guidance

MRM—most commonly used in financial services—is the process of identifying, assessing, and mitigating the risks associated with the use of models and especially from the use of inaccurate or poorly designed models in decision making. The financial services industry, by its very nature, is of course intensely focused on risk management. Banks make judgments about borrowers' creditworthiness every day, insurance companies assess individuals' life expectancy, and traders need to be able to predict trends in the stock and commodities markets. This gives the industry a wealth of experience in developing frameworks for managing risk—models that can be applied to other industries and other types of enterprises, and to the new risks introduced by AI. Let's take a look at one of the most important relevant model risk management frameworks that is being used to guide responsible AI implementation.

In 2011, the Federal Reserve Board released supervision and regulation Letter SR 11-7: Guidance on Model Risk Management (*https://oreil.ly/D68EW*). This has been authoritative guidance for assisting financial institutions in assessing the management of model risk. The established principles and guidance set a framework that can be adopted for AI models, encompassing robust model selection, development, implementation, effective validation, model challenging, and of course governance including policies and controls. These guiding principles, broken down more granularly, can be readily adapted to apply to AI risk:

Establish an appropriate governance framework for MRM

Strong governance is essential for the effectiveness of the model risk management. It involves establishing policies, procedures, resource allocation, and documentation. An appropriate governance framework for model risk management should be established and aligned with other risk practices in the enterprise, including clear roles and responsibilities for all relevant stakeholders. In terms of AI risk, this would clearly require significant expertise in AI techniques, including advances in generative AI and the LLMs they're based on, as well as the current and anticipated legal and regulatory environment surrounding the use of AI.

Adopt a risk-based approach to MRM
The specific risks associated with an MRM model should be assessed, and appropriate controls should be implemented to mitigate those risks.

Ensure that the data used to develop and calibrate models is sound
AI, perhaps more than any other technology, depends for its outputs' accuracy on the quality of the data it uses for input. The enterprise must have robust data management processes in place to ensure that the data used is accurate and reliable—likely an exceptionally difficult task when applied at the scale and velocity AI brings with it.

Develop and validate models rigorously
Enterprise AI initiatives will require sound statistical methods for their risk models, and the models will need to be tested on an ongoing basis.

Use models prudently
This means that an enterprise's risk model should be used in ways that are consistent with its established risk appetite and risk tolerance, which in terms of AI are likely to be recent in development and subject to ongoing and often sudden change.

Monitor the performance of models on an ongoing basis
There must be processes in place for identifying and addressing problems with the AI risk models in use. This is a particularly urgent concern with AI models, because AI itself, and its underlying technologies and data sources, are constantly changing.

Have robust processes in place for managing model changes
The unending changes in the way AI works and the way it's applied mean that changes will almost certainly need to be made to the associated risk models. The enterprise must establish a sound process for managing these changes.

Have contingency plans in place in case of model failure
Enterprises must always recognize the possibility that their risk models—in any area, but particularly in one as volatile as AI—will prove inadequate or will fail completely. They must have plans in place to address the broad range of risks associated with model failure or simply with the failure of a model to perform as expected.

Communicate effectively about model risk
Everyone with a stake in AI risk should be informed, in an appropriate and ongoing manner, about the enterprise model risk.

Have appropriate resources and expertise in place to manage model risk
This means appropriate resources and expertise—internal, external, or both—must be available to develop and validate AI risk models and use them effectively.

Conduct regular reviews of the MRM framework
Regular reviews of MRM frameworks will be needed to ensure that they are effective—a particularly important issue, given how rapidly AI and AI risk change.

Key AI Implementation Concepts and Frameworks

No one is expecting you to be an expert in AI, but there are certain concepts that are particularly relevant to AI and AI risk. Many of these concepts, like the standards and principles we've discussed throughout this book, are defined by regulatory agencies and governance bodies. Let's take a look at some of the most important AI-related concepts and the frameworks surrounding them.

Fairness and the risk of bias

There's no standard definition of the term *fairness* in a business context, but there are certain widely accepted views of the concept, and some apply directly to AI. The definitions are generally based on some combination of three basic principles—equality, transparency, and accountability—and those principles seem a solid starting point for this discussion. Equality means essentially that enterprises should treat all customers, employees, and other stakeholders equally; transparency holds that they should provide clear and accurate information about the practices and policies to all stakeholders; and accountability means the willingness to take responsibility for any harm the enterprise causes.

It's easy to see the impact AI will have on fairness and why a number of organizations have begun developing fairness standards and principles focused intensely on AI. Here are a few of the most important organizations and initiatives:

- The Algorithmic Fairness and Accountability Working Group (of the AAAI), which was formed in 2016 and has written a number of articles on fairness (*https://oreil.ly/jZfqt*)

- The Partnership on AI (*https://partnershiponai.org*), which promotes fairness, accountability, and transparency in AI

- NIST (*https://oreil.ly/TKWEH*), which established a resource center for trustworthy and responsible AI

These organizations' and others' views of AI practices are often based on two commonly recognized dimensions of fairness:

Individual fairness
This is the idea that similar individuals should be treated similarly by AI systems—and, crucially, that systems should not make decisions based on factors such as race, gender, or sexual orientation unless there is a sound ethical reason to do so.

Disparate impact
> This principle states that the AI system should not have a negative impact on any particular group of people.

Note that fairness principles may also consider other factors, like robustness, explainability, and accountability, all of which we'll discuss.

Soundness

Soundness can be thought of as the quality of being well-founded, sensible, and reliable in decision making, and considering factors like feasibility, viability, sustainability, and ethics. In terms of AI, this requires the consideration of two critical factors:

Accuracy (data integrity and quality)
> This requires careful and ongoing attention to the quality of the data used to train AI models, the choice of algorithms and techniques used to build those models, and the ways the model is implemented and used.

Consistency
> AI systems should provide consistent results, producing the same results from the same input data.

There are specific technologies, techniques, and processes that can be used to improve the soundness of AI systems. They include data cleaning (removing any data from training datasets that's "noisy" or contains outliers); algorithmic adjustments (making ongoing changes to AI algorithms to make them more sensitive to noise and outliers); and postprocessing (which involves adjusting the actual outputs of the AI systems to make them more accurate and more consistent).

Robustness

This is the ability of an AI model to maintain its performance and accuracy even when faced with unexpected or adversarial data inputs. The model should be able to handle outliers and noise in the data, and it should be able to adapt to changes in the environment without significant impacts on its performance.

A number of common robustness principles have been established for AI. These principles are designed to ensure that AI systems are resilient to attacks and failures, and that they continue to function correctly even when they're exposed to unexpected or adversarial inputs. Here are some of the most common principles:

Input validation
> AI systems should validate all input data before it's used and check it for errors or malicious content.

Error handling

Errors should be handled gracefully. In practice, this means an AI system shouldn't crash—or, far more importantly, produce incorrect or simply different results—if it encounters an error.

Fault tolerance

This means that the system should be able to recover from a failure without losing data or functionality. This might be a straightforward system failure or a more pervasive failure of the system's model (as was reportedly seen in a decline in the accuracy of ChatGPT's outputs in the months following its public launch).

Security

AI systems should be secure from attacks. This means that the system should be protected from unauthorized access, modification, or destruction.

A number of technologies and techniques are in place that can be used to improve the robustness of AI systems, including:

Data augmentation

The size of the training dataset can be artificially increased by the deliberate addition of noise or outliers, which makes the system more robust to real-world noise and outliers.

Ensemble learning

This technique involves combining the predictions of multiple AI systems to produce a more robust prediction, making the system more resistant to errors in any individual system.

Adversarial training

Training AI on adversarial examples—inputs that have been modified to cause it to make errors—makes AI systems more resistant to attacks by malicious actors.

Explainability

Explainability, simply stated, is the ability to understand why an AI system has made a particular decision or taken a particular action. It's an important concept, because explainability builds trust in the system, contributes to legal and regulatory compliance, and helps improve the performance of the system itself.

There are a number of basic subcomponents of AI explainability:

Purpose

An AI system's explainability should always be aligned with its intended purpose. For example, if the purpose of an AI system is to make predictions about customer behavior, then the explanations should be focused on the factors that are most likely to lead to changes in that behavior.

Accuracy

The explanations should be accurate, reflecting the actual reasons the AI system made a particular decision. This means they should be based on the actual data the AI system used to train and make predictions.

Transparency

Transparency—the ability to see the data and algorithms an AI system uses—is an absolutely critical component of explainability. It's especially important when third parties, like business partners and model providers, are involved.

Relevance

The explanations should focus on the factors that were most important in the decision-making process.

Sufficiency

Humans should have enough information to understand why the AI system has made a particular decision.

Context

An explanation should consider the specific situation in which the AI system made a decision, and should also be tailored to the audience and the reasons the explanation has been requested.

Auditability

Regular audits—the systematic examination of algorithms and data inputs and outputs—represent the backbone of trust and confidence in AI systems, ensuring compliance with ethical norms, regulatory mandates, organizational policies, and ethical standards.

Beyond AI: The Digital Frontier Never Stops Moving

So much attention is being paid to AI these days that it's easy, and tempting, to think that it's the final technological development that risk management needs to be concerned with. And there's no question that it's almost certainly going to be a top-of-mind risk concern for years to come. But the reality is, change just keeps coming, and it isn't going to stop. An extraordinary range of new technologies, and new use cases for those technologies, continues to emerge. And they will all have risk management implications.

There are so many emerging technologies competing for attention today that it's almost impossible to be aware of them all, much less to have a detailed understanding of them all or how they'll eventually work together as they evolve and mature. That is, of course, one of the key reasons enterprises need a comprehensive CRMP, working in alignment with other mature enterprise risk management programs. And that doesn't just mean technological change, but all the types of change we've been discussing throughout this book—social, economic, political, cultural, and more—that impact the enterprise risk environment. But there's no question that advances in technology will continue to be one of the most urgent risk management concerns for enterprises worldwide.

It's impossible to say with any certainty what the next "next big thing" will be, but one revolutionary technology—quantum computing—definitely holds the potential to transform computing, cybersecurity, and risk management as dramatically as AI is currently doing, if not more so. Quantum computing is an emerging field of computing that uses the principles of quantum mechanics and tiny, unstable units of data called qubits to perform complex computational tasks that "normal" computers can't and at radically increased speed.

Here's one spectacular example of the possibilities that quantum computing may open up: Google announced (*https://oreil.ly/ESmke*) in 2019 that its artificial intelligence division had created a quantum processor, called Sycamore, that could complete in 200 *seconds* a task that a state-of-the-art supercomputer would have taken 10,000 *years* to perform. And in 2021, the company announced an upgrade to Sycamore that made it 350 million times more powerful than the original version. What this means is that Google's quantum computing initiative and many others (from established players like IBM, Honeywell, and Microsoft; well-funded startups; and nations that are adversaries of the US and its democratic allies) have the potential to make computing billions of times faster and more powerful than it currently is.

The transformational potential of quantum computing will unquestionably bring radical—and impossible-to-predict—advances in a broad range of disparate fields. For example, financial institutions could use it to develop new predictive models for market trends and optimize investment portfolios. Pharmaceutical manufacturers could simulate molecular behavior, rapidly and accurately, in order to develop new drugs and treatments. Manufacturers could use quantum-driven advances in materials sciences to design products that are stronger, lighter, more energy efficient, and more environmentally sustainable. In addition, transportation and logistics providers, from airlines to car rental agencies to shipping firms, could use quantum techniques to improve routing optimization and fleet management, reducing their energy costs and their carbon emissions. Perhaps the most interesting area to watch for the impact of quantum computing is the technology we've focused on for most of this chapter: AI. Quantum computers could be used to train AI models and LLMs more quickly, efficiently and accurately, leading to far more accurate, and far more useful, AI decision making.

Quantum computing doesn't just present opportunities, of course. It will inevitably also introduce unique challenges that necessitate thoughtful and forward-looking risk management, in areas including:

Cryptographic risks

Quantum computers could theoretically break widely accepted cryptographic algorithms—like those used to protect sensitive personal information and online transactions.

Operational complexity

The intricacy of quantum computing systems requires specialized expertise. Without proper knowledge and handling, the complexity of these systems may lead to operational risks.

Regulatory compliance

As quantum technology continues to evolve, it may shape new regulatory frameworks. Adherence to these changing laws and standards will require vigilant risk management, constantly adjusting and aligning the program to ensure compliance.

Strategic alignment

The integration of quantum computing into business processes must be in sync with the organization's overall strategic direction and risk appetite. Any misalignment can lead to financial, reputational, or strategic risks.

To navigate these challenges, organizations must embrace a comprehensive risk management program tailored to the unique risks posed by quantum computing.

The Bottom Line

We began this book by detailing a set of critical enterprise risks—represented by damaging events such as a worldwide pandemic, plane crashes, and cyberattacks—that we believe require an evolved and mature approach to risk management. And we're ending it with even newer risks, introduced by technological and other developments, like AI and quantum computing, that make the adoption of a comprehensive, robust coordinated risk management program even more urgent. Enterprise decision makers today must address an astonishing range of risks—some as old as human history, some so new that they don't even have names yet.

A cyber risk management program builds on long-established principles of risk establishment—most importantly, the recognition of the need to balance risk against reward to protect the enterprise against threats while ensuring that it remains viable and competitive—and extends them into a world that's changing at the speed of digital technology. The reason a cyber risk management program is relevant is the pervasiveness of digitalization. This means everything we do today introduces a cyber related threat, and a new opportunity, and that in turn means that every risk, and every risk management decision, has a cyber risk component, including being more competitive in a marketplace.

In this final chapter, we've demonstrated that change is coming so fast that it's impossible to predict, and that it's equally impossible to predict its impacts on enterprises, industries, or individuals and the risks they face. New technologies are emerging constantly, of course, but the changes to the risk environment extend far beyond technology. Fundamental changes in the way we live and work, in societal expectations of how enterprises conduct themselves, and in the legal and regulatory landscape are making risk more difficult than ever to identify, address, mitigate, and take advantage of.

There is endless opportunity ahead, and it's an exciting time to be in risk management, especially in the security space. The formal cyber risk management program will allow for a forward-looking, strategic, interconnected function, and will lead strategic engagement and remain adaptable and flexible for a future-proof approach.

The Cyber Risk Management Program Framework v1.0

In the ever evolving landscape shaped by digital transformation, it's critical to recognize that cybersecurity is not just an IT concern but rather an intrinsic part of business strategy and decision making. With this realization comes the need for enterprises to operationalize a comprehensive cyber risk management program within their business operations. This Appendix introduces a framework designed to holistically establish a cyber risk management program (CRMP), from governance to operational escalation and disclosure.

Purpose and Context

Recent years have brought an extraordinary surge in cyber threats and incidents. Authorities and regulatory bodies have highlighted the pressing need for organizations to strengthen their cybersecurity postures, and to ensure effective communication to stakeholders about cyber risks. Boards and executives must be able to provide proper oversight of their cyber risk environment. Many existing standards and references, when viewed in isolation, may fall short of providing a comprehensive program that truly serves the requirements of the business. This gap underscores the critical need for a unified framework that harmonizes and interprets the authoritative guidance, regulations, and standards, ensuring that businesses can properly manage and oversee their cyber risks.

The CRMP framework synthesizes insights from leading practices and standards, providing a structured and comprehensive approach to a CRMP. The program can be tailored to the unique needs and regulatory landscape of each enterprise. It serves as a guide to operationalize a cyber risk management program, enabling businesses to make informed risk decisions and evolve their security strategies to survive and thrive in the digital age.

Structure of the Cyber Risk Management Program Framework

The framework is organized into four core components:

- Agile governance
- Risk-informed system
- Risk-based strategy and execution
- Risk escalation and disclosure

Each of these components is further broken down into multiple supporting principles, which provide considerations for implementation. To facilitate practical application and deeper understanding, the principles within these components are then mapped to relevant informative references.

Informative references are drawn from established authorities, including:

2023 SEC Final Rule: Cybersecurity Risk Management, Strategy, Governance, and Incident Disclosure (https://oreil.ly/o2TGU)
The 2023 SEC Final Rule serves as a comprehensive guide outlining the essential disclosure requirements that registrants must adhere to in managing and reporting cybersecurity risks and incidents. It encompasses several components focusing on risk management, governance protocols, and incident disclosure, with detailed insight into the board's responsibilities and specific filing requirements in the event of a material cybersecurity incident. By addressing both the strategic and operational aspects of cybersecurity risk management, this rule facilitates the development of robust cybersecurity frameworks within enterprises, promoting transparency and consistency in disclosures, and thereby aiding in informed investment decision making.

2023 NIST CSF 2.0 Initial Public Draft (https://oreil.ly/xngbU)
The updated NIST Cybersecurity Framework (CSF) 2.0 aims to provide enterprises with a set of industry standards and best practices for managing and reducing cybersecurity risk. It builds on its predecessor by introducing refined guidelines that encompass evolving cyber threats and technologies. The framework, while flexible, encourages enterprises to align their cybersecurity strategies with business objectives, fostering a proactive cyber risk management culture.

2023 NACD Director's Handbook on Cyber-Risk Oversight (https://oreil.ly/8enA4)
This handbook serves as a comprehensive guide for company directors to navigate the complex landscape of cyber risk oversight. It provides insights into and recommendations on how directors can foster a cyber-savvy boardroom, emphasizing the importance of collaboration between directors and management in creating resilient cyber risk strategies. Through this guide, directors are equipped with the necessary tools and knowledge to oversee and guide their enterprise's cybersecurity initiatives effectively, thus safeguarding shareholder value and corporate reputation.

ISO/IEC 27001:2022 (https://oreil.ly/0ID28)
This international standard outlines the requirements for establishing, implementing, maintaining, and continually improving an information security management system (ISMS). The standards within ISO 27001 provide a framework for safeguarding information through a risk management process, offering a systematic approach to managing and protecting sensitive information using risk management processes, physical security protocols, and business continuity plans. It facilitates the secure and reliable handling of information, bolstering the enterprise's defense mechanisms against cyber threats.

NISTIR 8286 (https://oreil.ly/WOC5f)
The National Institute of Standards and Technology Interagency Report (NISTIR) 8286 focuses on integrating cybersecurity risks within the broader landscape of enterprise risk management. It outlines the benefits of aligning the enterprise's cybersecurity activities with its enterprise risk management (ERM), emphasizing the reciprocal relationship between cybersecurity and ERM, where understanding and managing cybersecurity risks influence and are influenced by broader enterprise risks. This guide seeks to foster a comprehensive risk management approach, where cybersecurity is not seen as a separate entity but as an integral part of the enterprise's risk management practices. By doing so, it encourages enterprises to make informed decisions grounded on a comprehensive understanding of the risks and their potential impacts on the enterprise, facilitating the development of robust and resilient cyber risk management strategies.

2020 IIA Three Lines Model (https://oreil.ly/0OAQ6)
The 2020 update of the Institute of Internal Auditors (IIA) Three Lines Model serves as a comprehensive guide for enterprises to structure their risk management and governance strategies. This model encourages enterprises to delineate responsibilities across three lines: management control; risk management, compliance, and other oversight functions; and internal audit. It emphasizes the collaborative and synergistic working of these lines to achieve organizational objectives, ensuring a streamlined approach to risk management and governance. The model encourages adaptability, offering enterprises the flexibility to apply it

in a manner that aligns with their specific goals and operational structures. In the context of cybersecurity, this model can facilitate a well-structured approach to identifying, assessing, and managing cyber risks, promoting a holistic and integrated risk management culture.

2018 SEC Commission Statement and Guidance on Public Company Cybersecurity Disclosures (https://oreil.ly/SVwOx)

This 2018 statement by the SEC offers guidance on the disclosures that public companies should make concerning their exposure to cybersecurity risks and incidents. It emphasizes the necessity of having well-established cybersecurity policies and procedures, encouraging companies to be proactive in evaluating and upgrading their disclosure controls with respect to cybersecurity threats. Furthermore, it provides insights into the roles of directors and officers in managing cybersecurity risks, ensuring a transparent and timely communication of material cyber incidents and risks to the investors.

ISO 31000:2018 (https://oreil.ly/vuqzY)

This provides guidelines on risk management, offering a universal standard that can be applied to any type of risk, including cybersecurity. It outlines principles, a framework, and a risk management process that helps organizations identify, analyze, and mitigate risks in a methodical manner. By adhering to this standard, enterprises can cultivate a risk-aware culture where timely and informed decisions are made based on a comprehensive understanding of risks and their potential impacts.

2017 AICPA Description Criteria for the Entity's Cybersecurity Risk Management Program (CRMP) (https://oreil.ly/d5n8o)

The AICPA's criteria for a cybersecurity risk management program offer a structure that entities can use to describe their cybersecurity risk management programs and against which CPAs can examine and report. This framework emphasizes the critical role of senior management and the board in overseeing an entity's cybersecurity measures, stressing the importance of a comprehensive risk management program that encompasses prevention, detection, and response strategies to mitigate cyber threats effectively. It thus facilitates the establishment of resilient and robust cybersecurity infrastructures, fostering trust and confidence among stakeholders.

These references offer insights and practical guidelines, enhancing the robustness and applicability of the CRMP framework.

Note: Framework Disclosure

While the framework aligns closely with these references, it's important to recognize that no single standard or guidance can comprehensively cover all facets of a mature cyber risk management program as required for today's environment. Thus, the motivation behind developing this framework and writing this book is to provide a holistic, synthesized view that integrates insights across multiple sources. Depending on the specific circumstances and nuances of your organization, you might find relevance in other standards or additional mappings.

In sum, this Appendix seeks to encapsulate the essence of a comprehensive CRMP as guided by authoritative sources. It serves as a guide, aiding enterprises and their decision makers in understanding, implementing, and operationalizing a CRMP. The guide also ensures enterprises can remain resilient and adaptive in the face of digital challenges while it also protects them from evolving liability and regulatory risks. As you navigate the intricacies of the framework, remember that its ultimate goal is to provide clarity, align with industry standards, and empower the business to make better decisions and thrive securely in the digital age.

Component	Principle	Informative reference
Agile governance	Principle 1: Establish Policies and Processes *Enterprise-wide policies and processes must be in place for establishing a cyber risk management program.*	• 2023 Draft NIST CSF 2.0 GV.PO-01, GV.PO.02 (*https://oreil.ly/xngbU*) • ISO/IEC 27001:2022 5.2 (*https://oreil.ly/0lD28*) • ISO 31000:2018 6.1 (*https://oreil.ly/vuqzY*) • 2018 SEC Commission Statement and Guidance on Public Company Cybersecurity Disclosures Page 18 Paragraph 2, 3 (*https://oreil.ly/SVwOx*) • 2017 AICPA CRMP Description Criteria DC4, DC7, DC19 (*https://oreil.ly/d5n8o*)
Agile governance	Principle 2: Establish Governance and Roles and Responsibilities Across the "Three Lines Model" *Cyber risk governance must be established with clearly defined roles, responsibilities, and outputs across the "Three Lines Model."*	• 2023 SEC Regulation S–K Item 106(c)—Governance and Form 20-F (*https://oreil.ly/o2TGU*) • 2023 Draft NIST CSF 2.0 GV.RR (*https://oreil.ly/xngbU*) • 2023 NACD Director's Handbook on Cyber-Risk Oversight Principle 6 (*https://oreil.ly/8enA4*) • ISO/IEC 27001:2022 5.1, 5.3 (*https://oreil.ly/0lD28*) • ISO 31000:2018 5.2, 5.4.3 (*https://oreil.ly/vuqzY*) • 2020 IIA Three Lines Model Principle 2–4 (*https://oreil.ly/OOAQ6*)
Agile governance	Principle 3: Align Governance Practices with Existing Risk Frameworks *Cyber risk governance practices should be aligned with any existing enterprise or organizational risk frameworks.*	• 2023 NACD Cyber Risk Oversight Handbook Principle 1, 4 (*https://oreil.ly/PWOm6*) • 2023 Draft NIST CSF 2.0 GV.RM-03 (*https://oreil.ly/xngbU*) • NISTIR 8286 (*https://oreil.ly/WOC5f*)
Agile governance	Principle 4: Board of Directors and Senior Executives Define Scope *The scope of an enterprise's cyber risk practices should be defined and approved by its board of directors and senior executives.*	• 2023 Draft NIST CSF 2.0 GV.OC-01, GV.RR-01 (*https://oreil.ly/xngbU*) • ISO 31000:2018 5.2 (*https://oreil.ly/vuqzY*)

Component	Principle	Informative reference
Agile governance	**Principle 5: Board of Directors and Senior Executives Provide Oversight** *The board of directors and senior executives should provide proper oversight of the enterprise's cyber risk practices.*	• SEC Regulation S–K Item 106(c)—Governance and Form 20–F (*https://oreil.ly/o2TGU*) • 2023 Draft NIST CSF 2.0 GV.RR-01 (*https://oreil.ly/xngbU*) • 2023 NACD Director's Handbook on Cyber-Risk Oversight Principle 3 (*https://oreil.ly/8enA4*) • 2020 IIA Three Lines Model Principle 1 (*https://oreil.ly/00AQ6*) • ISO 31000:2018 5.4.2 (*https://oreil.ly/vuqzY*) • 2017 AICPA CRMP Description Criteria DC8 (*https://oreil.ly/d5n8o*)
Agile governance	**Principle 6: Audit Governance Processes** *Audit processes should provide appropriate review and assessment of the enterprise's cyber risk governance practices.*	• 2020 IIA Three Lines Model Principle 4 (*https://oreil.ly/00AQ6*) • 2018 SEC Commission Statement and Guidance on Public Company Cybersecurity Disclosures Page 18 Paragraph 3 (*https://oreil.ly/SVwOx*) • ISO 31000:2018 5.6 (*https://oreil.ly/vuqzY*) • 2017 AICPA CRMP Description Criteria DC15 (*https://oreil.ly/d5n8o*)
Agile governance	**Principle 7: Align Resources to the Defined Roles and Responsibilities** *Appropriate resources and skill sets should be aligned to the defined roles and responsibilities with ongoing training in place.*	• 2023 Draft NIST CSF 2.0 GV.RR-03 (*https://oreil.ly/xngbU*) • ISO/IEC 27001:2022 7.1 (*https://oreil.ly/0ID28*) • 2023 NACD Director's Handbook on Cyber-Risk Oversight Principle 3 (*https://oreil.ly/8enA4*) • 2017 AICPA CRMP Description Criteria DC10 (*https://oreil.ly/d5n8o*)
Risk-informed system	**Principle 1: Define a Risk Assessment Framework and Methodology** *A risk framework and methodology must be defined and executed on to identify, assess, and measure cyber risk within the organizational context.*	• SEC Regulation S–K Item 106(b)—Risk Management and Strategy (*https://oreil.ly/o2TGU*) • 2023 NACD Director's Handbook on Cyber-Risk Oversight Principle 1, 4, 5 (*https://oreil.ly/8enA4*) • Draft NIST CSF 2.0 GV.RM, ID.RA (*https://oreil.ly/xngbU*) • ISO/IEC 27001:2022 6.1.2, 6.1.3 (*https://oreil.ly/0ID28*) • 2017 AICPA CRMP Description Criteria DC11 (*https://oreil.ly/d5n8o*) • ISO 31000:2018 6.1 (*https://oreil.ly/vuqzY*)
Risk-informed system	**Principle 2: Establish a Methodology for Risk Thresholds** *An approved and repeatable methodology for acceptable risk thresholds—both appetite and tolerance—must be established.*	• 2023 Draft NIST CSF 2.0 GV.RM-02 (*https://oreil.ly/xngbU*) • 2023 NACD Director's Handbook on Cyber-Risk Oversight Principle 1, 5 (*https://oreil.ly/8enA4*)
Risk-informed system	**Principle 3: Establish Understanding of Risk-Informed Needs** *The governance body should be identified and engaged in establishing a comprehensive understanding of its cyber risk–informed needs.*	• 2023 Draft NIST CSF 2.0 GV.OC-02 (*https://oreil.ly/xngbU*) • 2017 AICPA CRMP Description Criteria DC13 (*https://oreil.ly/d5n8o*) • 2020 IIA Three Lines Model Principle 1 (*https://oreil.ly/00AQ6*) • ISO 31000:2018 6.2 (*https://oreil.ly/vuqzY*)

Component	Principle	Informative reference
Risk-informed system	Principle 4: Agree on a Risk Assessment Interval *The risk assessment process should be performed according to an agreed-on interval with its results regularly evaluated.*	• SEC Regulation S–K Item 106(b)—Risk Management and Strategy (*https://oreil.ly/o2TGU*) • 2023 NACD Director's Handbook on Cyber-Risk Oversight Principle 5 (*https://oreil.ly/8enA4*) • 2023 Draft NIST CSF 2.0 ID.RA, ID.IM (*https://oreil.ly/xngbU*) • 2017 AICPA CRMP Description Criteria (*https://oreil.ly/d5n8o*) • DC11, DC12, DC15 (*https://oreil.ly/R7N1q*)
Risk-informed system	Principle 5: Enable Reporting Processes *Reporting processes should equip the governance body with insights on the impact of cyber risks on existing practices and strategic decisions.*	• 2023 Draft NIST CSF 2.0 GV.OV (*https://oreil.ly/xngbU*) • 2023 NACD Director's Handbook on Cyber-Risk Oversight Principle 5 (*https://oreil.ly/8enA4*) • 2017 AICPA CRMP Description Criteria DC13, DC16 (*https://oreil.ly/d5n8o*) • 2020 IIA Three Lines Model Principle 6 (*https://oreil.ly/00AQ6*)
Risk-based strategy and execution	Principle 1: Define Acceptable Risk Thresholds *Acceptable cyber risk thresholds must be clearly understood, established, and approved by the risk owners based on the risk framework and methodology.*	• 2023 NACD Director's Handbook on Cyber-Risk Oversight Principle 1 (*https://oreil.ly/8enA4*) • 2023 Draft NIST CSF 2.0 GV.RM-02 (*https://oreil.ly/xngbU*)
Risk-based strategy and execution	Principle 2: Align Strategy and Budget with Approved Risk Thresholds *The cyber risk treatment plan and budget should be aligned with the approved risk thresholds.*	• 2023 Draft NIST CSF 2.0 GV.RM-04 (*https://oreil.ly/xngbU*) • 2023 NACD Director's Handbook on Cyber-Risk Oversight Principle 1 (*https://oreil.ly/wTGwV*) • ISO 31000 6.5.1, 6.5.2 (*https://oreil.ly/vuqzY*) • 2017 AICPA CRMP Description Criteria DC17 (*https://oreil.ly/d5n8o*)
Risk-based strategy and execution	Principle 3: Execute to Meet Approved Risk Thresholds *The cyber risk treatment plan should be executed to meet the approved risk thresholds.*	• 2023 Draft NIST CSF 2.0 GV.RR-03 (*https://oreil.ly/xngbU*) • ISO 31000 6.5.3 (*https://oreil.ly/vuqzY*)
Risk-based strategy and execution	Principle 4: Monitor on an Ongoing Basis *The execution of the cyber risk treatment plan should be monitored on an ongoing basis with established performance indicators and operational metrics.*	• 2023 NACD Director's Handbook on Cyber-Risk Oversight Principle 5 (*https://oreil.ly/8enA4*) • 2023 Draft NIST CSF 2.0 GV.OV (*https://oreil.ly/xngbU*) • 2017 AICPA CRMP Description Criteria >DC15, DC16 (*https://oreil.ly/d5n8o*)
Risk-based strategy and execution	Principle 5: Audit Against Risk Thresholds *The audit function should review and assess proper execution of the cyber risk treatment plan based on the approved risk thresholds.*	• 2020 IIA Three Lines Model Principle 4 (*https://oreil.ly/00AQ6*) • 2017 AICPA CRMP Description Criteria (*https://oreil.ly/d5n8o*)
Risk-based strategy and execution	Principle 6: Include Third Parties in Risk Treatment Plan *The cyber risk treatment plan should consider third parties including partners, suppliers, and supply chain participants.*	• 2023 Draft NIST CSF 2.0 GV.SC, ID.IM-02 (*https://oreil.ly/xngbU*) • SEC Regulation S–K Item 106(b)—Risk Management and Strategy (*https://oreil.ly/o2TGU*)

Component	Principle	Informative reference
Risk escalation and disclosure	**Principle 1: Establish Escalation Processes** *Formal cyber risk escalation processes must be established.*	• SEC Regulation S–K Item 106(c)—Governance (*https://oreil.ly/o2TGU*) • 2023 NACD Director's Handbook on Cyber-Risk Oversight Principle 2 (*https://oreil.ly/8enA4*) • 2018 SEC Commission Statement and Guidance on Public Company Cybersecurity Disclosures Page 18 Paragraph 3, Page 20 Paragraph 1 (*https://oreil.ly/SVwOx*) • 2017 AICPA CRMP Description Criteria DC13, DC16 (*https://oreil.ly/d5n8o*)
Risk escalation and disclosure	**Principle 2: Establish Disclosure Processes—All Enterprises** *The enterprise's cyber disclosure processes should address its specific risk factors, organizational context, and requirements.*	• 2023 Draft NIST CSF 2.0 GV.OC-03 (*https://oreil.ly/xngbU*) • 2023 NACD Director's Handbook on Cyber-Risk Oversight Principle 2 (*https://oreil.ly/8enA4*) • 2017 AICPA CRMP Description Criteria DC6 and DC14 (*https://oreil.ly/d5n8o*)
Risk escalation and disclosure	**Principle 3: Establish Disclosure Processes—Public Companies** *Public companies must disclose their material risks, risk factors, cyber risk management processes, governance, and material incident reporting.*	• 2023 SEC Final Rule Cybersecurity Risk Management, Strategy, Governance, Incident Disclosure Rule (*https://oreil.ly/o2TGU*) • 2023 Draft NIST CSF 2.0 GV.OC-03 (*https://oreil.ly/xngbU*) • 2018 SEC Commission Statement and Guidance on Public Company Cybersecurity Disclosures Page 4 Paragraph 1, Page 6 Paragraph 3, Page 7 Paragraph 4, Page 11 Paragraph 1 (*https://oreil.ly/SVwOx*)
Risk escalation and disclosure	**Principle 4: Test Escalation and Disclosure Processes** *Cyber risk escalation and disclosure processes should be challenged, tested, and updated on an ongoing basis to incorporate lessons learned.*	• 2023 SEC Final Rule Cybersecurity Risk Management, Strategy, Governance, Incident Disclosure Rule (*https://oreil.ly/o2TGU*) • 2023 Draft NIST CSF 2.0 ID.IM (*https://oreil.ly/xngbU*)
Risk escalation and disclosure	**Principle 5: Audit Escalation and Disclosure Processes** *Audit should review and assess the enterprise's cyber risk escalation and disclosure processes to ensure their effectiveness, consistency, and compliance with relevant regulations and policies.*	• 2020 IIA Three Lines Model Principle 4, 5 (*https://oreil.ly/OOAQ6*)

Index

bug bounty programs, 43
business continuity, 91
business continuity management (BCM), 159
business leaders, xii, 10
business resilience, 152
business growth, 149

C

Canadian Securities Administrators (CSA), 102
Capability Maturity Model Integration (CMMI) Model, 138
Caremark International, 34
Carnegie Mellon Software Engineering Institute, 138
CFOs (chief financial officers), 7
CFPB (Consumer Financial Protection Bureau), 111
chatbots, 171
ChatGPT, 82-84
  as generative AI, 167
  predictions of job loss, 171
chemical sector, 10
Chernobyl nuclear power plant, 161
chief financial officers (CFOs), 7
chief information security officers (see CISOs)
chief risk officers (see CROs)
China Securities Regulatory Commission (CSRC), 102
China, People's Republic of, 109
CISOs (chief information security officers)
  ad hoc role of versus CRMP role, 152
  assessment interviews with, 129
  defining enterprise governance posture, 55
  evaluating risk tolerances, 80
  liability, 38-39
  risk-related roles and responsibilities of, 10
  starting cyber risk management journey questions, 127
civil fines, 34
civil judgments, 20
clean technologies, 87
cloud computing, 86, 108
CMMI (Capability Maturity Model Integration) Model, 138
code
  ChatGPT writing, 82
  future of programming, 86
collaboration, as principle for Agile governance, 43

Colonial Pipeline ransomware attack, 112-113
commitment, 46
communication sector, 10
company-specific risks, 103
compliance activities, 145
compliance managers, 10
computer modeling, 142
confidential information, 171
consistency, 30, 164, 178
Consumer Financial Protection Bureau (CFPB), 111
consumer trust, 150
context, AI explainability, 180
contingency plans, 176
corporate culture
  cyber risk management journey causing changes in, 127
  governance defining, 25
  governance policy statement aligning with, 49
  governance setting tone of, 44
  risk escalation helping, 104
corporate officers (CxOs), xi, 10
cost savings, 104
courts
  accountability of decision-makers emphasized by, 104
  expectations for enterprises, 32
  expecting good-faith efforts, 20
Cox, Erin Nealy, 24
creative destruction, 6, 85
criminal fines, 34
crisis management, 159
CRMP.info, 12
CRMPs (see cyber risk management programs)
CROs (chief risk officers)
  assessment interviews with, 129
  starting cyber risk management journey questions, 127
cross-selling, 111
CRQ (cyber risk quantification) software applications, 132, 141, 143
cryptographic risks, 182
CSA (Canadian Securities Administrators), 102
CSRC (China Securities Regulatory Commission), 102
current disclosures (incident disclosures), 16
current-state risk levels, 90
CxOs (corporate officers), xi, 10

risk-based strategy and execution, 144
risk-informed system implementation,
   135-136
timeframe, incident disclosure, 17
timeliness, 30
Toyota shutdown, 61
training program, 131
transparency, 27
   AI, 171, 177, 180
   disclosure practices of public companies,
      119
   governance initiative addressing, 133
   material risk, 103
   SEC viewpoint on, 101
   Tylenol poisoning crisis, 45
transportation and logistics sector, 10
trust, 17
   enterprises gaining public's trust, 109
   with external parties, 150
   risk disclosures maintaining, 100
   value to enterprise, 150
trust architectures, 86
trusted outputs, 31
2022 Global Security Outlook survey, 132
Twitter, 41
Tylenol poisoning crisis, 45

U
Uber hack cover-up, 38, 41, 43

V
velocity, 4, 159

Verizon Communications, 107
virtual assistants, 171
voice assistants, 171
voice recognition, 171
volatility, 4
vulnerabilities
   digitalization introducing, 28
   unpatched vulnerability, impact of, 87

W
weaknesses, risk escalation and disclosure pro-
   cess, 123
WEF (World Economic Forum), 3, 9, 23
   2022 Global Security Outlook survey, 132
   Agile governance definition, 42
Wells Fargo scandal, 111
Wells notices, 38
Windows OS, 161
Witte, Greg, 92
workforce volatility, 171
World Benchmarking Alliance, 16
World Economic Forum (see WEF)

Y
Yahoo! data breach, 106

Z
zero-risk environment, 6, 26

About the Authors

Brian Allen was the chief security officer for Time Warner Cable, a critical infrastructure Fortune 130 enterprise. He worked for EY as the subcompetency lead for their cyber risk management program efforts, presenting to dozens of boards and C-suite executives at some of the largest global organizations. Today, Brian works at the Bank Policy Institute as the SVP, Cybersecurity and Technology Risk Management, working with bank executives (CEO, GC, CRO, CISO), advocating for the industry in front of regulators, legislators, law enforcement agencies, and the intelligence communities. Mr. Allen has worked on several industry and government coordinated critical infrastructure groups including the executive committees of the Comm-ISAC and Comm-Sector Coordinating Council. He was appointed by the FCC Chairman to represent the communications industry in working with NIST on the development of the Cybersecurity Framework. Mr. Allen is an author of two enterprise security risk management books, an adjunct professor at the University of Connecticut's MBA Financial Risk Management program, teaching cybersecurity risk and enterprise risk management concepts, and has spoken globally on the topic, including multiple keynote addresses. He holds multiple industry certifications and is a member of the New York State Bar Association.

Brandon Bapst is a cyber risk advisor in EY's cybersecurity practice. He works closely with executives, CSOs, and CISOs on developing mature cyber risk programs. He has worked with Global Fortune 100 companies to transform tactical security programs into holistic enterprise security risk management practices enabled through data driven insights and technology. Brandon is a Certified Information Systems Security Professional (CISSP), Certified Information Security Manager (CISM), and Certified Information Systems Auditor (CISA).

Terry Allan Hicks is a longtime business and technology writer, focusing primarily on the interrelated areas of financial services, information security, and regulatory compliance and corporate governance, with experience including more than twenty years as a senior writer with Gartner, the world's leading IT research and advisory firm. He is also the published author of more than twenty books.

Colophon

The animal on the cover of *Building a Cyber Risk Management Program* is a yellow-footed tortoise (*Chelonoidis denticulatus*), one of the largest types of tortoises on Earth. They can live for longer than 50 years, be over 3 feet long, and weigh more than 100 pounds.

The yellow-footed tortoise is native to the South American rainforests. It feeds on fallen fruits, low-lying vegetation, and occasionally carrion and insects. Their eggs incubate for one hundred to two hundred days and vary in size in accordance with the size of the female laying the eggs. Males are typically larger than females and have a longer tail and a distinctively curved shell. Yellow-footed tortoise young are self-sufficient at birth.

The IUCN considers yellow-footed tortoises vulnerable to extinction due to human activities. Many of the animals on O'Reilly covers are endangered; all of them are important to the world.

The cover illustration is by Karen Montgomery, based on an antique line engraving from *Brehm's Lexicon*. The series design is by Edie Freedman, Ellie Volckhausen, and Karen Montgomery. The cover fonts are Gilroy Semibold and Guardian Sans. The text font is Adobe Minion Pro; the heading font is Adobe Myriad Condensed; and the code font is Dalton Maag's Ubuntu Mono.

Printed in the USA
CPSIA information can be obtained
at www.ICGtesting.com
JSHW061511220124
55856JS00020B/96

9 781098 147792